READING
24

Reading Contemporary Television
Series Editors: Kim Akass and Janet McCabe
janetandkim@hotmail.com

The Reading Contemporary Television series aims to offer a varied, intellectually groundbreaking and often polemical response to what is happening in television today. This series is distinct in that it sets out to immediately comment upon the TV zeitgeist while providing an intellectual and creative platform for thinking differently and ingeniously writing about contemporary television culture. The books in the series seek to establish a critical space where new voices are heard and fresh perspectives offered. Innovation is encouraged and intellectual curiosity demanded.

READING

24

TV AGAINST THE CLOCK

EDITED BY
STEVEN PEACOCK

I.B. TAURIS

LONDON · NEW YORK

Published in 2007 by I.B.Tauris & Co Ltd
6 Salem Road, London W2 4BU
175 Fifth Avenue, New York NY 10010
www.ibtauris.com

In the United States of America and in Canada distributed by
Palgrave Macmillan, a division of St Martin's Press
175 Fifth Avenue, New York NY 10010

ISBN 978 1 84511 329 2

A full CIP record for this book is available from the British Library
A full CIP record for this book is available from the Library of Congress

Library of Congress catalog card: available

Typeset in Goudy Old Style by Steve Tribe, Andover
Printed and bound in the United States

CONTENTS

ACKNOWLEDGEMENTS

I would first like to thank the authors – Daniel Chamberlain, Scott Ruston, Michael Allen, Deborah Jermyn, Jacqueline Furby, Paul Woolf, Daniel Herbert, Anne Caldwell, Samuel A Chambers, Torin Monahan, Sharon Sutherland, Sarah Swan, Douglas L Howard, Janet McCabe, Joke Hermes, Tara McPherson, Paul Delany, Christopher Gair, and David Lavery – for providing insightful, engaging, and distinctive contributions, adhering to time-sensitive deadlines, and corresponding with boundless energy and enthusiasm.

The idea for this collection developed out of equally energetic discussions at the international conference on 'American Quality Television' at Trinity College, Dublin, in 2004. Thanks to Joke Hermes, for her encouragement and belief in the project, as well as her invaluable support in the early stages of the project's genesis.

Special thanks go to the series editors, Kim Akass and Janet McCabe. It is a pleasure and a privilege to work closely with two such supportive, generous and enthusiastic people. Their good humour, counsel and encouragement were crucial throughout all stages of the project's development.

At I.B.Tauris, special thanks also go to Philippa Brewster for her patience and guidance. Additional thanks go to David Lavery for being extremely generous with his time.

I would also like to thank all members of the Departments of Film Studies, and Film and Television Studies at Southampton Solent University, especially Karen Randell, Jacqueline Furby, Darren Kerr, David Lusted and Claire Hines. Equally, I am indebted to Sarah Cardwell at the University of Kent for giving me the opportunity to discuss *24* in the form and forum of undergraduate lectures and seminars. This leads me to another special thank you, to my students at both Southampton Solent and the University of Kent. Their enthusiasm for 24 sustained my belief in the project, and their insightful observations and sensitive criticism of the series inform my introduction and chapter.

My friends and family are a crucial source of inspiration: thank you to Thalia Baldwin and Matthew Roach, to my parents, and to my brother, David, whose view is always the clearest.

This book is dedicated to Leigh, with love.

CONTRIBUTORS

MICHAEL ALLEN is a lecturer in film and electronic media at Birkbeck College, University of London, where he teaches masters students on the MA course History of Film and Visual Media. His publications include the books *Family Secrets: The Feature Films of D. W. Griffith* (BFI, 1999) and *Contemporary US Cinema* (Longman, 2002), as well as numerous articles on the history of media technologies. He is currently working on a book detailing the relationship between film, television and the Space Race of the 1960s.

ANNE CALDWELL is an assistant professor of political science at the University of Louisville. She writes on contemporary theory and feminist studies and has published work in *Hypatia* and *Theory and Extent*. Her current research projects focus on the use of the concept of the exception to understand sexual difference, and the ways states invoke human rights to expand their own power.

DANIEL CHAMBERLAIN is a doctoral student in the Critical Studies division at the University of Southern California's School of Cinema-Television. His research is focused on the cultural impact of film, television, and new media, particularly on how emergent media technologies produce new types of urban spaces. He previously earned a Master's degree in Critical Studies from USC and a Bachelor's degree in Economics from the University of Michigan.

SAMUEL A CHAMBERS is a senior lecturer in Politics at Swansea University. He writes widely in contemporary political theory, with particular interests in language, culture, and the politics of gender and sexuality. His first book, *Untimely Politics*, was published by Edinburgh and New York University Presses in 2003. He is currently working on two books on the political theory of Judith Butler (both with Terrell Carver), and a third book on the queer politics of television.

PAUL DELANY taught English at Columbia in the 1960s and from 1970 at Simon Fraser University, Vancouver, where is now an emeritus professor. His books *D. H. Lawrence's Nightmare* (Harvester, 1978) and *The Neo-Pagans* (Macmillan, 1987) are studies of English writers around the time of the First World War. With George Landow, Delany edited *Hypermedia and Literary Studies* and *The Digital Word* (MIT Press, 1991 and 1993). His recent books are *Literature, Money and the Market from Trollope to Amis* (Palgrave, 2002) and *Bill Brandt: A Life* (Jonathan Cape, 2004). He is completing a biography of George Gissing.

JACQUELINE FURBY is a senior lecturer in film studies at Southampton Solent University. She is co-editor, with Karen Randell, of *Screen Methods: Comparative Readings in Film Studies* (Wallflower Press, 2006), and author of 'Rhizomatic Time and Temporal Poetics in *American Beauty*' in *Film Studies* (winter 2006). She is currently planning a co-edited collection, with Claire Hines, *A Queer Feeling: Reading Film against the Grain*.

CHRISTOPHER GAIR is a senior lecturer in the Department of American and Canadian Studies, University of Birmingham. He is the author of *Complicity and Resistance in Jack London's Novels* (Edwin Mellen Press, 1997), of *The American Counterculture* (Edinburgh University Press, 2007), and of numerous essays on American literature and culture. He has recently edited *Beyond Boundaries: C. L. R. James and Postnational Studies* (Pluto, 2006) and is the editor of the journal *Symbiosis*.

DANIEL HERBERT is a PhD student in Critical Studies at the University of Southern California. He has written reviews and essays for several journals, including *Film International*, *Film Quarterly*, and *Millennium Film Journal*. He is working on a dissertation about contemporary 'transnational remakes'.

JOKE HERMES' research interest is in issues of gender in popular culture and in cultural citizenship. Her latest book is *Rereading Popular Culture* (Blackwell, 2005). For over a decade she has co-edited the *European Journal of Cultural Studies*, founded by Pertti Alasuutari, Ann Gray and herself. At

Inholland University, Amsterdam, Netherlands, she develops qualitative research in public opinion formation.

DOUGLAS L HOWARD is assistant chair in the English Department at Suffolk County Community College in Selden, NY. His work has appeared in *Literature and Theology*, *The Chronicle of Higher Education*, PopPolitics.com, *The Gothic Other* (co-editor and contributor) (McFarland, 2000), and *This Thing of Ours: Investigating the Sopranos* (Wallflower, 2002).

DEBORAH JERMYN is a senior lecturer in film and television studies at Roehampton University. She has published widely on the representation of crime in film and television and is currently completing a book on real-crime TV, *Crime Watching* (I.B.Tauris, forthcoming). Her co-edited collections include *The Audience Studies Reader* (Routledge, 2002) and *Understanding Reality Television* (Routledge, 2004).

DAVID LAVERY is professor of English at Middle Tennessee State University and will soon join the Faculty of Film and Television at Brunel University in London. He is the author of over one hundred published essays and reviews and author/editor/co-editor of eleven books, including *Full of Secrets: Critical Approaches to Twin Peaks* (Wayne State University Press, 1995), *Reading* Deadwood: *A Western to Swear By* (I.B.Tauris, 2006), and *Reading* The Sopranos: *Hit TV from HBO* (I.B.Tauris, 2006). He co-edits the e-journal *Slayage: The Online International Journal of Buffy Studies* and is one of the founding editors of the new journal *Critical Studies in Television: Scholarly Studies of Small Screen Fictions*.

JANET McCABE is a research associate (TV drama) at Manchester Metropolitan University. She is author of *Feminist Film Studies: Writing the Woman into Cinema* (Wallflower, 2004), and is co-editor, with Kim Akass, of *Reading* Sex and the City (I.B.Tauris, 2004), *Reading* Six Feet Under: *TV to Die For* (I.B.Tauris, 2005), and *Reading* The L Word: *Outing Contemporary Television* (I.B.Tauris, 2006). She is managing editor of the new television journal *Critical Studies in Television* (MUP) as well as (with Akass) series editor of *Reading Contemporary Television* for I.B.Tauris.

TARA McPHERSON teaches courses in new media and popular culture in the University of Southern California's School of Cinema-Television. Before arriving at USC, McPherson taught literature, film, and popular culture at MIT. She is author of *Reconstructing Dixie: Race, Gender and Nostalgia in the Imagined South* (Duke UP, 2003), and a co-editor of the anthology *Hop on Pop: The Politics and Pleasures of Popular Culture* (Duke UP, 2003). Her writing has appeared in numerous journals and in edited anthologies. She is currently co-editing two anthologies on new technology, working on a book manuscript exploring the multimedia work of Charles and Ray Earnes, and recently launched *Vectors*, a new multimedia peer-reviewed journal. Co-organiser of the 1999 conference *Interactive Frictions*, McPherson is among the founding organisers of *Race in Digital Space*, a multi-year initiative supported by the Annenberg Centre for Communication and the Ford and Rockefeller Foundations. She is a member of the Academic Advisory Board of The Academy of Television, Arts and Sciences Archives, has served as an AFI (American Film Institute) Television Awards juror, is a member of HASTAC (Humanities, Arts, Science, and Technology Advanced Collaboratory), and is on the boards of several journals.

TORIN MONAHAN is assistant professor of justice and social inquiry at Arizona State University. Trained in the field of science and technology studies (STS), he researches the politics and design of technological infrastructures. He is author of *Globalization, Technological Change and Public Education* (Routledge, 2005) and editor of *Surveillance and Security: Technological Politics and Power in Everyday Life* (Routledge, 2006).

STEVEN PEACOCK is a senior lecturer in film and television studies at Southampton Solent University. He is the co-editor, with Sarah Cardwell, of 'Good Television?' for the *Journal of British Cinema and Television* (Edinburgh University Press, July 2006), and the author of *Colour: Cinema Aesthetics* (Manchester University Press, 2007).

SCOTT RUSTON is a PhD candidate in the Critical Studies division of the University of Southern California's School of Cinema-Television, where his research focuses on narrative forms of mobile and computational media, their intersection with cinema and television, and their potential in entertainment and education contexts. He holds an MA in Critical Studies from the University of Southern California and a BA in English from Northwestern University.

SHARON SUTHERLAND, BA, MA, LLB, LLM, is clinical instructor in dispute resolution at the University of British Columbia, in the Faculty of Law. She teaches mediation, negotiation and contract law, and practises as a child protection mediator. Sharon has collaborated with Sarah Swan on several other topics related to law and popular culture including papers on *Angel*, *Alias*, and *Trailer Park Boys*. Sharon's current research examines applications of drama and theatre to conflict resolution pedagogy and practice.

SARAH SWAN, BA, LLB, is a practising lawyer. She has collaborated with Sharon Sutherland on a variety of other law and popular culture topics, including essays on *Angel*, women lawyers on television, and *Alias*.

PAUL WOOLF is currently in the Department of American and Canadian Studies at the University of Birmingham (UK), where he is writing a PhD about depictions of Anglo-American love affairs in nineteeth-century fiction. His MA thesis looked at early detective stories and he has since published articles about Wilkie Collins, Arthur Conan Doyle, and film adaptations of Edgar Allan Poe's 'The Murders in the Rue Morgue'. Before returning to academia, Paul worked in the television industry, developing documentaries and entertainment programmes for, among others, the BBC and Discovery Channel, something he continues to do part-time.

REGULAR CAST LIST

Tony Almeida	Carlos Bernard
Jack Bauer	Kiefer Sutherland
Kim Bauer	Elisha Cuthbert
Teri Bauer	Leslie Hope
Bill Buchanan	James Morrison
Michelle Dessler	Reiko Aylesworth
Chloe O'Brian	Mary Lynne Rajskub
Curtis Manning	Roger R Cross
Nina Myers	Sarah Clarke
Mike Novick	Jude Ciccolella
David Palmer	Dennis Haysbert
Sherry Palmer	Penny Johnson Jerald

There will be time, there will be time
To prepare a face to meet the faces that you meet;
There will be time to murder and create,
And time for all the works and days of hands
That lift and drop a question on your plate;
Time for you and time for me,
And time yet for a hundred indecisions,
And for a hundred visions and revisions,
Before the taking of toast and tea.

T. S. Eliot (1888–1965)
'The Love Song of J. Alfred Prufrock', 1917
Prufrock and Other Observations

00.00
IT'S ABOUT TIME

STEVEN PEACOCK

00:00:00: STARTING THE CLOCK

It is fitting to start at the beginning, with a series of firsts, for this first critical collection on *24* (Fox, 2001–). First episode, first season, first sights and sounds of *24*. The programme has just started. It begins with little flashes and fragments, quickly collecting into a bigger picture. A sound strikes up: a clipped, rhythmic, repeated blip, like an electronic alarm clock chiming out seconds of time. A pulse of yellow light follows: single dashes flashing and forming into an LCD whole, into a display of multiple, digital '8's. Flares of light accelerate: there are fleeting signs of different numbers – '1', '5', '0'. Sound and light build in speed and intensity, growing from a blip and dash to glowing yellow digits and a fierce electronic fizz of white noise. The number '24' burns into the screen, instantly *branded* in the memory.

In seconds and in concentrated form, *24* announces many of its key concerns and distinctive features. It accentuates its interest in aspects of speed, intensity, precise measurements (of time), all expressed in a high-octane formula of visual and aural force. Even the style and type of the digits on display is precisely expressive of one of *24*'s chief preoccupations: the ubiquitous presence of the digital clock and associated forms of technology; their possibilities and limitations; our reliance on computers to mark and inform our daily duties. As Eliot's Prufrock measures out his life with coffee spoons, 24 shows us the necessity and dangers of living by the glare of liquid crystal.

A voice is heard. The gruff, low tones are distinctive, and faintly familiar. We know the voice, but cannot, just yet, place the face. (We only learn later, by association, that it is the voice of Kiefer Sutherland as central protagonist Jack Bauer.) Again, 24 hints at a concern to come, foregrounding questions of identity. At the same time, it annunciates its interest in the human voice. From this moment on, voices in 24 will be filtered, faked and sounded on myriad mobile phones or audio-links; recordings will be dubbed and doctored; words will seek to start and stop international wars. Equally, by privileging the use of the voice, 24 plays with established notions of television's form. Traditionally, as a descendant of radio, television is seen to place emphasis on the spoken word (over and above the image). Whilst asserting the voice, 24 places into disarray the idea that the TV image cannot hold its own, opening up a world of visual intricacy and intensity. Further, the words of the gruff, as yet nameless voice form a direct address to the viewer, another feature normally associated with television (seen and heard in all news and most documentary reports). Immediately then, 24 shows itself as skilfully taking advantage and pushing the boundaries of TV's features and formats.

As the first words of 24 are sounded out, corresponding text appears, in the same deep yellow hue of the numbers:

THE FOLLOWING TAKES PLACE BETWEEN MIDNIGHT AND 1:00 A.M., ON THE DAY OF THE CALIFORNIA PRESIDENTIAL PRIMARY.

Again, the programme announces its concern with specifics: of a particular time, period of time, place, and event. While the voice lends a sense of intimacy to the proceedings, the scale of the series' world is cast as increasingly expansive in space and status: the individual state of California; the election of a future President of the United States of America.

By dealing in the details, 24 takes a trick from Hitchcock. In *Psycho* (1960) and after Bass's credit sequence (another work of strips and streaks, of thrusts of light and sound), Hitchcock opens the film with the expansive view of a modern cityscape, and with the following titles, hurtling one after the other onto and off the screen:

PHOENIX, ARIZONA
FRIDAY DECEMBER 12
TWO FORTY-THREE P.M.

Hitchcock ties us, and the events of the film to follow, to a precise location, date and time. Senses are expressed of urgency, immediacy and, above all, suspense. On this day, in this town, something wicked this way comes, *just now*. And, just as we glide, inescapably, into the world of wickedness through the open window in *Psycho* (only to be released as a car is lifted from the muddy depths of a swamp in the closing moment), so too are we thrust, with urgency and immediacy, into the snare of *24*. First, the voice hails us, directs us, and *makes precise* the mechanics of the world. Then, it affirms that we will not be able to leave, to take a break or revisit less tense times, as it declares, 'EVENTS OCCUR IN REAL-TIME'. Even more so than in *Psycho*, we are to be caught and carried by a relentless momentum, a sustained movement forward, towards an inescapable end point, without prior knowledge of the shocks and surprises to befall us on the way.

While we quickly try to adapt to the promise and pressures of real-time, *24* hits us with a double-whammy, in its first glimpse of the wider world. A flourish of flutes and zithering strings announce the first images of the diegesis. A cityscape (*Psycho* again?) fills the frame in bold yellow shading. Again, *24* marks itself out through style, developing a distinctive palette of colours. Over the series and across seasons, *24* works with two overarching colour schemes, one for exterior and one for interior locales. As in this opening moment, exterior cityscapes are cast in amber, in dusty yellows and earthy tans, emphasising a sense of *exposure*, of being out in the open, or going to *ground*. When the action shifts inside, into the Counter Terrorist Unit's LA Headquarters, or into any number of offices, hideouts, sanctums and spy-holes, the colours shift accordingly, to deep blues and steely greys, in prisms of light and pools of darkness. These are *cool* spaces, defined by frosty *composure* and the latest blue-chip technology.

This time, an identity (of the city) is revealed, as the text states 'KUALA LUMPUR / LOCAL TIME / 4:00:29 P.M.' Perhaps as the first glimpse of its environs threatens to distract the viewer from the precision (and importance) of the time, *24* calls us back to the clock's counter with the shrill, metallic chime of seconds striking out. Matching this sense of tense assertion, the composition of the image is at once magnificent and foreboding. Two towers, twin towers, loom large in the centre of the frame. It is impossible not to see this moment of choice, this opening, as steeped in resonance. As will be explored in detail in the pages to come, 24 is, from inception, alert to the magnitude of feeling stemming from the events of 9/11. Through the seasons, it moves increasingly towards a direct address of this state, from a position of evocative closeness, from the outset, from the sight of these twin buildings.

As the credits begin to fade in and out (Kiefer Sutherland, Leslie Hope …), 24 asserts yet another, distinctive, hallmark strategy of style: the split-screen. For the viewer of this first episode, the effect is unexpected and surprising. The rug is being tugged away from under our feet (just as it will be pulled, time and again, with great force, in twists and turns of the narrative). All of a sudden, the full-screen image of Kuala Lumpur contracts to the top left-hand corner of the frame. 24 adds emphasis to this initial moment of movement by bleeding in a surging noise on the soundtrack, as if a heavy elevator door were quickly sliding shut, locking into place.

We're entering the world of 24. Predominant aspects and concerns of the series have asserted themselves, in crystalline form, in the opening moments. Key associations cluster together, at one and the same time: speed, intensity, questions of identity, the human voice, intimacy, immediacy, technology, exposure, composure, terror and terrorism, experimentation and innovation. Patterns gather again as the programme opens up its plot. As the right side of the frame opens up an image of the city's hordes bustling in a crowded marketplace, a single figure is picked out, moving into a murky hideaway. A tension makes itself manifest, between the ramshackle wooden surroundings of the hideout, and the sudden techno bleep of a laptop springing to life, and a phone connection being made. We hear the phone connect in a xylophonic scatter of electronic tones (just as we will come to know the distinctive ringtones and call signals of this ultra-connected world). In an atypical moment, 24 releases its earth-bound views to a shot of a satellite – taking and making the connection – as it arcs around the surface of the planet. Having seen this image once, we do not need to see it again to sense its significance: we are being watched, from afar, caught in a web of twenty-four-hour surveillance.

Crucially, the first diegetic word of 24 is a call for the lone figure to 'identify' himself. The above writing marks an attempt to give a preliminary account of some of the major points of 24's individual, ground-breaking, identity. Meanwhile, in Kuala Lumpur, the man with the laptop taps the keys, the signal is transmitted, and the plot begins.

Over the next 24 episodes, and across each season, we will encounter kidnapping, assassination attempts, nuclear detonations, political machinations, campaigns for international war, deadly viruses, and terrorism from around the globe. Each obstacle will be met by Jack Bauer as he crosses and recrosses the vistas of LA (and further afield), racing against the clock to save the day, each day. The purpose of *Reading 24* is to consider the dynamics, impact, status and forms of this most distinctive television drama, to chart these ebbs and flows, and, to mix metaphors to risk a final pun, to see what makes it *tick*.

01:00:00: CREDITS

Put simply, *24* is a cultural phenomenon. From the outset, the series garnered near-unanimous acclaim from critics and viewers alike. Chapter One of this collection begins by noting the series' measure of success in the USA; as such, I will not recount these details here. Rather, to give a sense of *24* as a cultural sensation, I offer an account of an exemplary, 'flashpoint' happening in Britain, encapsulating the series' impact. The broadcast and far-reaching influence of *24* led to the production, in 2002, of the BBC documentary *24 Heaven* (directed by Annabelle Waller). This 'one-off' documentary explores the zeitgeist quality of the show, examining the pop-mania effectuated by the series' arrival, the way *24* taps into the (inter)national psyche by taking the pulse of contemporary culture, and its garnering of both cult status and mainstream appeal. Indeed, the crossover ranking of *24* as both 'cult' and 'mainstream' continues to inform the wealth of fanzines, blogs and websites set up by devoted fans to discuss the show (examples of which are listed in the index; I encourage an hour or two spent exploring the passionate exegeses of the series offered by many of these sites).

The vast appeal of *24* and its ever-growing army of fans have also inspired spin-offs in other forms of media. Titan Books publish the UK edition of the US graphic novel of *24*, an official bi-monthly magazine, and an episode companion. If the collation of the DVD collection, favourite websites, graphic novels and magazines does not suffice, the fan can now also purchase *24* the Computer Game (Sony Playstation; Imagine Television; 20th Century Fox): 'Marksman, close-combat expert, ruthless interrogator, high-speed driver, counter-terrorism agent and protective father. Can you fill Jack Bauer's shoes?' Across all forms of entertainment media, the loyal fan is brought ever nearer to the hugely successful and influential world of 24, closer to 'being Bauer'.

02:00:00: TRUST NO ONE

But who exactly *is* Jack Bauer? For the characters of 24, the loyalty of the avid fan is replaced with a constant sense of disloyalty, distrust, deception and betrayal. You can never be sure who to trust; the 'true identity' of all players in the duplicitous war-games of 24 is never clear. Someone you were led to trust in the first two or twenty hours (two or twenty episodes) of the series may turn out to be a terrorist, a power-hungry turncoat, or, worst of all (in the world of 24), a mole. 24 is charged with multiple investigations into aspects of identity. Individual characters assume alternate identities to infiltrate the criminal lairs; equally, the many roles of the protagonists are held in tension and called into question – as parent, lover, leader, loyalist, liar – overlapping and clashing throughout. More implicitly, broader questions of identity are presented for our scrutiny. Social and sexual markers of identity inform the series, just as the series may appear *ill* informed in its location and handling of such matters. Female characters may appear to be placed in constant peril; anyone outside the WASP's nest may be stung by the series. As 24 is alert to its presentation of contemporary fears of terrorism stemming from 9/11 and the 'war on terror', it presents a fractured picture through the looking glass, appearing to tightly intertwine religious fervour and non-western characterisation. Yet, on closer inspection, it may be that 24 offers more than dastardly stereotypes of social, racial and sexual banding.

All of these matters are brought to the fore, of 24's style, status and sensibility, in the pages that follow.

03:00:00: ABOUT TIME

Part One of this anthology, 'Splitting the Screen: Rewriting Television Conventions', focuses on the dynamic aesthetics of 24, exploring particular aspects of its distinctive shape, structure, and style. Daniel Chamberlain and Scott Ruston start by situating 24 within the contemporary television landscape, considering its relationship with established notions of 'quality TV'. In doing so, they discover that whilst 24 does not share many of the generic traits that serve as markers for 'quality television', it challenges the existing definitions that inform this label, through its insistent use of certain stylistic and structural techniques, as well as in positing a particular ideological standpoint. Taking up the notion of 'all things televisual being potential markers of quality', Steven Peacock next provides a close, critical analysis of 24's points of style. Rather than meretricious flourishes standing at the behest of the narrative, 24's markers of style – split-screen, real-time, the appearance of the digital clock – are seen as crucial, expressive elements. Further, Peacock draws on textual readings of moments from the series to suggest that through a sensitive deployment of these stylistic strategies, 24 explores its status as a television programme. The next three chapters of the first section lead out of considerations of 24's style *in toto*, to address individual elements in detail. Michael Allen investigates the historical antecedents of the use of split-screen, as a means of better understanding the formal strategy and its particular application in 24. Deborah Jermyn also scrutinises the use of split-screen, but from a different perspective: considering how the stylistic device links spectator and characters, and promotes particular aspects of realism. Concluding this section, Jacqueline Furby investigates the demands that 24's real-time format makes on its audience. Through her analysis, Furby questions our understanding of time in television, and sees the use of real-time as central to 24's pervasive senses of pressure and anxiety.

Season One of 24 premiered only days after the terrorist atrocities of 11 September 2001. The series takes a 'no-holds barred' approach to reflecting and commenting on the atmosphere, post-9/11, of America's role on the world stage. Through each season, 24's plotlines engage directly with the 'war on terror', and the Republican administration's perceived 'agenda' in both domestic and foreign affairs. Part Two, entitled 'America under Siege: Terrorism, Globalisation and the Politics of (American) Morality', deals equally as directly with these matters of cultural currency. Paul Woolf starts the section with a revealing reading of the series' corporate sponsorship, as indicative of its relationship with matters surrounding the 'war on terror'. Woolf places 24 in the context of the heightened and ongoing post-9/11 political debate, and sees the debate as connecting US military action in Iraq, its dependence on foreign oil supplies, the environmental policies of its government, and the consumer habits of its population with regard to automobiles. Intertwining these various argumentative strands, Woolf considers 24 as entering most explicitly into the controversy and debate in its second season; as such, the chapter holds its attention there. Daniel Herbert also addresses Season Two, but from a distinct perspective. Addressing the overarching issue of 24 mirroring real-world political issues, Herbert considers the series as a 'nuclear narrative,' centring attention on Season Two's handling of the threat, and effectuation, of a nuclear explosion. Akin to Michael Allen's strategy of furthering an understanding of 24's forms by reaching back to earlier works, Herbert compares the series as 'nuclear narrative' via a previous television example: *The Day After*. A revealing historical shift is noted through the comparison, and in the narrative and aesthetic differences of the two works. The next two chapters are also bound as a 'diptych' of sorts, in their investigations of 24 as invoking a political 'state of exception'. Again centring attention on the second season, Anne Caldwell and Samuel A Chambers observe how, when read together, 24 and the theory of exception show us how American domestic politics and foreign policy function in a post-9/11 world. Taking up the debate, Torin Monahan adds considerations of how the current states and networks of neo-liberalism and global politics are explored in 24. In Monahan's chapter, the world of 24 (as our world) is seen as a place of 'absolute insecurities', constant crises, and extreme actions. The question of 'extreme action' is considered in greater detail in the final diptych of the section. From the perspective of legal scholars, Sharon Sutherland and Sarah Swan address the 'situational morality' on display in 24, as informing its depictions of extreme action as murder, self-defence, 'necessity for violence', vengeance and torture. Douglas L Howard concludes the section with a comprehensive cataloguing of the acts of torture that are performed in the world of 24. Addressing the registers and effects of physical cruelty that marble the series and seasons, Howard's chapter closes by questioning the moral implications inherent in the *escalation* of torture in 24. Whilst mirroring present-day political anxieties, 24 might be seen to offer 'fear-based wish fulfillment' of the darkest order.

Part Three attends to the unmasking of identities, investigating 24's representations of sexuality, the men and women of the series, and its handling of 'difference'. Starting from the assertion that Kim Bauer is a truly irritating character, seemingly possessing the most negative characteristics of the melodramatic 'damsel in distress', Janet McCabe argues that 24 provides more for the feminist television scholar than stock female protagonists. Tracing through the series, McCabe explores the struggle for female narrative authority, suggesting the battle faced by women in 24 as symptomatic of an uneasy post-feminist condition of cultural activism. Whilst sustaining the premise of 24 as a useful text for the feminist scholar, Joke Hermes turns attention to the male characters of the series, and in particular to that of Jack Bauer. Drawing together aspects of gender and genre, Hermes explores how 24's status as a generic hybrid (collating tropes from the Western, action movie, and noir thriller, to name but a few) informs and constructs Bauer's masculinity in unexpected ways. Holding attention on the forms of masculinity and hybridisation on display in 24, Tara McPherson sees the series as a 'techno-soap'. McPherson's chapter queries what role this new inflection of male melodrama might play in at once fixing and troubling masculinity in the era of global capitalism and national insecurity. In a change of tack, Paul Delany focuses on a minor female character, Chloe O'Brian. Focusing on O'Brian allows Delany to interrogate and question 24's handling of those existing on the boundaries, or standing outside the 'norm'. Unmasking different sets and markers of identity, the contributors to this final section draw on many distinct forms of identification within television: genre, gender, culture, race, nationality, stereotypes and 'stock figures', all as constructing borders and boundaries of difference. To bring the section, and the collection, to a close, Christopher Gair discusses the 'postnational American identities' on display in 24. The closing chapter binds the concerns of all three sections: aesthetic and structural, socio-political and cultural, in an analytical view of the principles and *values* on display in 24. A personal view of the series, from David Lavery, ends the anthology. With wit and flair, Lavery sees the series as a maddening, brilliant celebration of television, constantly 'jumping the shark' in its ascendancy.

As is expressed in the above overview, the concerns of each section and chapter will meet, from time to time, across the collection. This fact serves to show how the forms and issues of 24 work in *synthesis*: no one point of style or substance is divorced from the next; all work together in this fascinating and dynamic drama.

PART ONE
SPLITTING THE SCREEN
REWRITING TELEVISION CONVENTIONS

00.01

24 AND TWENTY-FIRST CENTURY QUALITY TELEVISION

DANIEL CHAMBERLAIN
AND SCOTT RUSTON

The television programme *24* is one of the rare series to enjoy critical and commercial success from its inception. Heralded by critics as 'engaging', 'innovative', 'stylish', and 'compelling', *24* was considered the best new programme in 2001 by *TV Guide*, earned a number of Golden Globe and Emmy nominations (winning an Emmy for Drama Writing), and has always performed satisfactorily in the ratings game, drawing over 11 million viewers for its premiere, around 8.6 million viewers each week in its first season and nearly 12 million viewers in subsequent seasons (James 2002a; Vogt 2003; Weeks 2001; 'Calendarlive' 2003). Stylistically bold, narratively engaging, culturally relevant, and blessed with commercial and critical success, *24* would seem to be a prime candidate for the canon of 'quality television' (Feuer 1984; Mulgan 1990; Thompson 1996), yet the programme has generally been left out of this category. Indeed, this chapter originated as a panel debate arguing *24*'s status as quality television at the American Quality Television Conference convened at Trinity College Dublin in April 2004. What became immediately apparent was that each of us could readily marshal arguments and rebuttals supporting our respective positions in the debate, but collectively found ourselves only circling the heart of the conundrum: 24 both seems like quality television and the farthest thing from it. In our discussions following the conference, we settled immediately upon two points of agreement: first, 24 is something different from its television peers, be they standard dramas or recognised quality programmes; second, the principle of a quality television genre was unsatisfactory, either as a method of inquiry into 24 or into the contemporary television landscape more generally.

The present chapter, then, is an exploration of 24's relationship to traditional notions of quality, arguing that while the show may fail along certain recognisable registers of quality, it should instead be seen as a programme that is actively challenging established markers for quality television in a manner that extends the genre. In so doing our chapter will also address the work that the designation 'quality' performs, both within the mainstream reception of television programmes and within the field of television studies.

The chapter focuses on three primary areas of consideration: the stylistic, the structural, and the ideological. We begin by situating 24 within the televisual landscape, examining how the programme's excessive style layers familiar cinematic tropes within a framework of contemporary videographic preoccupations. Next, the serialised and multi-threaded structure of the narrative is interrogated with regard to the trade-offs between open-endedness and closure. Finally, we analyse how the style and structure work against a seemingly conventional narrative to resist simple ideological closure. To varying degrees in each of these three cases, we find that 24 represents a break from traditional academic discussions of quality television. It does not share many of the generic traits which often serve as markers for quality television, and it is often fantastic and excessive in spite of its appeals to realism. 24 does, however, challenge the existing definitions of quality television through its insistent and innovative use of stylistic and structural techniques. By combining these formal machinations with contemporary ideological interventions, 24 effectively strikes new ground for quality television.

Before turning specifically to an analysis of 24, it will first be useful to briefly lay out the specific historical trajectory and familiar criteria of the term 'quality television'. The term first came to common usage by critics seeking to valorise the 'turn to relevance' that characterised the CBS programming of the 1970s and the Mary Tyler Moore shows of the 1970s and 1980s; this initial deployment of the term quality was explicitly normative, insisting that certain programmes were better than others (Williams 1994: 143; Thompson 1996). The term 'quality television' took on a more specific meaning when it was taken up by television scholars within the academy, as they attempted to determine the defining characteristics of programmes earning the quality distinction. Criteria for quality television range from the textual self-reflexivity and liberal humanism offered by Jane Feuer in MTM: *Quality Television*, to the ensemble cast, hybridity of serial and episodic structure, rich narrative complexity and bardic voice noted in such 1980s programmes as *Hill Street Blues*, to the 'wonderfully cinematic' qualities of the programmes of the late 1990s – like *The West Wing* and *The Sopranos* – praised by David Lavery at the 2004 American Quality Television Conference (Feuer 1984; Lavery 2004; Williams 1994). Robert Thompson, writing in *Television Quarterly*, concludes that by the 1990s 'quality television' had moved beyond a critical term negotiating economics and aesthetics and become a genre in and of itself. He further offers a lengthy and detailed list of the features of quality television, citing, in addition to the features mentioned above, the pedigree of a programme's producers, an appeal to a wealthy demographic, a notable diegetic history and memory, and a clear emphasis on realism. Beyond this, arguing that quality television had achieved a degree of maturity and stasis as a genre, Thompson writes, 'All of the innovative elements that have come to define 'quality TV,' even its unpredictability, have become more and more predictable. By 1992, you could recognize a 'quality show' long before you could tell if it was any good' (1996: 76–79). With this historical and critical backdrop, we can read *The Sopranos* and *The West Wing* as the quintessential example of the mature quality television genre. Both exhibit a decidedly cinematic visual style, hybridity of structure, a rich and complex character-based narrative, a generally liberal humanist presentation, the engagement of controversial and/or social issues, and a degree of textual self-reflexivity.

STYLE: RECUPERATING THE VIDEOGRAPHIC

The cinematic visual style is perhaps the most immediately evident characteristic of quality television, and one that is directly contested by 24's distinctive aesthetic style. In his book *Televisuality: Style, Crisis and Authority in American Television*, John Caldwell describes two types of visual style – the cinematic and the videographic – which had supplanted narrative depth as the primary feature of the majority of American television by the late 1980s and early 1990s. Generally speaking, exemplars of the mature quality television genre have announced their distinction with a clearly identifiable cinematic visual style that can be read as an intentional contrast to the videographic or blank style of standard television programming. 24, in contrast, deploys and emphasises both cinematic and videographic techniques in its style. If Caldwell is correct in asserting that 'style itself became the subject' of American television by the early 1990s (1995: 5), 24 is perhaps the salient example of this tyranny of style in the twenty-first century.

24's attention to cinematic style is immediately apparent in almost every scene. To begin with, the show is shot on 35mm film and framed for 16:9 widescreen presentations, media and format still more commonly associated with cinema than with the 4:3 aspect ratio of US television (Bankston 2004: 46–53). Like most contemporary Hollywood films, 24 is also free of the constraints of the stage. Approximately 70 per cent of the programme is shot on location, generally in locations in or near Los Angeles (Bankston 2004: 43). Even in those scenes shot on the stage, broad interior shots depicting office activity are juxtaposed with extreme close-ups in a manner that tends to emphasise the cinematic. Chiaroscuro lighting and masking shots accentuate many of the interior scenes as well, such as Jack Bauer framed by his office window (1.1) or Gael Ortega (Jesse Borrego) partially obscured by shadow in a stairwell while he plots his subterfuge (3.5). Such high production values for this type of series are not cheap, as evidenced by the approximately $4 million production budget for the pilot episode (Gallo 2001: 2). Even the production schedule attempts to employ cinematic references, as 24 is shot two episodes at a time, so that the crew is effectively making twelve 90–minute films each season (Bankston 2004: 43). As these examples suggest, 24 is clearly invested in presenting the cinematic visual features often praised in traditional 'quality' television.

What makes 24 unique, however, is the producers' embrace of videographic style. As understood by Caldwell, the videographic, which has its 'origins in electronic manipulation', exhibits hyperactivity and an obsession with effects; this style can readily be found in the layering of talking heads, graphics and backdrops on cable news providers such as CNN or MSNBC, in the information-dense presentation of sports on television, or in the hyper-edited sequences of so-called reality television programmes (Caldwell 1995: 12). Right from the start, 24 impressed audiences and reviewers with the foregrounding of video effects such as digital clocks, on-screen text, split-screens, and especially three, four, and five-image screens. Often in the four and five frame sequences, two of the frames show the same scene (Bauer at CTU Headquarters, for example) from different camera angles (medium long shot in profile and close-up frontal view), an arrangement that offers little additional narrational or character information, instead serving only to emphasise the extreme videographic style of the programme.

On the surface, it would seem that 24's embrace of the videographic would disqualify it from the canon of quality television. As the quality genre has taken shape, it has become axiomatic that quality television aims for an association with cinema as a superior art form to television. 24, on the other hand, seems to revel in its association with other media forms, particularly such cultural staples as news, sports, and 'reality' programming, as well as newer media forms such as the web page.

24's use of split-screens, for example, evokes television news and live sportscasts. Both of these forms use the split-screen to emphasise simultaneity of experience, whether during a crucial point of the game, or to unite geographically distant guests of a news programme. 24's on-screen clock is another obvious stylistic marker associated with live sports programming. Of course, 24, as a programme that purports to present its action in real-time, benefits from these televisual associations because these are the very types of programming that best support the ideological 'liveness' of television. As she deployed the term 'liveness' to emphasise television's fundamental disposition, Jane Feuer observed that the word live 'reverberates with suggestions of "being there ... bringing it to you as it really is"' (Feuer, 1983: 14). While obviously not live, 24 aims to forge what might be called a 'reality effect' by combining the visual markers of live television with a real-time narrative structure, attempting to connect the programme more closely with the rhythms of the viewer's life.

There is also an apparent correspondence between 24's appearance and an Internet web page aesthetic. In both cases, the screen bombards the viewer with information. A web page might have graphic hyperlinks, digital images, text and multiple hypertext links all vying for attention and implying that the viewer can access all of the world's information with a series of mouse clicks. Similarly, 24's split-screen bombards the viewer with information and carries a similar sense of hyperactivity. While it is tempting to read this as an example of television's anxieties regarding its own aesthetics, one instead might ask if the cable news programming and 24 are remediating the Internet web page aesthetic, or whether the Internet is simultaneously remediating videographic television and the newspaper. Recall that Caldwell identified a heavy emphasis on graphic effects, logos, and picture in picture, such as CNN's penchant for 'electronic feeds, image-text combinations, videographics, and studios with banks of monitors' (1995: 13) in the 1980s and early 1990s, long before the World Wide Web was a cultural phenomenon and object with its own aesthetics. As part of this television-Internet remediation loop, 24 emphasises videographic techniques that not only further 24's reality effect but also stylistically reference media forms – news, sports, reality shows, the Internet – which have not previously been associated with quality television.

24 may be the most videographic contemporary dramatic television programme because it not only deploys videographic elements as its signature style, it even goes so far as to feature its cinematic tendencies within a videographic framework. In 24, the cinematic sequences are often treated videographically, either divided on screen or overlaid by electronically manipulated graphics. The ticking clocks and split-screens, which found their way onto the show primarily to emphasise the real-time structural conceit and to make myriad telephone calls seem more interesting, are the core elements of a style that employs videographic elements not only as a distinctive stylistic flourish, but also directly in the service of the narrative structure. Indeed, these are the elements that set the programme apart from its peers and commanded early critical attention; the highly choreographed and explicitly cinematic shooting style is crucial to 24's visual impact, but it is the videographic stylistic markers that highlight the programme's ambitions. By foregrounding these visual elements, 24 actively promotes the videographic as a marker of its own quality, and thus troubling a definition of quality that privileges the cinematic. Moreover, 24's recuperation of the videographic goes beyond suggesting new markers of quality television, as these stylistic tropes can be further understood as a kind of televisual stylistic reflexivity. Instead of reaching toward another cultural form for legitimation, 24's deployment of excessive videographic style is an engagement and critique of twenty-first century television. If in the past television programmes had to pretend to be cinema in order to be considered worthy of distinction, 24 announces that televisual techniques have advanced to the point where quality can be found in televisual style itself.

STRUCTURE: PLAYING WITH TIME

Beyond 24's privileging of style, the programme's challenges to the norms of dramatic television go beyond the merely visual. Indeed, 24's narrative exhibitionism rests even more directly on the structural underpinnings of its real-time claims. The programme's coincidence of narrative hour and televisual programming hour hinges on a strictly serial presentation, as the last minute of each episode is understood to yield directly to the first minute of the next. Whereas the quality television genre has been recently made up of programmes exhibiting a hybrid of serial and episodic programming structures, 24's super-textual structure is staking a strong claim for the viability of a quality programme which emphasises seriality over the episodic. Ultimately, 24 goes so far to emphasise this structural conceit at every turn because the show's narrative tension is driven much more by its structure than through the complexity of its characters or plot.

First of all, the very title of the show, 24, privileges the hyperkinetic narrative structure. From *Hill Street Blues* to *St. Elsewhere* to *The West Wing* to *The Sopranos* typical quality fare emphasises the title characters or the ensemble linked by common mission and place (police precinct, hospital, White House or titular crime family). Notably, the show is not named *CTU* or *Agent Bauer* or any other subject, location, or organisation-type name. This may seem simple, but no 'quality' television programme comes immediately to mind in which the title doesn't foreground the *content* in some way. *Northern Exposure* and *Six Feet Under*, two examples that deviate somewhat from the place/character pattern, at least give some indication or comment on the content of the programme. In the case of 24, the emphasis of the title is on the narrative structure, the events of one day told one hour at a time.

Furthermore, the opening intertitle and voiceover reminds viewers 'Events occur in real-time.' Viewers cannot escape the emphasis on real-time, whether from the intertitle and voiceover, the ticking digital clock before commercial breaks, or the metronymic sound effect that accompanies the clock. This emphasis on time, accomplished largely through visual and auditory stylistic devices, is done to achieve a heightened sense of anxiety and suspense. Of course, real-time is also a conceit achieved through parallel editing and split-screens. In order to accommodate for the uninteresting real-time tasks, such as Bauer driving from one side of Los Angeles to another, the show shifts focus to one of any number of developing subplots, such as the intrigue between President David Palmer and his wife Sherry, the kidnapping of Kim Bauer, and CTU's office politics. Eliminating the real-time structure would not necessarily change the narrative content at all, but would significantly change the flavour of the show, eliminating one of its primary distinctions: the anxiety associated with the frenetically paced, networked, just-in-time lifestyle of the twenty-first century. The split-screens help navigate the rapid shifts across the network of subplots – the separate segments of any given storyline are usually played out in two- to three-minute blocks of screen-time spread across each episode – and the digital clock emphasises every passing second, all contributing to a hyperactive narrative style a step beyond Caldwell's notion of visual stylistic excess.

The intense pacing, emphasis on real-time and ticking clock all serve to bridge the week-long gap between episode broadcasts and keep the narrative unified in a serial manner. While early discussions of quality TV marginalised the serial form, particularly the melodrama or soap opera, in favour of more explicitly episodic programming, recent discussions have inverted this argument to show how serials can extend notions of quality. Betsy Williams has noted that a serial structure allows for richer character development on *Northern Exposure*, and suggests that most quality television since *Hill Street Blues* has been characterised by a hybridity of serial and episodic structure (1994: 148). This argument has held up well over the past decade, as the hybrid form has become the defining structural form of evening quality programming, evident in such celebrated hybrids as *The West Wing*. While these serials include regular episodic closure within broad story arcs, *24* strongly favours the serial over the episodic.

What sets *24* apart from other serial programmes, however, is that its serial format is circumscribed by its own promised closure. At the broadest level, the programme is repeatedly and forcefully insistent that each television season covers a single day of story time, so every narrative element of each season is constantly working with this closure in mind, in contrast to the open diegetic frontier available to other quality dramas. Complicating this promised closure is the emphasis on narrative openness that propels the story within and across consecutive episodes. In any given season of *24*, the programme is constantly inscribed by the tension between the openness of the two or three driving storylines for the entire season, the two or three ongoing minor storylines which get resolved and replaced every few episodes, the hour-by-hour cliffhangers timed so that multiple events coincide, and the closure promised by the completion of the day/season. This opposition of openness and promised closure (how many arcs can be opened when they must be closed by the end of the season?) creates a tension through structure, just as narrative creates a tension through plotting. Indeed, these are the very tensions that both drive and are underscored by the programme's aesthetics: split-screens reflect multiple storylines and narrative ruptures; ticking clocks and regular pronouncements of the show's real-time premise drive a sense of urgency and insist upon impending closure. This novel structural form, drawing on the openness of the traditional serial and the promised closure more common to episodic television or film, marks 24 as distinct from other TV programmes. Just as 24's stylistic tropes can be read as innovative pretensions toward the quality register, the foregrounding of the programme's structural parameters are also an attempt by the show's producers to mark their programme with distinction. As is the case with 24's style, these structural novelties put pressure on existing definitions of quality and can be read as a reflexive deployment and critique of broader twenty-first century television structures. In this manner, 24 calls attention to the obsessiveness of televisual time constraints and the compulsiveness with which these constraints are regularly attended.

IDEOLOGY: RESISTING CLOSURE AND EXPECTATIONS

Even as the stylistic and structural excesses of 24 may be understood as a unique form of self-reflexivity, an analysis of the narrative content reveals that, in this aspect more than any other, 24 deviates from the strictures of the quality television genre. As suggested at the beginning of this chapter, the quality television label has long been associated with programming that emphasises complex character-based narratives, a liberal humanist outlook, and the engagement of controversial issues. Such programmes typically present and develop their protagonists in a manner such that the viewer essentially trusts the characters to do what is right, and believes that the characters have a genuine interest in seeing that society is on a constant and progressive path toward improvement (exhibited, for example, in the education and enlightenment of Joel Fleischman [Rob Morrow] in *Northern Exposure* or the sure-handed guidance towards a better tomorrow of President Josiah Bartlett [Martin Sheen] and his staff in *The West Wing*). In turn, these characters are frequently seen addressing social, familial or political challenges within the space of a single episode. 24, on the other hand, provides a unique engagement with contemporary social issues explicitly because it rejects the familiar liberal humanism and narrative depth common to quality television. In the case of *24*, the narrative style, with its breakneck pacing and over-determined emphasis on liveness and simultaneity, tends to sacrifice depth, both of character and of story.

Yet *24* manages to use its thin narratives to great effect, particularly as it is able to provide an alternative perspective on the current events the programme continually evokes and evades. In terms of thematics and basic plots, each season of *24* has been concerned with an existential threat of great magnitude, from presidential assassinations to biological and nuclear warfare. Clearly operating in the shadow of the 9/11 attacks, and emerging at a time when society was consumed by the fear of global terrorism, *24* can even been read as the fictional treatment of the crisis of global terrorism in catastrophic terms; that is, the programme chooses not to present global terrorism as a crisis of consequential duration, and instead collapses it into a real-time, day-long catastrophe.

Moreover, while *24* generally approaches its themes of global terrorism and political repercussion within familiar registers of containment, the show recognises the complex and dispersed nature of these contemporary threats and resolutely refrains from offering complete, orderly solutions. Instead, the programme thematically foregrounds difficult choices and their conse-quences, emphasising the fractured nature of these threats with its stylistic and formal conceits. Just as global terrorism requires resistance at a multi-plicity of locations, so must *24* seek to contain its multiplicity of narrative threads – the programme literally splits the screen in order to accomplish this. All of this occurs within the compelling yet limiting context of a fiction-al television serial, one that is constantly inscribed by the tension between the openness granted by the show's serial nature and the promised closure that completes each season. As an extension of contemporary spy fiction (as with *Alias* for example), the show turns its gaze inward to suggest that the government may be too caught up in its own bureaucracy and self-interest to be unquestionably trusted with the protection of the citizenry from new glo-bal threats. As a technology-steeped melodrama (such as *The West Wing*), *24* explores the boundaries between public and private spaces, particularly con-cerning governmental use of surveillance technologies and the suspension of civil liberties. As a 'ripped-from-the-headlines' narrative of social rupture (like that of *Law and Order*), it collapses public threats with private interests to suggest that resolutions to such crises are problematic, and not without collateral damage. And as a programme with claims on the real – like the vast slate of reality television – it engages these issues in a formally progressive manner, marrying style and structure with content in a long-standing tradition of 'quality' or merit-worthy art. Further, in its hybrid relationship to these and other contemporary works of television, 24 both extends and complicates the assumptions surrounding 'quality' programming.

Rather than offering tidy solved-it-in-sixty-minute solutions to seemingly intractable problems, 24 instead prefers to hint at moral dilemmas, to suggest that all political actions have consequences, and to raise questions about whom to trust in a political crisis. Bombs explode on 24; citizens die; suspects are tortured; and naked political machinations lurk behind most decisions. This might not be a very humanist manner of engaging with contemporary world issues, but it does suggest the gravity of the stakes and the consequences of our political choices.

CONCLUSION: CONTESTING QUALITY TELEVISION'S BOUNDARIES

24 is full of excesses, with its demonstrative emphasis on style, its eponymous and continuously referenced structure, and its convoluted and irresolute narrative. 24 could be accused of elevating style over substance, sacrificing character development even to the point where the structure of the narrative becomes more important than the content of the narrative itself. Yet the tug-of-war within each of these registers also indicates how 24 taps into the multiple modes and affordances of the televisual medium. Geoff Mulgan writes: 'television can only escape from the problems of aesthetics when it erases its nature as a medium and offers unmediated access to such things as sport and political events' (1990: 17). On this count, 24 is trying to have it both ways, emphasising its aesthetics while simultaneously insisting on a reality effect and an illusion of liveness. In the process, not only does 24 demonstrate, even celebrate, the aesthetic range of television, it also reflexively highlights television's very nature as a medium.

Additionally, the stylistic experimentation of the show is exemplary of the traditional quality register of reflexivity, but instead of simply presenting textual references, the reflexivity in 24 can be located in its hyper-awareness of its status as Internet-age television. Enacting the networked and real-time lifestyle of the twenty-first century, 24's reflexive 'knowingness' is not simply a wink to previous television shows (like *Arrested Development* or the aggressively intertextual and self-reflexive *The Simpsons*) or pop culture (like *Gilmore Girls*) or even to itself (like *The OC*), but a more encompassing deployment of the serial format, a mobilisation of the ideology of liveness, and capitalisation of the excess of televisual style all marshalled in a direct challenge to the predictability of the quality television genre.

Ultimately, the term 'quality television' is a judgemental one, whether deployed in a critical context or within academic considerations of television genres. *24* is of interest to this debate not because it fits neatly with pre-existing notions of quality, but precisely because it challenges and extends the space of the term 'quality television' itself. In this expanded space we must not only consider new markers of quality, such as videographic styles and narrative structures, but we should attempt to gauge how these formal features might yield fresh ideological and reflexive perspectives. More directly, this argument raises questions about how the embrace of 'televisuality' can shatter the deference to cinema and the consequences of all things televisual being potential markers of quality.

24: STATUS AND STYLE

STEVEN PEACOCK

TELEVISION AS TELEVISION

The concerns of this chapter stem from two overarching claims for particular accomplishments of the serial drama *24*. First, that the series achieves richness from the way it embraces the attributes of its status as a television programme. Elements such as the strictness of hourly slots in the schedule, the sense of the broadcast's 'immediacy', and the interposition of commercial breaks are not considered by *24* as restraints, or as traces of television to be concealed in order to attain 'quality' status via a connection with 'the cinematic' (Caughie 2000: 132). Rather, they are seen as valuable factors of presentation, crucial to the development of the programme's concerns, and bound by a careful handling of its points of style.

This leads to the second claim, for the dynamic and expressive use of stylistic techniques in *24*. Whilst praising *24* for its innovative structure and fast pace, many critics discuss the programme's style in a somewhat cursory (if not pejorative) manner. In *Sight and Sound*, Rob White suggests that, 'The visual techniques in *24* – particularly the use of split-screen – are purely functional, subservient to the onward rush of the story' (2002: 7). Whilst acknowledging that the programme's stylistic strategies contribute to the 'rush' of the series, this chapter claims a much more central role for these devices. Rather than appearing piecemeal as 'subservient' flourishes – to boost the drive of the narrative – the techniques form crucial, expressive elements. Particular points of style – split-screen, the use of real-time, the on-screen appearance of the digital clock – are shaped into precise arrangements, and used at specific points. Through its application and synthesis of these techniques, the programme expresses its thematic concerns.

Equally, and drawing the claims together, it is through a sensitive deployment of these stylistic strategies that 24 explores its status as a television programme. The style of the programme both highlights, and provides an inquiry into, certain aspects of television. In particular, and providing the focal point of the chapter, 24 shapes its style to draw on aspects of television's (sensed) liveness, immediacy, and, above all, the expressions of intimacy afforded by the TV image.

Particular points of style, and particular aspects of 24's expressive understanding of TV traits can be detailed through close analysis of moments from across different seasons of the series. In the first of these instances taken up by this chapter (from 1.2), 24 uses split-screen and real-time to convey the suddenness of shifting events. On the telephone, and attempting to convey the importance of tightening security around presidential candidate David Palmer, CTU agent Jack Bauer receives another incoming call on his cellphone from his boss, Richard Walsh (Michael O'Neill). The identity of the caller is unexpected; Bauer anticipates it to be his wife. Walsh has been ambushed, and calls for Bauer's assistance. As 24 moves through the moment in various combinations of split-screen panels, it conveys the characters' jolts of surprise, drive and anxiety. The full-screen image of Bauer only gives way when he recognises the voice (and tone) of the caller. As the screen splits to share the men's images, Bauer gives Walsh his *undivided* attention. As Walsh explains the full extent of his jeopardy, 24 doubles the images of the hunted agent. Finally, as a gunshot rings out, a split-screen of both men is suddenly broken as the image of Walsh vanishes to black.

To restate one key concern, I believe this moment exemplifies 24's precise arrangement and timing of the split-screen effect. The technique does more than contribute to the 'rush' of the story: it *is* the story. The programme chooses to use the technique at just this point, to weight the moment and to express particular ideas about the characters' relationships and situations. Most simply, the use of split-screen allows 24 to connect disparate spaces, places and characters in the same frame, at the same time.

This effect reinforces the sense of the scenarios' simultaneity. It bolsters the programme's use of real-time, declaring that all these events are happening at precisely the same time, are happening *now*: as Sutherland-as-Bauer states in voiceover at the beginning of the first series: '*Right now*, terrorists are plotting to assassinate a presidential candidate.'

At the same time, the moment is indicative of the way 24 plays with associations of television's liveness, or, more precisely, the 'assumed liveness' of the broadcast. As John Ellis declares, 'The broadcast TV image has the effect of immediacy. It is as though the TV image is a 'live' image, transmitted and received in the same moment that it is produced' (1982: 132). In the moment described, 24 points up the immediate transmission and reception of a television broadcast by emphasising, in tandem, corresponding factors of another form of electronic communication, the telephone. With directness and immediacy, the telephone connects the characters aurally as, for the viewer, the split-screen connects them through space, visually. Throughout the series, from season to season, 24 is particularly sensitive to the co-relationship of these matters. In the above instance, the abrupt introduction and connection of the image of Walsh also displaces the shot of Bauer. The quick shift suggests how Bauer is suddenly placed 'off-course' by the call (expecting, as he does, to hear his wife's voice on the end of the line). The unexpected interruption of Walsh's cry for help is expressed as a visual irruption into the space on screen. Equally, at the end of the sequence, Walsh is abruptly 'cut off' from the call. As the connection suddenly vanishes in a rattle of gunfire, so too does the image of Walsh from the split-screen. In turn, the abrupt loss of a link between two characters is coupled with the viewer's own sense of momentary disengagement from the sight of the person on screen. The force of the disconnection emphasises the fragility of a live telephone link, and the strength of the characters' dependency on this form of communication.

In this way, the split-screen is used not only to create links and connections, but also to emphasise, at precise points, the physical distance between the characters. 24 uses the assertion and disruption of a direct (live) connection to point up a sense of the characters' helplessness, of their fear of not knowing, and of not being able to see, what is happening to their friend, or partner, or daughter. Through a careful juxtaposition of style and situation, the programme gives the viewer a sense of the immediacy of this experience, whilst expressing the characters' own shifting sensations of closeness, distance, frustration and separation.

A further set of examples illustrates a corresponding use of the split-screen, expressive of the way 24 handles the point of style to convey its characters' sense of their own predicaments. In 3.1, despite heralding a new beginning and long-awaited return to our screens, the series holds off its hallmark use of the split-screen until halfway through the episode. Even then, it limits the strategy to envision only phone-calls between key characters. In each case, a full-screen image of Bauer retracts, shrinking in size, moving into the top left of the frame, to make way for multiple panels of disparate events and characters: the President's limo in a cavalcade; CTU headquarters; drug baron Ramon Salazar (Joaquim de Almeida). As well as bringing the protagonists together, the synchronous reduction of space for Bauer's image and the addition of surrounding scenarios expresses a sudden, mounting sense of pressure for the CTU agent. This is perhaps best demonstrated in the scene where Bauer retreats to his office, desperately fighting to resist injecting himself with heroin (a habit picked up whilst working undercover with the Salazars). Shrinking the frame of Bauer's view to make way for further, split-screen images, 24 captures overlapping expressions of pressure: the impulsive, addicted contraction of thoughts (to nothing but the drug); a claustrophobic sense of restriction, before the release of the fix; a sense of shame, of being *belittled* to and by this situation. Further, the conjoining split-screen images all speak of Bauer's mounting responsibilities: Palmer; his daughter, Kim; Salazar. In these instances of its use of split-screen, 24 gives us Bauer's world-view, as it alters, moment by moment.

In the closing shots of all the above examples, the clustering of split-screen panels also introduces another crucial point of style in 24: the appearances of the digital clock. The clock appears at regular intervals, before and after commercial breaks, and through fades. Most simply, it reminds us of the time, of 24's use of real-time (just as the characters do – to us, to each other – when they declare specific pieces of information and business will be ready 'within the hour'). The clock shows us how much time has gone in the hour of the episode, and thus increases the sense of urgency. Yet, I claim that the clock does more than this, that the appearances themselves of the digital display are carefully timed. I want to make two particular points here, about the use of the clock in the programme as a whole.

First, we can note how the sight and sound of the clock reappearing after each commercial break most often coincides with a re-grouping of all the different scenarios and principal characters of the programme into different blocks of one, split-screen. Whilst the use of the clock reminds us of, and builds up, the pressures of time, *24* concurrently *compresses* the action, clustering the characters together. Secondly, we can also consider the programme's decision to bookend the commercial breaks with the appearance of the clock. The appearance and reappearance of the clock before and after the breaks shows us that the digits appear to change in accordance with the length of the commercials. This fact creates a significant tension between the (diegetic) activities of the characters, and our own activity, of watching the television. That is to say, under normal circumstances, the announcement of a commercial break signals an opportunity for us to detach from the programme, to re-settle, or chat, or make a cup of tea, or even, heaven forbid, mark time by watching the commercials! However, *24* twists this conventional situation, to a subtly unsettling effect. There is a sense of the world of *24* carrying on 'behind the veil' of the commercials. So, if we accept this effect (whilst acknowledging the distinction of matters factual and fictional), it suggests that whilst we yawn or make that cup of tea, CTU and myriad innocent bystanders are still in danger, with Jack Bauer still running, as the clock ticks down.

The most striking example of this tension occurs in 1.9. Whilst being held in captivity, Bauer's wife, Teri, is raped by one of her captors. *24* chooses to elide the scene but, on returning from the commercial break, makes clear that the attack has taken place. The viewer watches the commercials knowing that time is still ticking away in the world of *24*, and knowing the dreadful truth of Teri's ordeal. Far from diluting the effect of the situation, the programme's handling of the scenario lends it an even more disquieting edge. Our commonplace activities – making snacks, throwing off-the-cuff jibes at the inanity of the commercials – are now held in simultaneous tension with the unseen, unspoken terror of the assault. Again then, *24* is not only aware of its status as television, but uses certain attributes of the medium to expressive effect. That is to say, the stipulation that all (American) network television programmes must accommodate the intrusion of commercial breaks becomes a positive factor in *24*, contributing directly to the serial's form and content.

Yet, *24* is not just alert to the expressive potential of television's 'assumed liveness', or the simultaneity of events on and off screen. Other, related achievements of the programme can be highlighted through a return to the ideas of John Ellis, who notes that, 'The immediacy of the broadcast TV image does not just lie in the presumption that it is live, it lies more in the relation that the image sets up for itself. Immediacy is the effect of the directness of the TV image, the way in which it constitutes itself and its viewers as held in a relationship of co-present intimacy' (1982: 132). In 2.24, the series creates a moment that draws upon these ideas, of the 'directness of the TV image', and 'the way in which it constitutes itself and its viewers as held in a relationship of co-present intimacy.' In this climactic moment, all attention focuses on a 'sting' operation, organised by Bauer, involving Palmer's (now ex) wife Sherry. The duplicitous and desperate Sherry must work to extract a confession from the criminal kingpin, Peter Kingsley (Tobin Bell), of his involvement in a plot to overthrow Palmer's presidency and to start an international war. Bauer and Sherry use the whereabouts of another man – Alex Hewitt (Rick D Wasserman) – as a bargaining tool.

As the scenario unfolds, 24 emphasises a sense and threat of exposure in its choice and handling of location. Whereas many events and affairs of the programme take place in the spot-lit spaces of CTU headquarters or under cover of night, here the climactic moments come in the harsh morning sunshine, and in the open expanse of an empty sports arena. Sherry, seeking to expose Kingsley's criminal involvement is herself an (unwitting) open target of a sniper, positioned atop the arena. If Kingsley admits responsibility (into the hidden microphone), his position will be exposed to all the key players of CTU and the US government, all listening in on an audio-link. If Sherry falters in her act of bargaining with the (dead and absent) figure of Hewitt, she will be assassinated.

Again, 24 draws on a sense of liveness to add to the suspense and urgency of the moment. As the substitute president, Jim Prescott (Alan Dale), declares, he'll abort a military attack, 'if we've received confirmation that this [conversation between Sherry and Kingsley] is in fact live ... ' 24 bolsters the effect by clustering the characters together in split-screen. The choice to move to split-screen at just this point stresses not only the simultaneity and connectedness of the protagonists' situations, but also emphasises the shared nature of the point of focus, with all involved concentrating intently on the intricacies of Sherry's negotiations. Here, viewer and characters come together, as *24* increases the impact of the moment (as an apogee) by emphasising the *shared* attention of all those involved in its broadcast and reception. As we, as viewers, tune in at a specific time to watch together as the events of the climactic episode unfold, the central protagonists of the second series gather together, all connected by their 'live audio-links', listening to Sherry's dealings with bated breath. As the television audience hangs on every word of the conversation, so too does the sniper atop the pillar, and the amassed agencies of power awaiting their cue. In this way, *24* orchestrates a moment of global proportions in an intimate fashion. Those viewing and those being viewed connect as part of a co-present, unseen audience, all monitoring (aurally, visually) Sherry's attempts to stop a war.

WAYS OF VIEWING

As the above analysis has shown, *24* demands and rewards our close attention to detail. Whilst following some of John Ellis' claims regarding broadcast TV, *24*'s own attention to detail troubles his assertions on the nature of the viewer's relationship with the TV image. Ellis states that, 'TV does not encourage the same degree of spectator concentration [as cinema]. There is no surrounding darkness, no anonymity of the fellow viewers, no large image, no lack of movement amongst the spectators, *no rapt attention*' (1982: 128). Ellis is describing a particular kind of relationship between viewer and television that, 'implies that no extraordinary effort is being invested in the activity of looking' (1982: 137). *24* demands a renegotiation of this relationship. It encourages the viewer, moment to moment, to pay close attention to all details on display, placed across the split-screens. In the continuing twists and turns of each season, *24* entreats us to focus on each fleeting glimpse and glance, on décor, trappings and gestures, on passing features and facial expressions.

A case in point is the series' handling of its greatest villainess, Nina Myers. As David Thomson remarks of Season One (in a suitably oblique style), 'Watch Nina's face, it is the mouse in this computer' (2002a: 4). So, let us play cat to the mouse, and consider two passing views of Nina from 1.1. The first moment occurs as Bauer enters CTU headquarters for the first time. On seeing Nina as he walks in, he ends a telephone conversation with his wife. He then issues orders to Tony Almeida to collate 'detailed biographies of everyone on Senator Palmer's staff, *now*'. In an oft-repeated bit of business in *24*, orders are first debated (as to how they might be construed) and then, begrudgingly yet skilfully, followed. As Bauer moves away from the workstation, Nina pauses under the blue glow of a display screen, eyes darting down and left. In her hands she slowly, methodically tilts and twists a pen (just as she will turn the screw on Bauer, for two seasons to come). In a later moment, a split-screen shows Bauer (left panel) again on a mobile phone talking to his wife (right panel). In the background (left panel), Nina slowly slides into view, positioned (for the viewer) between husband and wife, eyes tilting up into the glare of an overhead light and quickly down again. A flicker of divisiveness is marked, even as it passes.

In both instances, the programme integrates the sight of Nina in 'the bigger picture' whilst allowing us, if alert, to *be* alert to the illumination of her eyes. On both occasions, Nina is positioned within the harsh architecture of CTU headquarters, surrounded by the fracturing geometrical lines of steel columns and glass divides. Pools of light allow for bright spots and shadows, to point up and conceal each agent's business as they work. In both moments, 24 further fragments this high-tech mosaic of lines and lights, by splitting the screen into distinct panels of activity. Within all the splits and divides, Nina is positioned in front of a brightly lit LCD screen (blue and green, displaying a map of LA – further fragmented into blocks and borders). Equally, whereas Bauer's face remains darkened as he stands in a pocket of shadow, Nina stands in the glow of the beam. Thus, particular points of illumination are fleetingly noted, amidst the obstacles, designs and *trappings* of the surrounding décor.

In both instances, 24's decision to include a fleeting glimpse of Nina's glance raises complex questions of interpretation. To put it most simply, what is the cause of Nina's furtive look, and how do we interpret the look itself? To offer a few readings: on one level, Nina is apparently curious about the state of Bauer's relationship with his wife, due to the fact that Nina and Bauer have had an affair. So the glance may be tinged with bitterness or jealousy. On another level, Nina's reaction to events can be seen to reflect our own. Standing under the glare of the HQ lights, she is being 'kept in the dark' by Bauer. It could be argued that, at this point of Season One, and in the way that the moment is handled, we are aligned with Nina. Yet, oh yes, with the glorious benefits of hindsight, there are other, lurking reasons for that dart of the eyes, reasons that become piercingly clear as the series develops and concludes. The nuances of a single glance from Nina can only be fully appreciated if *we* stop glancing at the television screen, and start paying it close attention. *24* disallows casual viewing, requiring and rewarding our sustained focus.

An understanding of Nina's glance also points to two other related achievements of the programme. First, that *24* intelligently and meticulously constructs each moment to contain the possibility of multiple readings. That's to say, the programme captures a sense of ambiguity and a threat of duplicity in each passing instant. It balances each moment to allow for, and to encourage, many different interpretations of a single action. Second, that *24* creates each scene so as to be dynamic on a second or third viewing. The more information I have of individual scenarios, and of the outcome of the 24 hours, the more the morals and motives of each character shift kaleidoscopically around.

These opportunities for multiple viewing opportunities are made ever more readily available to the contemporary TV audience. First, an episode may be viewed again in the form of repeat broadcasts on network television (with repeats of the latest *24* instalment running almost daily, at the time of writing, on Sky One in the UK). Secondly, there is the availability and increasingly popular option of purchasing and viewing the entire series on DVD. Next, the Internet offers the chance to download episodes to view at leisure. Further, with the technological advancements and possibilities offered by digital home systems such as Sky Plus, the viewer is presented with the opportunity of pausing live television, and rewinding to watch a moment again (and again). In returning to *24* on repeat broadcast, disc, download, or instant rewind, the viewer can appreciate more fully the attention to detail in the series' visual compositions. Pausing and rewinding points of the series, shuttling to and from different moments, we can discern how (and savour the sense of knowing that) a detail or gesture caught on the periphery of the frame (a glance, a glimpse of information) becomes crucial to the unfolding scenarios of the series; equally, we can appreciate the way *24* builds to pivotal twists and turns, thickening the plot and heightening the tension, taking a scenario to breaking point before performing a volte-face for characters and viewers alike.

In this sense, *24* is instructive in the ways we watch and talk about television. In rewarding close attention and multiple viewings, the series negates the 'glance' relationship historically ascribed to the television viewer and the small-screen image. Moreover, the programme's concentration of detail encourages us to involve ourselves in a concentration *on* detail, to hold attention on the particular stylistic strategies and achievements of the series a little longer (even as the drama rushes on). In this way, we can consider the intricacies of *24*'s designs, appreciate its sensitivity to the relationship of form and content, and understand more fully the series' handling of its status as a work of contemporary television.

00.03
DIVIDED INTERESTS
SPLIT-SCREEN AESTHETICS
IN 24[1]

MICHAEL ALLEN

INTRODUCTION

24's split-screen technique has been hailed as one of the show's more innovative and interesting features. American television critic David Bianculli has linked its use to the show's excessive narrative demands: '24 is so crammed with action, information, subplots and subtext that the screen barely can contain it all. Lots of times, in fact, the images separate, breaking into split-screen to impart even more events, points of view or camera angles at once' (2001: 100). The series has also been likened to recent films such as Mike Figgis' *Timecode* (2000), made the year before the first season of 24 aired, which showed its four, simultaneously unfolding, narratives in split-screen quadrant panels and in continuous time (Talen 2002).

Seen by some critics, such as Tim Goodman in the *San Francisco Chronicle*, as an audacious gimmick to attract attention, others, like Sean Weitner, claim 24 presented something new and interesting:

> I'm not sure how well all this split-screen works. I commend the audacity of the filmmakers to try it, and, to be sure, having more than one camera capturing the same movement is proving to be effective at a strictly graphic level. I doubt we can expect transcendent use of split-screen, but, again, points for audacity. [2001]

To be sure, the foregrounding of such an aesthetic, in partnership with its central real-time-pressure concept, was undoubtedly a strategy designed to make 24 stand out from other quality American television dramas as a distinctive product at the start of the new millennium. But I hope to prove that the aesthetic has a more serious purpose and a far richer heritage than the situating of it as a gimmick would suggest.

Stephen Boyd Davis argues that:

> The attributes of television news space include the following:
> symmetry: pairs of presenters sit together at a desk, or as a diptych
> where a presenter and a correspondent each occupy their own
> frame ... multi-segmentation: the display comprises more than
> one component, organised both as panels across the surface and
> in layers; multimodality: a typical display uses text, graphics, film,
> animation and so forth. In addition, many television news pictures
> are ambiguous, toying with our inability to work out exactly what
> we see or precisely where things are, whether something is real or
> a pictorial fiction, flat or three-dimensional. Above all, it is overtly
> representational: viewers cannot possibly forget that they are being
> presented with the material. It is often remarked that the pace of
> television news has altered in the last, say, thirty years ... perhaps
> justifying John Caldwell's epithet of 'acute hyperactivity'. But
> equally significant, as Caldwell extensively documents, is the shift to
> 'excessive stylisation and visual exhibitionism.' [2003]

Boyd Davis neatly itemises many of the visual characteristics of 24: the double panel of news anchor and field reporter in discussion (for which read two characters talking face-to-face or conducting a phone conversation); the mix of multiple images and text (the moving image panels and digital clock, or the many diegetic screen displays); visual ambiguity (panels often show partial objects or uncertain movements); and its overtly self-referential nature in terms of its foregrounded graphic qualities and its furious and relentless pace (an explicit feature of the show). In all of these features, 24 could be seen to be explicitly mimicking the televisual format closest to its own subject matter: twenty-four-hour rolling news reportage.

This aesthetic approach shares similar qualities with other multi-screen displays and visual iconography of the modern media age. 24's split-screen aesthetic can also immediately be seen as a representation of the multi-screen surveillance technologies that are central to the operations of both CTU and the enemies it is attempting to defeat. Mugshots of the terrorists are displayed in the separate windows of a CTU computer database; unfamiliar landscapes are negotiated using handheld GPS (global positioning system) devices; debriefing interviews are recorded using multiple camcorder video screens. The co-ordinator of the villain's plot, Ira Gaines (Michael Massee), is shown at one point in the first season to have remote control over the four-panelled CCTV system at the hospital where Teri Bauer and 'Alan York' (Richard Burgi) are searching for their daughters; this enables him to force Jack Bauer to leave the hospital and submit to his demands (1.6). To such an extent, therefore, the split-screen aesthetic of 24 can be seen to simply be echoing the media-rich, technological world of the show itself, in which everyone is making use of multiple window imaging systems to keep track of everyone else.

Focusing primarily on Season One, this chapter argues that the use of split-screen in 24 is both strategic in support of its narrative and character concerns, and that this usage draws upon a long lineage of multi-panel aesthetics stretching back centuries within western culture. As such, 24 becomes the latest incarnation of a specific way of reading meaning between discrete framed images that is quite distinct from the linear single-frame narrative image that has come to dominate western film and television dramatic forms.

MULTI-PANELS I: DIPTYCHS, TRIPTYCHS AND POLYPTYCHS

In his article on television news aesthetics just cited, Boyd Davis makes reference, almost in passing, to the medieval diptych, a two-panel visual representation of an aspect of medieval power relations or religious belief. The panels of a diptych, triptych (three-panelled) or polyptych (multi-panelled) are designed to fold out, gradually revealing the narrative progression across all panels. For example, in Grunwald's *Isenheim Altarpiece* of 1515, its closed position shows the Crucifixion in the central panel and saints in flanking panels. Opening the panels reveals representations of stages in Christ's narrative, such as the Annunciation and the Resurrection (Mellinkoff 1988: 4–6). Although the 'action' of the narrative is sequential, in that it describes stages in the story of Christ, rather than suggesting simultaneous time as in 24, the process of inferring narrative connection across the guided revelation of events framed in panels is similar.

Many diptychs took the form of two painted panels hinged together which when opened would allow a cord to be strung between them. With the aid of hour lines stamped into the surface of the panels, the diptych could, when oriented correctly in terms of the sun, be used to tell the time. Here we find an intriguing combination of visual image and timepiece used to represent a summation of temporal condition and worldly reality. There is a close correlation, I would argue, between this and the multi-panelled images and digital clock which regularly recapitulate the current status of the 24 narrative; they are separated by several centuries but essentially performing similar tasks in terms of telling time within a specific visual context.

Intriguingly, the diptych could also be used for writing, the two hinged panel tablets holding a layer of soft wax onto which messages and records would be temporarily etched using a small stick, before being smoothed clean, ready for the next entry. More ambitious records could also be stored with the addition of extra panels to form triptychs, or even polyptychs. It is tempting to see this written usage as a precursor to the multi-panelled screens accompanying the digital clock which ushers in each post-advert break of each episode of 24; the summary record of 'the story so far' appearing temporarily, before being replaced by new events, only for those events to appear summarised in multi-panel form after the next commercial interruption.

MULTI-PANELS II: EARLY CINEMA

In the early, more formally open (because not yet strictly systematised), era of cinema, directors would often experiment with frames within frames as a means of negotiating the conceptual problems of how to represent space and time in cinematic terms. This becomes especially intriguing in terms of 24 when telephones are used to link the spaces and suggest simultaneous time. In the 1901 British film Are You There?, for example, two lovers, supposedly far apart, talk via the telephone as the wall edge cuts the frame into left and right halves, producing the effect of a split-screen. The technique is found again, more fully developed, in the film Suspense (1913), the drama of a woman threatened by an intruder, phoning her husband to come to her rescue. At the film's climax, the frame divides into three triangles, each showing one of the three central protagonists: the woman and her husband helpless at either end of the telephone while the intruder approaches the house. The tension is heightened by the viewer's ability to simultaneously see all three characters; to witness that which is invisible to the couple talking on the phone.

The foregrounded use of the telephone as a mechanism to quickly connect disparate narrative elements and thereby forward the plot, has a striking parallel to 24, where landline and mobile phones are continually in use to keep characters and plot strands interconnected: 'Director Stephen Hopkins says he first got the idea for 24 because "there were so many phone calls in the script that these people would never share any screen-time together … I loved the idea of showing what people were saying on the phone but also what they didn't want other people to see"' (Talen 2002).

In all of these examples, the temporal simultaneity of communication enabled by the telephone – still a novelty in 1901, and even by 1913, as mobile phones might be said to have still been in 2001 – is figured in the use of split-screen, to show both parties existing and interacting *at the same time* within the same frame, rather than consecutively as in traditional film grammar. This temporal simultaneity, a pleasure of convenience in the Williamson example, becomes, as in *Suspense*, an urgent necessity in 24, in which characters' lives depend upon their ability to reach one another by phone; a pressure which is dramatically figured in the splitting of the normally unified single television frame into two or more panels as the characters conduct their vital and intense conversations.

A final example from early cinema is the formally adventurous Abel Gance film *Napoleon* (1927), in which he experimented with the possibilities offered by the multiple panel:

> A simple panoramic vision was not the sole aim of Gance's device. He wanted to extend the emotional and psychological range of montage, and compare and contrast images across the three screens. It was thus not only a technical step forward, but an aesthetic leap as well. [Brownlow 1983: 132]

Gance's formal complexity enabled him to explore how the film's emotional power could be intensified by breaking the frame into separate spaces and allowing a more complex meaning to be constructed by multiple juxtapositions of images and actions. A similar use of the technique in 24 enables the construction of complex relations between its various narrative strands, such that actions in one strand are seen to have a connection with, and potential effect upon, events in the others.

Frames within frames were also used in early cinema to represent dreams, visions or memories; the smaller inset frame showing the mental image being 'conjured up' by the character seen in the main image. Such projections can be seen, for example, in the opening shot of *Life of an American Fireman* (1903), where a dozing fire chief seems to be thinking of a woman and child who appear in a circular inset above his head. The identities of the woman and child remain ambiguous, however – perhaps his own wife and child, perhaps a universalised representation of the mother and child who will be rescued in the film's climax (Musser 1991: 223–4). While such imagined projections seem a far cry from *24*'s gritty realism and emphasis on fact and literal truth, the two might not be so far apart after all; a hypothesis I will explore further towards the end of this chapter.

The split-screen technique would periodically resurface in American filmmaking, as in *The Boston Strangler* (1968), which used multiple panels within the film frame to represent a range of objective and subjective viewpoints of the murderous actions taking place. More significant, perhaps, was the conscious design of the panels, both in terms of their arrangement on screen and the timing of their appearances relative to one another, as is explained by the film's cinematographer, Richard Kline:

> I learned how to make the audience look at the panel that was most important at the time, and shift their eye as critical action occurred from panel to panel. It taught me that you have to guide the audience's eye to what you want them to specifically see in each frame. It can be done with colour and light density, with a certain lens, or with camera angles or movement. There is no one right way to do it, but one way or another, you have to make the audience subconsciously look at a specific place within the frame, and not just at the frame in general. [Anon 1969]

The makers of *24* take up this strategy especially during the timed appearance of several panels around the digital clock that reintroduces the show following each advert break. Although the majority of the panels appear one after another in a clockwise direction, there are notable exceptions, generally used to surprise and unsettle the viewer by introducing the unexpected. For example, in 1.14, the return from the second advert break displays the panels as follows:

1. President Palmer with his staff in the upper right quadrant;
2. Nina Myers in the upper left quadrant (i.e., beginning to run counter-clockwise);
3. Kim Bauer in the lower right quadrant;
4. Jack Bauer being interrogated by head of CTU Ryan Chappelle (Paul Schulze) in the lower left quadrant.

Just prior to the break, Nina had discovered that an unfamiliar man at the hospital where Teri and Kim have been taken has been posing as an FBI agent. Showing Palmer in the first panel suggests the threat that this rogue figure poses is to the President, who is threatened with assassination throughout the series. The second panel showing a concerned Nina returning to Teri and Kim, with Kim subsequently being shown in the third panel, intermixes the political and personal; a tension then confirmed by Bauer being shown in the fourth. The unpredictable zigzagging of our attention back and forth across and down the screen represents this confusion between the two agendas: Nina as both a protector of and threat to Teri and Kim at the same time as, seemingly, also protecting Palmer while Bauer is powerless to help and protect either Palmer or his own family.

After the first few episodes of Season One, where the use of multiple panels showing several actions supposedly occurring simultaneously is quite widespread, most of 24 is shown single frame, with only momentary shifts into the multiple panel aesthetic at largely prescribed points: title sequences, phone conversations, returns from advert breaks, summations at the close of episodes. But even with this relatively systematised use of the technique, the presentation of several simultaneous events and the failure to adequately explain the current relationships between them heightens the sense that any strand of the narrative could quickly, easily and shockingly become the dominant one, overturning expectations and assumptions and sending the narrative as a whole on a new trajectory.

MULTI-PANEL III: COMIC BOOKS AND GRAPHIC NOVELS

According to Scott McCloud, there are six discrete relations between consecutive panels of a comic strip: *moment-to-moment* (effectively, continuous action); *action-to-action* (where the action in the second panel is directly caused by action in the first); *subject-to-subject* (two actions in a single location appear to be bound by some kind of relationship, but this is not made fully explicit); *scene-to-scene* (two actions have a relationship but are physically distant); *aspect-to-aspect* (images of a general or abstract state or condition – e.g., a summer's day); and *non-sequitur* (images appear to have little or no connection or relationship) (1994: 70–81).

Only some of these are employed in *24*, and generally in modified form, as befits a moving-image medium as opposed to a still-image one. Aspect-to-aspect and non-sequitur are never used, as *24* is overtly plot and action driven and not given to either contemplative representations of general states of being, or the juxtaposition of completely unrelated events and characters. Moment-to-moment relations between panels are used when two camera angles on an event are shown in two separate panels, as when the American spy at the very beginning of the first episode of Season One is seen walking down an alleyway in both close-shot and long-shot (1.1). But there is a modification of the simple continuous movement from panel to panel, with the action in the second panel of a comic book layout understood to be occurring momentarily *after* the action in the first. The spy's movements in the two panels are temporally simultaneous rather than continuous; they are two angles on the same action happening *at the same time*, mutually confirming their reality and, as such, they reinforce the believability of the fiction, expressly inverting the traditional way of looking at such foregrounded formal techniques which, as argued above, tends to break the illusion of the fiction being constructed.

Action-to-action occurs repeatedly; for example, when Bauer is pinned down by Gaines in the woods (1.13), their actions are directly linked, in their call and response over the walkie-talkies and in their gunfight interplay. Scene-to-scene relations are used repeatedly for dramatic effect, as the action of *24* persistently takes place simultaneously across multiple locations. In 1.14, for example, Tony Almeida tells Alberta Green (Tamara Tunie) that they haven't yet identified the third assassin while the second panel appears on screen to show Alexis Drazen (Misha Collins), the third assassin. The second panel is explicitly conjured up by Alberta asking Tony: 'And the other one?' They are also, of course, central to the multi-panel images that wrap around the digital clock as the programme returns from each advert break. Two, three, four, and even more images are shown together, each representing one of the many narrative strands, the suggestion being that the action contained within each panel is occurring at the same time as each of the others, and that all have some kind of significant interrelationship.

The layout of a comic's page has been referred to as its *mise-en-page*, a form which 'generates a phenomenon of multiple dialectics' (Barber 2002: 5), in which meaning is constructed through the relationship between the content of a panel and the arrangement of panels on the page. The page layout of a comic is different to the multi-panel displays of *24* in terms of the time duration of the reading. In comics this is determined by the reader as s/he chooses which panel to look at and in what order. In *24* it is determined by the length of time the images, and especially the full multi-panel arrangement, is on screen; more importantly, the order in which the panels are shown.

'Deliberate persistence' is the distinctive presentation of a panel (size, position, etc) so that it remains in the memory after it has gone. The biggest panel in a comic page layout tends to indicate the most important character and/or action. There is an equivalent to this device in *24* and it covers quite a range of effects. It features in a relatively inconsequential way in, for example, Bauer questioning Vincent (Gary Murphy), Kim's ex, when first trying to determine where she's run off to (1.1). It quickly assumes a more emotionally significant role when, for instance, the image of Teri sitting at their kitchen table dominates the two smaller panels showing Bauer arriving at CTU; the insinuation being that Teri at that point holds the moral authority over Bauer, who has elected to go to work at midnight rather than help his wife find their errant daughter. In terms of narrative, the device becomes central in the multi-panel/clock display which signals the return after the second advert break of 1.16, for example, when Bauer's panel is seen dominating the frame over two smaller ones showing Teri and Kim in the safe house and a dead guard in a van outside it. Bauer is setting up an important meeting between Palmer's aide and Alexis Drazen, the third assassin, in an attempt to capture the latter. His actions take precedence over the threat to his wife and daughter from the imminent attack on the safe house.

This last point suggests an ironic undercutting of the deliberate persistence model. While Bauer's command of the current situation (he has just persuaded George Mason [Xander Berkeley] to let him stage the risky meeting) seems strong, as is reflected in the relative dominance of his panel in the frame, his control is about to be substantially challenged, not only by the successful attack on the safe house and subsequent capture of Teri and Kim, but also by the spectacular failure of the set-up meeting, in which

Palmer's aide will be killed and Drazen will escape. Perhaps we see here a more subtle and challenging use of the deliberate persistence aesthetic; one suited to the twists and turns, repeated authority shifts and moral ambiguity that lies at the heart of the show, in which we as viewers never know who can be trusted, who is really in control, and who really demands our attention.

But one might perhaps also see the device of deliberate persistence in terms of the question of which panel is chosen to generate the return to the full-screen image as the programme's aesthetic returns to the traditional single-frame out of each advert break multi-panel display. Often the panel chosen has not been the largest or most dominant of the three or four that surround the clock. Through this strategy, the programme is perhaps consciously unsettling us, by repeatedly confounding our anticipation of which narrative strand will be picked up and developed at any one point. This is especially the case when none of the panels involved in an advert-break-return display proves to be the one that initiates the next section of single-image narrative.

The unappealingly named 'gutter' is the space between panels on a comic book page. McCloud argues that, 'Here in the limbo of the gutter, human imagination takes two separate images and transforms them into a single idea' (1994: 66). That is to say, the size and shape of the gutter, and the way in which it separates image panels, carries meaning. This operates at specific times throughout 24. While there is a standard size gutter between panels in the programme, this is replaced by a noticeably different kind at significant moments in the narrative. For example, with the return after the second advert break in 1.16, three panels appear: firstly Teri and Kim in the top left quadrant, then a dead guard in a van outside their safe house in the lower left quadrant and, finally, Bauer in a larger panel which occupies most of the right hand side of the frame. The gutter between Teri/Kim and the guard is the standard size, indicating spatial coherence (they are at the same location), as well as narrative significance (the dead guard indicates that Teri and Kim are in imminent danger). The gutter between Teri/Kim and Jack, however, is noticeably wider, suggesting that Jack's attention is away from his wife and daughter and focused on other matters; in this case, setting up the meeting between the third assassin, Alexis Drazen, and Palmer's aide. In this way, 24 consistently utilises one of the major features of the comic book layout aesthetic to reveal and substantiate narrative and psychological detail developed on other layers of the text.

SPLIT EMOTIONS: THE DOCTRINE OF SYMPATHY AND NARRATIVE SEPARATION

This idea of physical and emotional distance is played out using another formal mechanism borrowed from other media. The Doctrine of Sympathy was a theory of emotional sensitivity, part medical, part philosophical – for our purposes dramatic – which explained the potential for those emotionally close to one another – family members in the primary instance, loved ones more generally – to be able to sense the condition and situation the other was facing even when separated by physical distance. Examples can be found from antiquity through the Renaissance to the nineteenth century. Clifton Cherpack has detailed its use as a narrative staging device in French Neo-Classical tragedy, generally noting that 'it seems obvious that if sympathy was believed to act in these ways, it would not have been difficult for an author to suppose, and for an audience to accept, an instinctive recognition between members of a family ... ' (1958: 9). Similarly, Nicholas Vardac describes its use in a 1852 stage production of *The Corsican Brothers*, commenting upon the telepathic union effected between the brothers in terms of stage devices – isolating one brother on an elevated stage as the imagined mental image of his sibling – which gave the play a 'cinematic quality' (1949: 38–9). I have also argued elsewhere that American early film-maker DW Griffith regularly employed the Doctrine as a formal device to enable him to link characters in separate filmic spaces at a time in cinematic history when filmic grammar had yet to fully formally develop the structures to do so (Allen 1999: 54–5).

I would like to argue that 24 employs the Doctrine of Sympathy on many occasions through the use of split-screen, the different panels placing in juxtaposition the characters who have a particularly powerful relationship, and thereby suggesting that they are intuiting one another's physical or emotional situation, or at least thinking of one another. In 4.23, for example, after Almeida has been taken hostage by Mandy (Mia Kirshner) and she has phoned his wife Michelle Dessler to force her to reposition the CTU agents surrounding her in order to allow her to escape. A right-hand panel shows Michelle deep in thought, while a left-hand panel depicts him bound with his hands behind his back; the latter image easily readable as a representation of Michelle's anguished mental picture. In this way, the split-screen technique is used to emotionally unite those with the strongest bonds, creating a further layer of the text.

CODA: WAS IT ALL JUST BAUER'S IMAGINATION?

At the very end of 1.24, when Bauer has found Teri dead, he slumps to the floor with her in his arms. At that moment, the screen splits into two with Bauer framed in the left-hand panel. In the right are grainy black and white images of the very beginning of the first episode, of Kim telling her father that she's glad he moved back in before pretending to go to bed and then of Bauer and Teri going to Kim's bedroom to find her gone. This is the first time such black and white images have been used, and signal a different kind of representation. Most simply, they represent Bauer's memory; at the very moment he loses his wife and family life, he remembers it at its best, just before Kim's disappearance structurally triggers the events of the next twenty-four hours. But in another way, the conjuring up of the images sends the show back to its beginning and enables everything we have been watching to become a visualisation of Bauer's memory, of him mentally 'piecing it all together' to see how he has got to the present moment, with his wife lying dead in his arms. All of the multiple panels and shifts from split-screen to single frame thereby become readable as his mentally working through the events, all now 'previously on', following the logic of one strand and comparing it to others to arrive at the whole truth of the day. Through the introduction of the black and white flashback images, the first and only in a relentlessly forward moving narrative, the entire series is reclaimed as Bauer's memory from his point of collapse at its very end. In this, perhaps, we go full circle to connect back to the dream visions of early cinema, the non-formalised aesthetic of a new medium allowing plays of ambiguities denied its later systematised version.

CONCLUSION

The split-screen aesthetic used in 24 therefore calls upon a long lineage of similar multi-frame formats in a range of media forms. It moves from the highly ritualised arrangements of religious (and political) medieval altarpieces, through the experimental formal strategies of pre-classical filmmaking to the beguilingly complex reading processes involved in comic book page layout and the complex graphics of contemporary television news. Each of these media forms can be seen to influence, both consciously and unconsciously, the sophisticated role played by the multi-panelled image display used in 24. Its use lends complexity to the character interactions and to the power relations constantly oscillating between them. It helps persuade us that the events we are witnessing are really occurring ('taking place in real-time') while supporting and intensifying the delicious tension and suspense which are such central features of the fiction. Far from being a mere novelty made possible by modern digital graphic technologies and used to maintain ratings, the use of split-screen in 24 strengthens and enriches the show's textual layering by drawing upon centuries of alternative multiple-image display and the complex possibilities of reading, meaning and narrative control that they employ. As 24 goes into its sixth season, the constantly interesting formal qualities of the show, figured in the split-screen aesthetic, have ensured that a series whose conceptual premise might have militated against it being used more than once, has justified its position as one of the leading television drama series of recent years.

1. I would like to thank Janet McCabe for reading my early drafts of this chapter, and for improvements made due to her many invaluable suggestions.

00.04

REASONS TO SPLIT UP

INTERACTIVITY, REALISM AND THE MULTIPLE-IMAGE SCREEN IN 24

DEBORAH JERMYN

From its first appearance in 2001, 24 was enthusiastically received for its radical approach to televisual aesthetics and narrative, or, as David Thomson put it, for the 'exultant madness' of its form (2002b: 12). Taking the suspense, intrigue and cliffhanger device typical of the crime genre to new levels, 24's central conceits – real-time and a storyline played out over a 24 hour period – pushed the boundaries of TV drama and challenged complacency about the perceived limitations of small-screen storytelling. Central also, of course, to its inventiveness was its use of the split or multiple-image screen, where a number of viewpoints and/or planes of action were played out on screen at any one moment. Underlining 24's frenetic sense of action, multi-stranded plotting and paranoia, this device was central in two major ways. First, in a pragmatic sense, split-screen constituted a convenient mode of storytelling (for example, enabling simultaneous 'updates' or clarifications across numerous storylines and characters, particularly after commercial breaks and at the end of each episode); second, as a stylistic feature, it was pivotal in establishing the overall 'character' of the drama (namely dynamic, intricate, urgent). 24 was heralded as one of the most imaginative TV dramas to appear on our screens in years, and, in Mark Lawson's words, 'change[d] the rules of television by making format central to a drama' (2003). This chapter looks at the use of split-screen in Season One in order to examine more closely exactly what this 'change of rules' entailed.

Though in fact Lawson argues that the use of split-screen in the first season detracted from what he sees as the more interesting device of real-time, and though he notes that later series of 24 have utilised it less, the split-screen was very much part of the perceived aesthetic radicalism of 24's format. In Julie Talen's words, 24 was 'the first prime-time dramatic series to employ multiple screens as an active storytelling technique' (2002). Of course, the multiple-image screen is not 'new', with a history in cinema dating back to 1927 (Abel Gance's Napoleon), and notably enjoying considerable success, albeit briefly, in the 1960s with The Boston Strangler (Fleischer, 1968) and The Thomas Crown Affair (Jewison, 1968) and later in the work of Brian De Palma. More recently, Mike Figgis has made split-screen experimentation a growing feature of his work (most prominently in Timecode (2000)), while in regards to television the split-screen has been a central device in British screenwriter Lynda La Plante's ITV serial Trial and Retribution since 1997 (a point neglected by Talen (2002)). In an earlier article from 1984, Talen observed that the use of multi-screens and/or multi-monitors has a lengthy history in installation art, an aesthetic later embraced by music video. In addition, she noted too that for some time it had become commonplace for TV title sequences from Dallas to Freeman Reports on CNN to manipulate images of their stars in individual scrolling boxes, while sports promos had increasingly inserted reaction shots as the drama played out, or divided the screen up in order to feature an instant replay (Talen 1984: 69; see also Lury 2005: 170). Clearly, then, there are numerous precedents for 24's multiple-image screen. But how does 24 adopt and utilise the potential of split-screen in original ways; and what is significant about its revival and success at this particular time?

24's use of the multiple screen image and its relationship in particular with realism and interactivity in a multimedia age – with its visual echoes of live news broadcasts and CCTV surveillance cameras – adds to the programme's sense both of real-time immediacy and 'authenticity', borrowing an aesthetic which in these media has come to connote a privileged relationship with 'the real'. So too, then, does it engage with questions about how we look at these media. I want to argue here that 24 facilitates a critical spectatorial position in relation to a whole array of contemporary visual media which it self-consciously alludes to and incorporates; that it foregrounds itself as a reflexive televisual text which invites the audience, on the one hand, to align themselves with the hero and join in the frenetic, labyrinthine plot, but also, on the other, to question and probe the nature and truth claims of the technologies it utilises.

THE LONGEST DAY OF YOUR TELEVISION VIEWING LIFE

It has been argued that the multiple-image screen, familiar to us too now from computer screens, digital television, websites and video games, speaks of our inability to maintain a focused gaze or lengthy attention span in the multimedia age. Indeed, these technologies have been conceptualised as belonging to a wider 'glimpse-culture' (Talen 2002). This perspective on contemporary audiences and their viewing habits is arguably indebted to popular critiques and anxieties about the ubiquity of a '3-minute attention span' often attributed to the rise of MTV in the 1980s. And of course, beyond this, television itself was at one time conceptualised as a medium which requires only a 'glance' in contrast to the gaze necessitated by cinema (Ellis 1984).

Ellis' premise about the distinctiveness of the ways cinema and television are watched was arguably always a problematic one, and in the contemporary televisual landscape *24* illustrates the shortcomings of this position particularly well. One might argue that far from inviting us to merely glance at the screen or watch in a distracted fashion, in *24* the split-screen does quite the reverse. Instead, it invites the viewer to embrace the act of editing for themselves, mobilising them to actively engage with the screen and its drama by demanding they move between planes of action simultaneously. Rather than leading to a shortened attention span, the subsequent sense of continually running the risk of 'missing' something in this process arguably demands a *heightened* attention span from the audience. As Richard Fleischer said of his film *The Boston Strangler*, which utilised split-screen for approximately one third of its running time (Anon 1969: 202),

> [T]he total effect on the audience is wonderful, because it makes them work. It makes their eyes and ears explore the entire screen and keeps them very conscious of what is happening. So there's an added excitement in trying to follow and keep up with it, which is something you just don't get in a conventional film. [Fleischer cited in Anon 1969: 204]

For example, the 'cliffhanger' has long been recognised as one of the cornerstones of the serial form, but in 24 this device is rearticulated in ways which re-imagine its inexorable nature. When, in 1.14, we are left (as the episode ends) with screens featuring: Nina Myers, having just been unmasked as the 'dirty agent', still at CTU; David Palmer driving to a secret rendezvous; Bauer in his car, carrying the severed finger of an unknown hit man; and Teri Bauer still desperately searching for Kim – the audience is in effect left with *four* cliffhangers to juggle and preserve till the next instalment. Like Fleischer's audience, the audience for 24 must 'work' throughout its layering of screens and monitors; witness the moment in 1.6, when we watch a split-screen *within* the screen as villain Ira Gaines (Michael Massee) spies on Bauer at the hospital, forcing us to quickly scan and make sense of this new, unfamiliar set of screens even more rapidly in order to keep up with him. Furthermore, the very fact that one series of 24 requires a six-month commitment from the interested viewer, despite detailing just one day in the life of Bauer and co, clearly further undermines the notion that this splintering of the screen speaks of a text which could gratify a distracted or otherwise casual TV observer.

Indeed, the multiple-image screen is also masterfully utilised in 24 in the manner in which it embeds the spectator's position 'within' the sensory world of the protagonists. Through the use of split-screen, the spectator's experience comes to parallel that of the characters; forced to scan multiple frames for information, the viewer mirrors the agents' investigative pursuits – they must adopt the hero's sense of distrust and CTU's compulsion to remain alert. Beyond this, 24's frequently moving, shaky, hand-held camera, which may lurk near Jamey Farrell's (Karina Arroyave) desk one moment and career round to follow Tony Almeida the next, suggests a narrative point of view which is constantly assessing, moving and vigilant. This stylised camerawork constitutes an aesthetic *within* the text which again mirrors the look of the spectator *at* the text, who is obliged to move rapidly between the different components of the screen.

An interesting paradox emerges here, then. On the one hand, as outlined above, split-screen is arguably used by 24 to *enhance* the spectator's identification with the narrative and arguably with Bauer in particular who, rather like the viewer, has to juggle copious amounts of information about multiple plot strands and move through more of the different spaces in the plot than anyone else. Working in conjunction with one another, then, the programme's aesthetic devices, from real-time to the quasi-documentary camera style to split-screen, lead the spectator to experience some of the urgency and anxiety felt by Bauer and those around him. But at the same time, despite precedents elsewhere, split-screen remains an uncommon and strikingly unusual self-conscious technique within the realm of television drama, one which announces the text's own construction. For Lury, then, even despite the intimacy engendered by 24's camerawork, split-screen 'is still disorientating and its presence wilfully interrupts the coherence or integrity of the places represented on-screen and, potentially, disrupts the viewer's identification with the characters and events portrayed' (2005: 173). Arguably, what this leads to in 24 is a text rich in complexity and contradiction; one which uses split-screen to draw us into a spectatorial position which arguably aligns us with the characters (and hero in particular), while simultaneously manipulating the screen in a manner which draws attention to its own status as a constructed televisual text.

INTERACTION VERSUS DISTRACTION: SPLIT-SCREEN AND 'AMBIGUITY OF EXPRESSION'

There are intriguing connections here, too, between 24's split-screen and Andre Bazin's theories of the relationship between cinematic realism, editing and spectatorship. As Lury notes, 'In effect, the split-screen is a substitute or condensation of the common film practice of parallel editing' (2005: 171). Since DW Griffith, parallel editing has been a staple device drawn on in audio-visual media to produce tension or dramatic juxtaposition by cutting between events occurring in two or more spaces at the same time. But in 24, via split-screen, 'this dynamic tension can be organized within a single frame, making it both an economic and intense narrative' (ibid). The split-screen in 24 is more than a convenient device for rendering its multiple telephone conversations more visually dynamic, then. For example, when Alberta Green (Tamara Tunie) separates Almeida and Nina for questioning and attempts to break their resolve to protect Bauer with threats of prosecution and dismissal, the tension is rendered all the more palpable for seeing them both on screen at the same time despite their having been isolated (1.12); who, if either of them, looks likely to crack first? Similarly, in 1.14, after Nina leaves Teri's hospital room the two women's faces are juxtaposed in split-screen following an awkward exchange between them. In the tradition of soap opera, the camera lingers for a moment in close-up on them and we seek to 'read' their faces for emotion and information while pondering what their looks 'mean'; how much does Teri know about Bauer and Nina?; what do they both think of each other?; what does Nina really feel for Bauer now? These questions are made all the more inscrutable and challenging for the viewer, who has to 'read' both women simultaneously.

It was Bazin's premise that the practices of deep focus and of the long take enabled the filmmaker to circumvent montage and thus to produce a more sophisticated and complex relationship between the spectator, the text and its evocation of realism. In his words, which bear a striking and prescient parallel to Fleischer's claims for split-screen above, deep focus meant:

> Both a more active mental attitude on the part of the spectator and a
> more positive contribution on his [sic] part to the action in progress.
> While analytical montage only calls for him to follow his guide, to let
> his attention follow along smoothly with that of the director who will
> choose what he should see, here he is called upon to exercise at least
> a minimum of personal choice. It is from this attention and his will
> that the meaning of the image in part derives ... In short, montage by
> its very nature rules out ambiguity of expression. [1967: 35-6]

In the same vein, then, what are the implications of 24's invitation to the spectator to take more ownership of the 'editing' process through their evaluating of multiple screens? Does it result in a more active, open spectatorial experience and challenging representation of 'reality', replacing the didacticism Bazin alludes to above with a more potentially fragmented or polysemic outlook? Arguably the critiques originally made of Bazin remain true here too. To suggest that the long take and deep focus, or split-screen, give the audience an entirely open and undirected text with which to contend would be to misrepresent and overstate the 'freedom' these techniques endow the audience with. Bazin welcomes the opportunity for the spectator to pursue their 'personal choice' of what to concentrate on, but this 'choice' is nevertheless a restricted one, enacted within the realms of what the director has already placed on the screen. Significantly, unlike some earlier precedents in the use of split-screen, other than a brief moment at the series' climax when Jack remembers his now-dead wife (1.24), 24 also essentially respects the classical convention of linear temporality by choosing not to use split-screen as a means of contrasting different temporalities, subjective points-of-view or flashbacks. Furthermore, Lury argues that 24 manipulates sound levels in such a way that we are in effect 'directed' to focus our attention on one screen rather than another at any particular time: 'if we are with Jack, his voice and sound dominate; if we are with Teri, her voice and sound will dominate' (2005: 172). Indeed, Figgis uses this same technique in *Timecode* to avoid utter confusion across the four screens which he utilises for the entire duration of the film. For Lury, this means that sound disperses some of the potentially 'aggressive impact' of the split-screen in *24*. We might say, further, that it seeks to help unify a text which might otherwise be rendered rather more fragmented, ambiguous and demanding for the spectator; or, in other words, more like Bazin's vision.

Nevertheless, it is possible to argue that *24* does facilitate the 'more active mental attitude' and 'positive contribution' Bazin speaks approvingly of, by constituting a more 'interactive' spectatorial position than is typically the case in TV drama. Interactivity in its contemporary sense has of course been widely adopted to refer to audiences engaging with (increasingly, new media) technologies in order to intervene in some sense in the outcome(s) of a text. Furthermore, Spiro Kiousis has highlighted the importance of the notion of 'feedback' to interactivity: 'the ability for message receivers to respond to message senders' (2002: 359). The *24* audience is evidently not interactive in this sense in the way that, for example, the reality TV audience(s) for *Big Brother* or *The Salon* are (Holmes 2004), since clearly the *24* viewer has no voting power or bearing on the final outcome of the narrative. The programme has sought to exploit other associated interactive opportunities of course, including the Fox website (where, for example, one can access characters' desktops), numerous Internet discussion boards, 'episodes' texted directly to subscribers' mobile phones and, in the UK following Season Two, the BBC Three fan chat show, *Pure 24*. But this invitation to take up a kind of 'interactive' relationship with the programme is arguably written into the primary text too, rendered particularly salient by virtue of its split-screen.

The precise nature of what constitutes 'interactivity' remains a contested arena, marked by theoretical ambiguity (Jensen 1999; Marshall 2004: 13–15; Jermyn and Holmes 2006). Even in this digital age, it connotes more than the invitation to 'press the red button', still implying, more broadly, a heightened degree of connection between audience and text; certainly, to return to its etymological roots as P David Marshall does, 'interaction' amounts to more than 'feedback'. For Marshall, interactivity also importantly connotes a viewer or user who is engaged in choices about what they see, who is in some sense practising control over the 'time and images' they experience (though clearly this 'control' is predicated on a limited range of pre-designated options) (2004: 16). Interestingly, in an interview shortly before the release of *Timecode* in the UK, Mike Figgis critiqued the way that editing in mainstream film has become 'a huge series of gimmicks with which we've all become overfamiliar', leading to what he sees as a largely complacent audience. He continues:

> I find that really distressing. In America they eat and go for a piss and
> talk the whole time, and it's got something to do with the fact that
> *there's no interaction between them and the screen* any more ... This film is
> delivering constantly the idea that you might be missing something,
> so you can't afford to go and take a piss or take your eyes off the
> screen. People who watch it seem far more alert, whether they like it
> or not, because of the degree of attention required to watch the film.
> [Figgis cited in Williams 2000: 6, italics mine]

In Figgis' account, the multiple screen is again very much imagined as a technique which by its very nature requires a greater degree of engagement on the part of the audience. The alertness and attention necessitated by split-screen, the element of choice embedded within it, its requirement that we adapt 'our habits of perception' (ibid) all speak of a viewer who must intervene in the text in a heightened fashion in order to follow it; and who is in some sense, therefore, watching 'interactively'.

Rather than merely replicating a new media world and its interactive address, however, throughout Season One *24* also critiques and problematises the technologies it draws on. *24* both offers us the (surface) ambiguity of the multiple screen image and the 'openness' this allows, while emphasising how such images, along with screens and monitors everywhere, are manipulated and determined every bit as easily as conventional mono-vision. Throughout CTU, we see the ease with which agents dart between the screens on their monitors, using the technology as a 'smokescreen' to hide their (often treacherous) real activities. The unreliability of the multiple screen image is foregrounded when Almeida and Nina trick Gaines by putting the CCTV cameras at CTU on a loop (1.8). Far from offering authenticity, immediacy and realism as the popular depiction of CCTV would have it, the image here is a simulacra, a moment out of time, constructed and contrived to play with the naive investment we so often place in such technology. Despite the fact that, curiously, mobile phones never seem to suffer from battery failure in the world of *24*, the uses of the multiple screen image and its associated technologies are not idealised, made foolproof or revered as constituting 'progress' here. Quite the reverse, CCTV patently fails to protect Janet York (Jacqui Maxwell) from an assassin at the hospital (1.6); the satellite pictures mailed to Bauer fail to prevent Kim and Teri getting lost in the valley (1.13); the multiple hidden cameras and four screens recording Elizabeth Nash's (Kara Zediker) hotel tryst with Alexis Drazen (Misha Collins) fail to prevent their meeting ending in disaster (1.17). In short, no computer, no camera, no monitor can be entirely trusted or relied on in the world of *24*.

Through all this, *24* makes a virtue of split-screen. It elevates it to more than mere 'gimmick' or empty spectacle, instead rendering it an integral part of the storytelling process. It embeds split-screen as an aesthetic through which some of the core (and arguably topical) themes and issues raised by the programme, such as contemporary urban paranoia, political urgency, surveillance and 'infiltration' anxieties, can be powerfully evoked beyond and outside the mechanics and content of the actual narrative. At the same time, it reminds the audience continually of its own construction, self-consciously producing a text where screens and monitors are repeatedly layered, manipulated and repositioned in such a way that the integrity and truthfulness of the image is continually questioned. Through all this, *24* has revitalised both critical debate and the popular imagination regarding the ever-changing possibilities of televisual storytelling. In doing so, it constitutes a televisual text which invites us to think critically about signifiers of realism, about our engagement with new technologies and, indeed, about the ways we watch television itself.

00.05

INTERESTING TIMES

THE DEMANDS 24'S REAL-TIME FORMAT MAKES ON ITS AUDIENCE[1]

JACQUELINE FURBY

ABOUT TIME

24's real-time format, and a storyline in each series that covers a twenty-four-hour period in twenty-four one-hour episodes, demands a particular kind of relationship from its audience. The audience cannot view casually, but instead enters into a contract of intense involvement that endures over twenty-four weeks if viewed as originally broadcast, or for eighteen hours of viewing episodes on DVD or video. The temporal format, including the real-time conceit, is integral to this contract of extreme involvement, and in this chapter I argue that it is the programme's temporal structures that force the audience to view it as a compulsive text. I also consider the veracity of the claim for real-time from a number of angles and debate that the role of time may be considered subservient to the narrative but is also central to the programme's powerful effect.

REAL-TIME

Season One featured an announcement at the start of each episode: 'The following takes place between [nine a.m. and ten a.m.]. Events occur in real-time.' Since the first season the overt claim to real-time has been removed, perhaps because when the programme is aired on non-commercial stations or watched on DVD or video, time is missing where the commercial breaks would have been, and the 'hour' actually only lasts around 42 minutes. This clearly impacts on the programme's real-time status. The real-time conceit, however, remains central to the programme's aura of innovation, immediacy and excitement. We might usefully pause, therefore, to consider what this claim to real-time means. The Internet Movie Database cites thirty-seven texts made with recourse to real-time since 1948, the year of the release of Alfred Hitchcock's film *Rope*. Other examples in the list include *Nick of Time* (John Badham, 1995), and *Timecode* (Mike Figgis, 2000). Each of these films interprets the idea of real-time in a different way and can be used to clarify the use of real-time in *24*, so I will return to discuss them further in due course. In general, though, we can assume that, in real-time, each minute of screen-time corresponds to a minute in the plot and the story, and events are presented exactly in the order that they occur chronologically, without any edits or jumps in time. The exact time of the story action is therefore equal to the time it takes to view that action. To understand real-time, and how this differs from how time is usually presented in the visual text, we need to explore these temporal layers of time in the film or television text. These layers may be thought of as screen-time, story-time and plot-time. We should also consider how time might be treated and manipulated according to order, duration and frequency. (For a detailed discussion of these issues, see Genette 1972; Chatman 1978; Rimmon-Kenan 1983; Bordwell 1985; and Lothe 2000.)

SCREEN-TIME, STORY-TIME, PLOT-TIME: ORDER, DURATION AND FREQUENCY

The term 'story' denotes the underlying layer of events, occurring sequentially, which take place in linear chronological time. The events in story-time may be thought to occur in a natural series (*a-b-c-d-e-f-g*), in which the events actually took place, and may cover, say, a period of 70 years in, for example, *Citizen Kane* (Orson Welles, 1941), which covers the lifetime of its eponymous character. In the case of *24*, story-time is twenty-four hours. Screen-time is the time it takes to view the text – 119 minutes in the case of *Citizen Kane*, or twenty-four hours in the case of *24* when viewed with the original duration of commercial breaks intact. Under normal circumstances a text which seeks to tell a story where story-time is greater than screen-time will be selective about which events to refer to, and will also select the order, duration and frequency with which these fragments are narrated.

These temporally manipulated events are told in 'plot-time'. Plot-time may shuffle the order of story events, for example through the use of the flashback or flashforward. Story events may also be presented in the plot as taking more or less time than they would naturally. Montage sequences may condense time considerably – see again *Citizen Kane, Dr. Strangelove or: How I Learned to Stop Worrying and Love the Bomb* (Stanley Kubrick, 1964), and *Blow* (Ted Demme, 2001) – or slow-motion sequences may stretch time, as in *The Matrix* (Andy and Larry Wachowski, 1999). Events that happen more than once may be summarised or presented only once, so that frequency is distorted. An event that occurred only once may be replayed and revisited more than once for narrative or dramatic effect, as in *Pulp Fiction* (Quentin Tarantino, 1994).

Plot-time, then, is to be understood as the period of the events depicted in the text; it is the arrangement of the story material that the filmmaker chooses to present to the viewer. Few filmic plots made after 1908 present events precisely as they occur in the story. Instead, the viewer reassembles the story from the information given by the plot and reorders the story into a chronological sequence according to normal experience of the laws of cause and effect and the normal experience of (linear) time. To summarise, story-time may be reconstituted from plot-time plus that which the plot omits. Screen-time is the time that it takes for the plot to be shown. There are three relations that plot-time duration may have to story-time duration: plot-time may be equal to story time; plot-time may be greater than story-time; and plot-time may be shorter than story-time. Similarly, screen-time's relation to plot-time can be greater than, shorter than, or equal. Obviously, story-time and screen-time can also follow this set of relative durational differences and similarity. In real-time, order, duration and frequency in plot-time and screen-time are understood to be the same as in the story and there is no time manipulation. Pure real-time would allow the viewer to experience time as it unfolds for an individual character who is thus limited in terms of travel in time and space.

Rope follows this pattern and may be considered to be an example of real-time in its extreme form. The action throughout is cinematically continuous as the film is created without the use of narratorial editing. It is filmed using the long-take (usually referred to as the ten-minute take, although in reality most of the takes in this film last for approximately seven minutes) and, although the film plays for approximately 80 minutes, there are only ten cuts.

As VF Perkins has pointed out, only the first cut, which takes us from an external, establishing shot into the interior where all the subsequent action takes place, is made 'at the will of the director' (1972: 35). The remaining nine cuts are merely to change the film in the camera after ten minutes, and in the projector after twenty minutes. The overall effect is that of continuous action in real-time. No time is elided in service of the narrative; the moments that are lost during the necessary cuts (Perkins estimates the loss to be forty seconds) do not create gaps in the information flow, nor in the flow of action as there is only one plotline followed (ibid). Real-time is 'realistic' in that it runs according to the conventions of clock-time. It is usually, therefore, easy for the audience to follow and to understand.

An alternative model of the use of real-time is seen in *Nick of Time*. The film follows the dilemma presented to the main protagonist Gene Watson (Johnny Depp), whose daughter is kidnapped. The kidnappers give Watson a gun and a photograph of a person and he is told that if he hasn't killed that person in one hour and fifteen minutes, his daughter will be killed. The narrative then follows the single character's point of view (POV) through that period in real-time, using the race-against-time plot device and usual twists and blocks inherent in the thriller mode to heighten audience anticipation and suspense.

Timecode further complicates this real-time model by employing the split-screen to present four parallel-plotted, interconnected narratives on four screens simultaneously in continuous action with no edits. The four frames are on-screen throughout the film's 97-minute duration and the viewer is theoretically free to choose which frame of action to follow.

24 TIMES

It is certainly not unreasonable to suggest that *Nick of Time* and *Timecode* may have influenced *24*'s temporal structure and style, but *24*'s real-time is a version of real-time that owes little to the extreme paradigm offered by *Rope*. In this section I shall outline some key aspects of how time is dealt with in *24* and what relationship there might be to the real-time models discussed above.

In terms of continuous action with no durational gaps, *24*'s format both complies with and goes against the conventions of real-time. For example, due to the requirements of commercial television, each of *24*'s episodes elides around fifteen minutes of screen-time to allow for commercial breaks.

The plot is understood to continue to unfold during this time off-air (see Steven Peacock's discussion elsewhere in this volume). This, when viewed on commercial television, adds to the aura of real-time. This is because we understand that the story continues to be told, even though our viewing of the unfolding events is replaced with commercials. However, when the programme is screened in non-commercial formats, the real-time effect may be reduced by the temporal abridgement at these gaps since time is not felt to be continuous in the same way. Nevertheless, because the plot *allows* for gaps in the action to correspond with the temporal gaps, the sense of immediacy that accompanies the real-time strategy *is* maintained and the tension and anxiety of the race-against-time model is heightened.

Although the title of *24* draws attention to time as an essential element, and there is an intense sense of the pressures of time maintained throughout each season, and a consistent sense that perhaps time is as much the enemy as each of the antagonists, time in *24* might be considered to be subordinate to the storytelling. We are continually reminded of the deadlines (literal in that each season features a threat to life as the central problem to be overcome), and the race against time that is structurally central to each episode and each season. Each programme seems to feature dialogue that draws attention to the time-constraints, exemplified perhaps by Jack Bauer's petulant reminder in 2.6, 'We're fighting the clock here Nina', or Nina's comment in 2.7, 'We need a little more time', and her request to Bauer while interrogating Faheen (Anthony Azizi), 'Give me more time with him', to which Bauer replies 'You've had enough time', and shortly after announces 'We're out of time' (2.7).

Certainly, the real-time strategy seems to lose integrity when weighed against the exemplar offered by Hitchcock's *Rope*. Mundane details and action are glossed over in *24*, just as they are in conventional television drama and film that make no claim to real-time. Elapsed screen-time and represented plot-time are apparently equal and yet there is a sense of temporal distortion due to a number of factors. Firstly, there is clear manipulation of duration seen in the abridgement of action. Travel, for example, seems much more easily negotiated than in real life (irritatingly, Bauer seems to be able to drive across Los Angeles, even during peak traffic hours, with few hold-ups). Secondly, there is the feeling of multiplied time, or perhaps layered time, connected with the presentation of a variety of plotlines and the use of split-screen. Time may be continuous inside the diegetic world, but as viewers we do not follow the actions of a single character as in *Nick of Time*; instead we occupy different spaces as we follow the action that continuously crosses between alternative spheres of action. So much more seems to happen because we follow more than one story. Thirdly, there is an impression of temporal expansion through the charging of effect, which changes how the spectator feels time passes. In order to understand this last point it should be noted that the spectator's subjective perception of the duration of any programme is variable and linked to their experience of the action. During fast paced and exciting action time may seem to pass quickly, or conversely, time may seem to pass slowly during slow and tedious sequences. In addition, any period of extended waiting, paradoxically even through an exciting sequence, may feel like a long time to the viewer anxious for narrative closure. An example of this is the tension of the anticipation and suspense inherent in the race against time and thriller genres which, may, on a subjective level, make time feel stretched out. I will deal with issues two and three more fully in turn and argue that although *24*'s time-scheme may not seem to conform to a strict reading of real-time, such as that offered by *Rope* and other texts cited by the IMDb, there is a sense where time does *feel* 'real'. Crucially, time *feels* real in that it has many characteristics in common with how we experience time as members of modern western society, and how we feel the pressure of time in our everyday lives.

A strategy that militates against the real-time model, but that adds a great deal to the programme's sense of urgency and pressure of time is the use of multiple plotlines, which the viewer is privileged to cross between. The use of cross-cutting became an important aid to the atmosphere of suspense and expectancy in films that used deadlines as a motivational dynamic device (there are countless examples of this, starting with early chase films such as DW Griffith's 1908 film *The Fatal Hour*). Cross-cutting allows the viewer to see the action taking place at locations separated in space but linked together in time (a serial version of the split-screen style seen sporadically throughout *24*, or continuously in *Timecode*). This method of presentation organises time and space so as to provide excitement whilst maintaining narrational continuity. The viewer is able to see events occurring consecutively along disparate timelines. From the viewing position, space-time is eviscerated: space behaves in a temporal manner, and time in a spatial one; events separated in space are seen in temporal sequence, and events separated in time are brought together spatially.

Cross-cutting is often an aid to durational economy in the narrative. Actions that are mundane or unnecessary are hidden in the transition from one spatial location to another. Cross-cutting also enables narrational, and spectatorial, omniscience. It contributes to the creation of suspenseful effect, and acts as a signalling device that heralds narrative closure. It also possesses an internal rhythm as it oscillates between time-lines, and can heighten the sense of urgency as we switch more rapidly from one story to another.

Each season, and every episode within that season, presents a set of cues, patterns, and gaps in information that shape the viewer's experience of suspense and anticipation that is a key functional device of the thriller genre. Viewing is an act of interpretation that involves identifying links between cause and effect and which is assisted or blocked, accelerated or retarded, by gaps and omissions in the presentation of information. Adhering closely to story order focuses the viewer's attention on the immediacy of events as they happen and encourages a suspenseful 'what's going to happen next?' enquiry. This natural chronological presentation of cause and effect seen in 24 enables the viewer to form clear-cut hypotheses about future events. The detective thriller, psychological thriller, science fiction, action adventure, or fantasy genres are particularly likely to delay the presentation of key images and information up until the final scene, or may include false or misleading information, which will cause the viewer to construct an inaccurate story until the moment when the complete information set is revealed.

In any real-time narrative the arrow of time points unremittingly forwards, and this dynamic is reinforced in 24 by the race-against-time plot and the viewer's desire to know the whole story. Time is, however, fractured by the many parallel storylines presented. The real-time format is supported by the on-screen clock, and the cause-and-effect relationship between the events taking place in various locations. Simultaneous action is presented in moments of split-screen narration, whereas the scene shifts are not to parallel action but action occurring sequentially; one thing happening after another. Sometimes these scene shifts are linked by cause and effect (often based on information transmission), and at other times there appears to be no direct cause-and-effect relation between zones of action, but all are linked in to the overall narrative trajectory of the race against time.

Many strategies are clearly designed to heighten the viewer's sense of time anxiety, yet the day's action also *seems* to go on forever because of the twenty-four episodes each presenting only one hour. Therefore, although there is a sense of urgency attached to the fast pace and rush of the story, time paradoxically appears to be stretched in comparison to the majority of films and television programmes that compress into the ninety-minute screen-time events that occur over a much longer period. Conversely, time within each episode seems to run at an accelerated speed because of the number of events crammed into the 'hour', and the multiple threads that the viewer is following.

THE IMPACT OF TIME

In general, then, the overall effect of the way that time works in 24 is that it appears hyper-real rather than real. It is like the time we experience every day in our relationship to external clock time, but speeded up and multiplied. In western society our usual experience of time is often a tension between having not enough time, or having too much. As human beings we are aware of our own mortality that limits our time on a large scale, and the pressures of everyday life that may limit our unstructured time on a small scale. Conversely, we may even feel threatened by the idea of unfilled hours or days. Tied up with the idea of mortality, with schedules, deadlines and periods of 'free time', is the awareness, often symbolised by a ticking clock, of time's inevitable flow and our subject position with regard to time. Time (and our time) is somehow 'owned' by the clock.

Developments in technology in the twentieth century, particularly during the last forty years, have engendered and nurtured the sense of a lack of available time. The idea that technology squanders rather than saves time is counter-intuitive. Many machines were initially developed and marketed on the strength that they were labour-saving (and therefore time-saving) aids to modern living. In 1999, James Gleick wrote 'we are in a rush. We are making haste. A compression of time characterizes the life of the century now closing' (1999: 9). Czech novelist Milan Kundera says that 'speed is the form of ecstasy the technical revolution has bestowed on man' (1996: 2), while Paul Edwards, chairman and chief executive of consumer consultancy at the Henley Centre, believes that a sense of time starvation is partly based in reality and that technology has engendered it. He says 'there's a perceptual thing about time – we think we have less of it than we have ... Regardless of the amount that we've actually got, almost everybody thinks we have less of it' (cited in Hurley 2001: 33). Mary Ann Doane, in her work on the representation of cinematic time, also discusses 'modernity's increasing understanding of temporality as assault, acceleration, speed', and writes that 'modernity is conceptualized as an increase in the speed and intensity of stimuli.' She continues by saying that in the late nineteenth and early twentieth centuries 'time emerges as a problem intimately linked to the theorization of modernity as trauma or shock', and that 'time is no longer the benign phenomenon ... but a troublesome and anxiety-producing entity' (2002: 33-4).

As a tool, the clock has been instrumental in the development and continuation of industrial and technological western society. We act according to what time the clock tells us it is. It is time to wake up; time to eat; time to go to work, school, or college. We 'watch the clock', and order our lives according to what it 'says'. Social theorist Barbara Adam sums up this dependency. She says that 'the members of such societies use the concept of time not merely to synthesise aspects of mind, body, nature, and social life, but they also employ it on a world-wide basis as a standardised principle for measurement, co-ordination, regulation, and control' (1990: 9). Clocks, therefore, have aided human beings' evolutionary journey, and clock time has made possible the transition to co-operative synchronous human societies. But, as Adam asserts, the drawback is 'we cannot escape the clock time that structures and times our daily lives ... As long as we remain part of a society that is structured to the time of clocks and calendars our activities and interaction with others can only escape its pervasive hold to a very limited extent' (1995: 107). A side effect of this dependent relationship, therefore, is a sense of time anxiety, and chronic temporal anorexia, engendered by a sense of being continually 'behind time', and a feeling that there is little free or unoccupied time.

Yet, when we view a film or a television programme, we are taking time out of everyday time symbolised by the clock. This experience is different from everyday time. We elect to spend a (predictable) period concentrating on story and entertainment. This different order of time may be thought of as 'lived time', 'lifetime', which, Jan Campbell says, *can* be tied up with public (clock) time, but 'might just as well be [time spent] dreaming or doing nothing' (2005: 175). In this case it might be thought of as time unstructured, and unharnessed from public clock time. During this unstructured time we can usually escape from the multi-tasking, or multi-focusing behaviour that is usual elsewhere in our daily lives. This time, therefore, is normally characterised by an energy that differs from time spent 'watching the clock'.

The experience of 24's time scheme, however, is very different from this low-energy model. The sense of the ongoing present moment, combined with the race against time, and the intense attention demanded by the complexities, and frequent twists and reversals, of the plot and layered sub-plots, allows no respite during the programme's duration for escaping from time anxiety or temporal anorexia. The nature of time that 24 imposes upon the viewer is easily as insistent and as anxiety-ridden as public clock time. Time in 24 is frenetically enhanced clock time and permits no moments for dreaming or doing nothing. This is 'leisure' time that allows no time for leisure.

The attention demanded by 24 is, thus, not characterised by the glance theorised to be part of television viewing, because a more active and faithful viewing position is required (Ellis 1984). The glance, which posits a three-minute attention span, is overridden by the information-dense plots and the rapid succession of scene shifts. In a forty-two minute show there may be as many as twenty-one scene shifts, so the average duration of any single scene is two minutes. In addition, Deborah Jermyn (elsewhere in this volume) argues that the split-screen in 24 works against the culture of the glance discussed by Ellis. She comments that 'rather than leading to a shortened attention span, the subsequent sense of continually running the risk of "missing" something ... arguably demands a *heightened* attention span from the audience.'

The intense viewing style demanded by the programme appears to be addictive. Vivienne Parry describes it in an article in *The Times* as 'gripping television', which she says is 'due, in part, to its format', and to the 'exploits of its hero Jack Bauer' (2006: 4). Parry asks 'can anyone stand this much adrenalin?' (ibid). The adrenalin effect noted by Parry transfers from the programme to the viewer and the effect may be addiction (or arguably rejection). If addicted, we become dedicated viewers, partly because of the compulsive viewing engendered by the way the programme sets up intrigue and suspense, and partly because we are aware of the twenty-four week format. We commit to the whole season, and commit therefore, to the particularly intense and attention-rich viewing style that the show demands. Daniel Chamberlain and Scott Ruston also comment (in this volume) on the 'addictive' effect that the 'break-neck pace of the narrative' and 'the sense of intrigue and suspense created by the serial's cliffhanger endings' has on the viewer. The effect of the real-time, race-against-time structure that endures through twenty-four shows, is a protracted sense of urgency, and a sustained sense of temporal anxiety and suspense, from which the addicted viewer is unable to escape.

The real-time conceit supports the race-against-time narrative motivation, and intensifies the suspenseful atmosphere and effect, keeping the viewer engaged, forcing an intensity of attention, and a commitment to loyalty. The viewer is required to schedule further viewing time in order to avoid missing vital action and the drip-feed of dense information that would make holes in their knowledge and understanding of the action. Although this is mitigated somewhat by the summary scenes that introduce each episode, which might suggest that, if one misses something one can catch up later, this 'taster' is not necessarily sufficient to satisfy the addictive effect set up by the complex narrative sutured to the hyperactive real-time structural conceit that is so central to 24. The show is driven by time, and drives towards the moment of dénouement, when all the information is complete and the action resolved. We know this will not happen until the final episode because closure is directly yoked to the clock, and that future moment when the day (and the day's events) has been lived through. The journey cannot be short-circuited, and viewer gratification is drawn-out and, seemingly, endlessly delayed.

The end is important, because that is what we are all inexorably heading towards, but we cannot arrive there without experiencing the journey itself. This is another way in which the real-time can be seen as real. It is not in the pretence that events are happening at the pace, or in the density, that they happen in real life, or in the parallel action – as we cannot, in everyday life, skip about geographically to view events occurring elsewhere. The real-time is authentic in that, owing to the nature of the show's heightened seriality, we cannot access the future, or the dénouement, without experiencing, or enduring, the sequential and linear series of 'nows', the present moments, that lead us to that future time. The intermittent presentation of the on-screen clocks grounds us in the present moment, and the illusion, of real-time (and the time of real life) in the continuous present. The structure of everyday life is therefore inscribed into the seriality. The series drives its overall narrative towards the dénouement that completes each season, which provides it with a future-directed trajectory, but each hour has its own sub-set of rhythms as some sub-plots are resolved and others are opened. The temporal beat of each show's idiosyncratic rhythm is further augmented by split-screen 'updates', or summaries, which punctuate the real-time segments. The periods of relative inactivity of some sequences, such as those which focus on conversations, appear slow (and tense) and are interspliced by the digital clock – which reminds us that time is passing – and by moments of fast action or spectacle and rapid relocation to a different sub-plot. This segmented presentation style offers a variety of rhythmic tempos that is like life, but speeded up, more frenetic, tense, and more anxious. This accelerated rhythm is often echoed in the soundtrack, which at moments of high tension features a burst of percussion suggestive of a rapidly ticking clock. The series, in this way, can be seen to possess a life cycle of its own that echoes idiosyncratic human rhythms – hourly, diurnal, annual, and lifetime rhythms.

So what has this argument done to the claim of real-time in *24*? The title of this chapter, 'Interesting Times', refers to a curse, commonly remembered as 'may he live in interesting times'. The term 'interesting', here, should be taken to mean 'dangerous', 'turbulent', 'chaotic' or otherwise unpleasant. And, however much we might understand the time in *24* to be like life, let's hope that the dangerous, turbulent, chaotic, and unremitting time lived by the characters does not closely resemble the time experienced by the viewer in their everyday life. In addition, we may not be able to easily recognise the paradigm of real-time offered by *Rope* in its leisurely unbroken action in a single continuous take, but the show's interpretation of real-time is real in many ways. It is real in that its style and form reflects the rhythms of human life. It is real in that it possesses an inherent pressure of time that echoes that of life in modern western society. And it is real in the sense that it is driven by the clock in the same way that the viewer is in everyday life, and real in that both programme and life are characterised by a heightened sense of time anxiety. But it is also hyper-real because all of these aspects – rhythm, pressure of time, the tyranny of clock time, and the heightened sense of time anxiety – are even more intense and given even more emphasis, and are even more 'interesting' (dangerous, turbulent, chaotic) in the show, than they are in real life.

1.   I should like to thank my third-year film students for their intelligent observations and enthusiasm in helping me to work through ideas for this chapter. My special thanks go to Claire Hines for her advice, support and encouragement.

PART 2

AMERICA UNDER SIEGE

TERRORISM, GLOBALISATION, AND THE POLITICS OF (AMERICAN) MORALITY

'SO WHAT ARE YOU SAYING? AN OIL CONSORTIUM'S BEHIND THE NUKE?'

24, PROGRAMME SPONSORSHIP, SUVS, AND THE 'WAR ON TERROR'

PAUL WOOLF

One does not need the investigative skills of a Counter-Terrorist Unit agent to see some connection between the enormous success of *24* in Britain and America, and the post-9/11 preoccupation in both countries with terrorism and the so-called 'war on terror'. The first season of *24*, which revolves around a terrorist plot to assassinate a presidential candidate, was in production when the attacks on the World Trade Center and the Pentagon took place. It began transmission just two months later, in November 2001, soon after the start of US-led military action in Afghanistan.

The makers of *24* certainly seemed to capitalise on the first season's unexpected topicality when preparing for its second season. Season One's DVD box set includes a trailer for Season Two in which the show's star, Kiefer Sutherland, directly addresses the viewer. In a scripted sequence, Sutherland promises for Season Two, 'a story that's literally been ripped from today's headlines'. Season Two, it turned out, featured Middle Eastern terrorists attempting to detonate a nuclear bomb in Los Angeles. Its transmission – from October 2002 in the US and February 2003 in the UK – coincided with the build-up to the predominantly Anglo-American invasion of Iraq and the ensuing conflict.

This chapter explores in more detail the relationship between 24 and the 'war on terror'. My aim is to place the show in the context of a debate that at the time of writing is increasingly preoccupying American politicians, commentators and citizens. This debate connects the country's military action in Iraq and elsewhere, its dependence on foreign oil supplies, the environmental policies of its government, and the consumer habits of its population, especially with regard to automobiles. I will argue that 24's engagement with this debate is made particularly problematic by the sponsorship of the series in the USA by the Ford Motor Company. 24 enters into the controversy most explicitly in its second series so I will concentrate primarily, although not exclusively, on that season.

It seems for most of Season Two that a fundamentalist Islamic organisation, motivated by ideological anti-Americanism, and apparently sponsored by three unnamed Arab governments, is responsible for the attempted nuclear bomb attack on Los Angeles. In Season One, although Jack Bauer saved the life of presidential candidate David Palmer, his own daughter was kidnapped and wife killed as a consequence. In Season Two, Palmer, now the President, calls Bauer, depressed and inactive since his wife's death, back into action to prevent the bomb being detonated. Bauer gets to work while Palmer reluctantly prepares for what promises to be devastating retaliatory action against the three Arab nations. As the series progresses through innumerable twists and turns, it ultimately becomes evident that one Peter Kingsley (Tobin Bell) is actually behind the terrorist scheme. Kingsley is the front-man for a group of 'major players in the oil industry' (2.21) which has 'ties to oil interests both here [in the USA] and abroad' (2.23). The aim of Kingsley's cartel is to provoke a war in the Gulf. Why? 'To improve the value of their oil in the Caspian Sea and to control the oil coming out of the Middle East', Bauer discovers, and tells Palmer (2.21). Palmer delays launching air-strikes to allow Bauer time to search for evidence of Kingsley's guilt. The situation is made especially perilous because Kingsley has recruited senior members of the government's own National Security Agency (NSA) to assist his plan. We discover that malcontent administration insiders view the bomb threat as a way of undermining Palmer's presidency, and the war that will inevitably follow as a means of legitimising increased spending on defence. An attack on the innocent Arab nations – in which we are told there will be local civilian deaths as well as American military casualties – seems certain. Between them, however, Bauer and Palmer just about save Los Angeles and avert war in the Gulf.

The picture that finally emerges in Season Two of 24 is one of ruthless oil industry leaders willing to destroy hundreds of thousands of lives for profit, and of high-ranking US government officials willing to collaborate with them for personal and political gain. Only Palmer's heroic insistence that no bombs should be dropped until he has incontrovertible evidence incriminating the Arab nations, and Bauer's superhuman efforts to provide that proof, thwarts the greedy oil tycoons and treacherous politicians.

To my knowledge, it has never been suggested that George W Bush or anyone in his government has ever plotted to explode a nuclear bomb in Los Angeles. However, like the head of the NSA in 24, President Bush and his closest colleagues have been accused of using a terrorist attack on America as 'an opportunity to pursue another agenda' (Unger 2005: 251). They have been charged with deploying 9/11 as justification for fighting wars overseas that actually have more to do with the administration's complicity with the oil industry than with homeland security. An article by Michael Meacher, a British MP and former cabinet minister, merely sums up widespread concerns that Bush's 'war on terror' is really a war for control of oil supplies (2003: 21). Meacher notes that the US government ignored numerous advance warnings of the 11 September hijackings, and continues:

> it seems that the so-called 'war on terrorism' is being used largely as a bogus cover for achieving wider ... geopolitical objectives ... [It] is not surprising that some have seen the US failure to avert the 9/11 attacks as creating an invaluable pretext for attacking Afghanistan in a war that had clearly been well planned in advance. [ibid.]

Meacher argues that the long-term aim of the war in Afghanistan was to enable the construction, for the benefit of US oil companies, of 'hydrocarbon pipelines from the oil and gas field' in the nearby Caspian Sea region that in 24 is potentially so precious to Peter Kingsley and cohorts. Meacher contends that the war in Iraq was similarly motivated by the USA and UK's desire to gain greater control of Middle Eastern oilfields at a time when both nations face 'increasing dependence on' the region's oil. For Meacher, and many others, the 'war on terror' is about American and multinational corporations trying to secure access to oil so they can maintain supplies to, and control prices in, their most lucrative market – the USA, a nation that, as the well-used statistic goes, has less than five per cent of the world's population but consumes 25 per cent of its oil.

In the years since Meacher's article, numerous books and articles have investigated the myriad personal and financial ties between the Bush administration, and the oil trade and related industries (Baer 2003; Klare 2004; Roberts 2005; Unger 2005). Such works have analysed everything from the high levels of campaign funding donated to Republican politicians by oil companies (Roberts 2005: 294–5) to, perhaps most famously, Vice President Dick Cheney's involvement with Halliburton, a company that supplies engineering and other services to oil firms. Cheney was once Halliburton's chief executive officer, and the corporation has more recently been awarded by the US government contracts for work in post-war Iraq worth hundreds of millions of dollars (Sadowski 2003; Briody 2004). It has been implied that key figures within and connected to the administration, including the Vice President and the President's own close family, effectively have vested financial interests in the success of pursuing strategies, such as the 'war on terror', that benefit the oil industry (Briody 2004; Davis 2005: 82; Unger 2005: 223–6). Even when President Bush took up office in 2001, it was clear from the CVs and stockholding records of numerous of his senior appointees that, 'Never before had the highest levels of an administration so nakedly represented the oil industry' (Unger 2005: 222).

In this light, it is perhaps difficult to see Season Two of *24*, with its depiction of warmongering politicians colluding with the oil industry, as anything other than a critique of US foreign policy and its commercial objectives. A speech delivered by Palmer in 2.24, an episode filmed during the first weeks of the war in Iraq, is especially striking. The dovish President admonishes his hawkish cabinet for their eagerness to attack the three Arab nations:

> We came dangerously close to war today. That all of you reacted emo-
> tionally to the nuclear detonation is understandable. But leaders are
> required to have patience beyond human limits. The kind of action

we nearly took should only be exercised after all other avenues have
been exhausted, after the strictest standards of proof have been met.

One can easily interpret this as a reprimand to the Bush leadership, a
condemnation of the suspicious urgency with which it pressed for an attack
on Iraq, without any proof of Saddam Hussein's involvement with al-Qaeda
or of the country maintaining Weapons of Mass Destruction, and as an
expression of dissatisfaction at the US administration's 'emotional' use of
9/11 to justify such a war.

Indeed, it is possible to see Palmer as a carefully constructed, anti-Bush
figure. Having established Palmer's liberal credentials in Season One,
through fleeting verbal and visual references to his policies on healthcare,
taxation, abortion and affirmative action, those credentials are confirmed
and re-enforced in Season Two, in which we learn that this is an eco-friendly
President. Palmer's presidency is to a large degree defined by his pro-green
stance, for this is the only thing we learn during the entire second series
about his domestic policies. One suspects that this President would not
withdraw from the Kyoto Protocol, as President Bush did. Palmer spends the
day preventing a nuclear holocaust and a world war, but he was supposed to
have been giving a speech about 'clean energy' instead (2.1). Palmer's goal is
to save the planet by advocating responsible energy policies; the oil industry
seems intent on diverting him from that work.

24 undeniably casts Palmer as a hero, second only to Bauer himself in
the heroism stakes. However, environmental groups might find a certain
irony in the fact that a series that so venerates an eco-friendly President was
sponsored by the Ford Motor Company, particularly given, as I now want
to explain, Ford's use of 24 to promote its range of Sports Utility Vehicles,
or SUVs.

Between the early 1990s and mid 2005, sales of these characteristically
colossal vehicles increased phenomenally, and America became a nation of
SUV-drivers. By 2003, the year in which Season Two of 24 was transmitted,
there were estimated to be more than 20 million SUVs on American roads
(Barnett 2003). Along with pick-up trucks, they accounted that year for
around half of all new vehicles sold in the United States (Roberts 2005:
155). Supplying profit margins 'roughly ten times greater' than smaller
cars (Roberts 2005: 262), SUVs were reported to 'produce half the profits
automakers earn' (Frank 2003) and 'are widely credited with having almost

single-handedly kept American car-makers out of bankruptcy court' (Roberts 2005: 262). The sense of safety derived from the vehicles' large frames and driver's high vantage point is, apparently, what appeals most to consumers about SUVs (English 2003). Of Ford's SUV range, one of the organisation's own documents reportedly notes: 'SUVs contribute more than any other vehicle to the company's bottom line' (Anon, 'Green Products: The SUV Question', 2006).

In 2002, Ford paid between $1.5 million and $5 million (reports vary) to Fox to sponsor Season Two of 24 (Cozens 2003; Graser 2002: 7). As part of the deal, 2.1 was broadcast in the USA – very unusually – without commercial breaks. Instead, two three-minute Ford advertisements were shown, the first leading into the programme, and the second immediately after the final scene. The popularity of 24 with affluent, 18–49-year-old viewers (Strachan 2002), a demographic group much craved by advertisers, was presumably what attracted Ford to the show; the series provided the perfect opportunity for the company to market some of its more expensive models. While the pre-show half of the advertisement included footage of Ford's sports cars, the latter segment concentrated for the first minute-and-a-quarter on SUVs, presenting images of the vehicles being driven along otherwise empty roads in scenic, mountainous locations, and of a happy-looking family packing items such as bicycles and canoes into an SUV, presumably in preparation for a vigorously healthy vacation. The sequence combines two typical tropes of SUV advertising. First, it proclaims the notion that SUVs allow you to explore America's expansive, unspoilt countryside. Second, it expresses the idea that they offer the opportunity for families to spend safe, quality time together.

Given that, in Season One, Bauer ultimately fails to protect his family, 24 might seem a risky choice of a programme for Ford to align itself with. But if it was a gamble, it paid off. An American media monitoring service reported that the pair of three-minute commercials, 'though never rebroadcast, were among the most-remembered ads of the year. No other automotive spots even placed' (Rose 2003). The association of Ford with Bauer – the man who strives heroically to keep both family and nation safe – satisfied the motor manufacturer to the extent that the deal with Fox was repeated in 2003 for Season Three of 24. Echoing the previous strategy, 3.1 was broadcast without commercial breaks, but was accompanied by a short film, The Donation, a parody of 24 in which a construction worker named Jeff Bauer is mistaken for Jack Bauer and kidnapped. Bauer outwits his terrorist captors with the help of his trusty F-150 truck, a Ford model originally built for commercial users but that by 2003 had been increasingly redesigned and marketed also as a 'personal use pickup truck' – effectively, an SUV (Ford 2003). Bauer has the terrorists arrested and even manages to take from them a briefcase full of money that he then donates to a local paediatric care centre threatened with closure. Even more deliberately than with Season Two, Ford here uses its privileged advertising position to imbue its products with the same values arguably espoused by 24 itself: a commitment to community, family and national security.

It was, though, not only extended commercials that Ford gained from 24 in return for its money. Ford products, most notably SUVs, are featured conspicuously throughout the programme itself, though Ford stopped short of making theirs the only vehicles used on the series. One of the company's executives commented: 'We think that might be stepping over the line' (cited in McCarthy 2003). Indeed, we see characters driving a variety of brands during Seasons Two and Three. In a show in which people are constantly mobile and are dependent on the speed and reliability of their transport, motor vehicles have an almost heroic role in 24. SUVs – in 24, the chosen conveyance of America's counter-terrorism services – are especially prominent. Of course, though, of all SUVs in 24, Ford's are seen to be the most heroic, appearing at critical moments in Season Two. The very first time we see Bauer he is getting into his Ford SUV (2.1). Later, Bauer and Sherry Palmer drive to a showdown with Peter Kingsley that will, they hope, prove the oil magnate's guilt and prevent America starting a world war (2.24). They are driving a General Motors SUV, one Bauer was using earlier, when, in a moment not entirely necessary to the plot, they crash and are forced to requisition a passing vehicle. Bauer and Sherry's new transport just happens to be a Ford SUV; more than once the familiar blue and white badge on its front grille is clearly visible. The Ford safely carries Bauer and Sherry to their – ultimately successful – confrontation with Kingsley. We are invited to see a Ford SUV helping to save the world from the oil industry, and the terrorists and the corrupt politicians in its pay.

It is here that any environmentalists watching 24 might have seen some irony. Pro-environment groups have long disliked SUVs for their high gas-usage, which by 2003 was on average almost twice that of the average petrol-fuelled family saloon car (Younge 2003). SUVs, environmentalists say, create pollution and contribute significantly to global warming and the depletion of the world's natural fuel resources. Campaigners in America have decried Washington's unwillingness to enforce higher fuel-emission standards, which would be expensive for automobile companies to implement, and have accused both major political parties of accepting large campaign donations from US motor manufacturers in return for legislative leniency (Huffington 2003; Younge 2003; Roberts 2005: 296). The current government's ties to the automobile industry have been especially scrutinised, with critics noting that Andrew Card, White House Chief of Staff, was previously a General Motors executive and a chief lobbyist for the so-called Big Three group of automakers, which includes Ford (Huffington 2003; Kennedy 2003). According to an article written by Robert Kennedy Jr., the help given in 2003 by 'administration lawyers' to General Motors and DaimlerChrysler in challenging 'a California law that rewards carmakers for selling low-emission, gasoline-electric hybrid vehicles' is just one example of the collusion between the Bush administration and the motor industry that has created an SUV-friendly automobile market (ibid).

By the arrival of 24, Ford had become, for a number of reasons, perhaps the primary target of anti-SUV environmentalists' hostility. The company was, for instance, being accused of covering-up substantial evidence of their SUVs' poor environmental and safety records (The Environmental Working Group's 'SUV Report', 2003). Campaigners claimed Ford was evading legal fuel-efficiency standards with the production of its Excursion model; the Excursion is *so* large that, although marketed as an SUV, it actually classifies as a light truck and is thus exempt from the same federal regulations as most other SUVs (Fisher 1999; Bradsher 2000). Even when Ford announced intentions to improve the fuel efficiency of its SUVs, some environmentalists reacted with scepticism (Huffington 2002a).

In 2003, around the same time Season Two of 24 was being broadcast, SUVs became the target of several high-profile campaigns by environmental activists. These ranged from a spate of SUVs being vandalised, to television adverts funded by an environmental Christian group bearing the slogan 'What Would Jesus Drive?' (Younge 2002; Plungis et al. 2003).

By far the most controversial of the anti-SUV campaigns was launched by an organisation called The Detroit Project. The group presented the argument over SUVs in new and provocative terms: The Detroit Project accused SUV-users of inadvertently financing anti-American terrorism. Its website and television adverts, which juxtapose images of American SUV-users with masked Arab men firing machine guns into the air, put forward the argument that, because SUVs consume so much petrol, they increase the USA's dependence on buying oil from countries whose governments intentionally or otherwise help to harbour and fund anti-American terrorists, such as Saudi Arabia, where fifteen of the 9/11 hijackers obtained their US visas (Sheridan 2001). Furthermore, insisted Arianna Huffington, The Detroit Project's co-founder, the US government was willing to send its troops to war in Afghanistan and Iraq in order to feed the country's SUV-driven 'foreign oil habit' (Huffington 2002a) – 'to protect our supply of cheap oil in vehicles that would be prohibitively expensive to operate without it' (Huffington 2002b). The Detroit Project reproduced on its website Robert Kennedy's article, cited above. In it, Kennedy claims that a law raising fuel-economy standards would save nearly two million of the 20 or so million barrels of oil used every day by the USA, enough to free the nation from its dangerous reliance on Middle Eastern oil (2003). But, Kennedy implies it would be against the financial interests of American oil and automobile companies to take such action and, so, going to war to protect and increase current oil supplies, rather than enforcing greater fuel efficiency, is the preferred tactic of a government favourable to both industries. The ultimate aim of The Detroit Project was clear: to persuade US consumers to switch from gas-guzzling SUVs to smaller, more fuel-efficient cars in order to help rid the world, and America in particular, of terrorism.

Huffington and her supporters turned vehicle choice into an issue about patriotism; 'if American car buyers want to do something truly patriotic, they have to buy Japanese,' (referencing more fuel-efficient vehicles produced by companies like Toyota) (Huffington 2003). There was an inevitable backlash, with pro-SUV groups like Sport Utility Vehicle Owners of America emerging to argue that SUVs are in fact environmentally friendly, and that it is, in any case, every American's entitlement to buy whatever vehicle he or she chooses. The SUVOA even has its own 'Bill of Rights,' containing the clause: 'I have a basic right to own and operate the vehicle of my choice and to use it for whatever transportation purpose I may choose'. The SUVOA's view seems consistent with that of the US government, at least as expressed by White House Press Secretary Ari Fleischer in May 2001. When asked by a journalist whether 'the President believe[s]' Americans 'need to correct our lifestyles' as a means of curbing the country's unrivalled per-capita energy consumption, Fleischer replied, 'That's a big no. The President believes that it's an American way of life, and that it should be the goal of policy makers to protect the American way of life' (2001). Fleischer effectively proclaimed the Bush government's intention to protect not only freedom of consumer choice from state regulation, but also the right of Americans to world-beating levels of energy consumption. It is worth noting that since 9/11 other key figures in the Bush administration have used the same phrase as Fleischer, arguing that the 'war on terror' is rightfully being fought to preserve the 'American way of life' – that 'way of life' presumably, then, includes high energy usage (Rice 2004; Ridge 2004). In one of a number of direct rebuttals of The Detroit Project by journalists, columnist Daniel Ruth proffered a complementary opinion, contending that, regardless of the fuel efficiency of a vehicle (or lack thereof), it was 'un American' of 'Huffington ... to threaten your freedom to drive whatever vehicle you want,' and labelling the group's actions 'as much of a threat to society as thugs in caves [i.e. terrorists]' (Ruth 2003).

This debate, like that over gun control, asks what constitutes 'true' 'American-ness': community-mindedness (eschewing guns and SUVs), or the assertion of individual rights (owning a gun, driving an SUV) in the name of protecting one's self and family. A similar debate over the compatibility of personal rights and civic responsibilities is played out, almost obsessively, in Seasons One and Two of 24, through both Bauer and Palmer. Can they protect their families *and* perform their social duty in protecting the nation? The climactic murder of Jack's wife (1.24), and Palmer being seriously hurt in another assassination attempt (2.24) both suggest that the writers of 24 think safeguarding oneself and one's family *and* defending the country are ultimately incompatible, that one must pay a heavy personal price for preventing the United States from coming to harm.

However, The Donation, the extended advert that accompanied the start of Season Three, says something different, showing that, as long as you drive a Ford, maintaining personal safety and contributing to the community *are* compatible, presumably a preferable message for Ford to convey. There are further contradictions between the programme and its advertiser. In Season Two, by implicating the oil industry and its government connections in America's perceived vulnerability to terrorism, 24 presents a message that both anti-war and anti-SUV lobbies might welcome. But the series also valorises and insistently promotes the use of SUVs, seemingly oblivious to the relationship between, on one hand, the high fuel consumption of

SUVs and, on the other, America's problem with terrorism and, as Season Two of the show itself indicates, the connection between terrorism and oil. Americans are encouraged by the series to continue to buy gas-guzzling vehicles. One could argue that the show reassures consumers that, to keep America free from terrorism, they need not after all make the sacrifice of switching to smaller, more fuel-efficient cars, for instead brave, self-sacrificing men like Jack Bauer are on hand to protect the country. In this sense, Season Two of 24 might be considered a perfect embodiment of the logic of Bush-administration policy and rhetoric: American consumers need not make changes to their lifestyle, for instance by adhering to higher fuel-efficiency standards for vehicles, because the brave, self-sacrificing men and women of the American intelligence services and armed forces are available to safeguard the nation and the 'American way of life' by fighting the 'war on terror'.

POSTSCRIPT

In Season Four of 24, broadcast in both America and Britain in early 2005, Bauer once more saves the USA from Middle Eastern terrorists. Again, Ford had an involvement in the series, not this time by sponsoring a commercial-free premiere, but by providing what the programme credits call 'promotional consideration'. During the season, the various government agencies involved in the fight to foil the terrorists all drive around in fleets of Ford SUVs. Even more so than in previous seasons, these vehicles play a conspicuously crucial part in the counter-terrorist effort. To cite just one example of their countless appearances, Bauer spends almost the entirety of 4.2 inside a Ford SUV as he trails a suspect, demonstrating as he does the vehicle's apparently infallible handling ability. Season Four, however, contains none of the uncomfortable contradictions of Season Two. There is no apparent relation between these terrorists and the oil industry; they seem to be motivated solely by anti-Americanism. This 'war on terror' is one in which a heroic America battles 'lawless, godless' ideological fanaticism, and in which human-rights organisations and peace campaigners with 'sixth-grade Michael Moore logic' impede the nation in its counter-terrorist efforts (4.1). In comparison to Season Two, this portrait is more in keeping with the depiction of the actual 'war on terror' – as a relatively straightforward confrontation of good and evil – that is usually offered by Fox, the 'voice of Bushian crusading democracy' (Bloom 2005).

Since Season Four ended, there has been a discernible shift in American attitudes towards the nation's oil usage, and its connection to the 'war on terror'. In the wake of Hurricanes Katrina and Rita, petrol prices hit all-time highs in autumn 2005 (Teather 2005), sales of SUVs fell dramatically, seemingly as a consequence (Vidal 2005), and Ford announced it would discontinue production of the Excursion, and increase by tenfold its production of more environmentally friendly hybrid vehicles (Healey 2005). In his January 2006 State of the Union Address even George Bush admitted, 'we have a serious problem: America is addicted to oil.' If in 2003 the Detroit Project's arguments were deeply contentious, by October 2005 *The New York Times* could confidently declare, 'There's no serious disagreement that two major crises of our time are terrorism and global warming. And there's no disputing that America's oil consumption fosters both' (Anon 2005). Whether, and to what extent, *24* responds to this shift remains to be seen.

00.07

DAYS AND HOURS OF THE APOCALYPSE

24 AND THE NUCLEAR NARRATIVE

DANIEL HERBERT

Even before it went on the air, *24* gained a reputation for mirroring real-world events and social issues. The show made its debut in November 2001 and featured a narrative about terrorist threats to the United States; it depicted Jack Bauer working to prevent the assassination of presidential candidate David Palmer. Following the attacks of 11 September, sensitivity to the programme's apparent socio-political relevance prompted the Fox network to re-edit a sequence from the pilot episode that depicted an airplane exploding (Rice 2001: 28; James 2001b: 21). Similarly, the third season of the programme recalled the anthrax scare of October–November 2001, as it dramatised a terrorist attack with a killer virus, which was visualised as a white powder. Perhaps most remarkably, however, the second season of *24* dramatised fears about nuclear weapons, as it depicted Bauer and CTU attempting to stop terrorists from setting off an atomic bomb in Los Angeles. The agents fail, however, and the bomb detonates, making *24* one of the few television dramas to depict a nuclear explosion. In this respect, the programme illustrated contemporary concerns with nuclear weapons, circumscribed as they were by the ideological parameters of the post-9/11 cultural moment.

Yet 24 follows a tradition of nuclear narratives, a genre of films and television programmes designed to dramatise nuclear anxieties. As its constitutive feature, the nuclear narrative depicts the detonation of a nuclear weapon within the *mise-en-scène* (Shapiro 2002: 10). In this respect, a nuclear explosion and mushroom cloud comprise the 'semantic elements' that define the genre, according to Rick Altman's theoretical model (Altman 1999: 219). The narrative structures that situate semantic units within relationships mobilised by the nuclear narrative are variable and change over time (Altman 1999: 219). Scholars have demarcated several historical periods for the genre, typically based on relationships between the films and their socio-political contexts (Evans 1998; Perrine 1998; Shapiro 2002). Thus, the changes in the genre indicate shifts in cultural attitudes regarding nuclear weapons, which accord broadly with changing historical conditions.

Under the logic of the cold war conflict between the USA and the USSR, which prompted the arms race that produced over 65,000 warheads, nuclear weapons were largely viewed under the policy of 'mutually assured destruction' (MAD) that promised the end of life on the planet (Norris and Kristensen 2002: 103). The use of any nuclear weapon would lead quickly and inevitably to a full exchange of missiles between the two superpowers. After the cold war, however, conceptions of nuclear weapons changed. Following the bombing of the Federal Building in Oklahoma City and the attacks of 11 September 2001, popular discourses about nuclear weapons turned from the binary totality of the US/USSR conflict toward notions of 'asymmetrical warfare' between opponents of notably disparate methods and capabilities, 'weapons of mass destruction' (WMD), and the 'war on terror'.

This historical shift is clearly demonstrated in the narrative and aesthetic differences between 24 and an earlier television nuclear narrative, the made-for-television movie *The Day After* (ABC Circle Films, 1983). Whereas *The Day After* presents nuclear weapons within the terms of 'mutually assured destruction' consequential of the cold war, 24 conveys concerns with terrorism via 'weapons of mass destruction', as a mentality born of post-9/11 anxieties. Generically, the narratives of *The Day After* and 24 share many characteristics of melodrama and in this regard both programmes situate nuclear weaponry as a pervasive problem that threatens the family (Boyd-Bowman 1984: 89–92; Shapiro 2002: 187, 190). However, *The Day After* and 24 feature significantly different narrative structures, which delimit the programmes' respective representations of nuclear weapons. Further, both programmes mobilise different aesthetic strategies aimed at immediacy and 'liveness' in order to convey the threat of nuclear weapons. Whereas *The Day After* emulates tropes of *cinéma vérité*, *24* connotes liveness through its signature 'real-time clock' and split-screen effects. These changes further shift the depiction of nuclear weaponry from the catastrophic, total annihilation seen in *The Day After* to the limited, containable, and survivable crisis depicted in the second season of *24*.

The American Broadcast Company (ABC) aired *The Day After* on Sunday, 20 November 1983. The made-for-TV movie tells the stories of several families, couples, and individuals living in Kansas during a crisis between the US and the USSR. These stories do not intersect; rather, the programme cuts between the respective narratives. Maintaining what David Thornburn calls the 'multiplicity principle' of television melodrama, the programme presents a seemingly large number of diverse characters and thereby claims to represent a broad social portrait (1994: 542). Further, the characters' dramatic crises conflate domestic issues with the growing political/military crisis. For example, Russell Oakes (Jason Robards) and his wife (Georgann Johnson) discuss the military stand-off as they lie down to sleep. They recall the Cuban Missile Crisis and its peaceful resolution. As they acknowledge that they conceived their first child at that time, the programme thematically aligns the continuation of the family with nuclear deterrence. Negotiating between the social and the emotional, *The Day After* depicts a world where nuclear weapons bear heavily upon daily life and, conversely, the programme infuses nuclear weapons with the emotional charge of family melodrama.

Halfway through the two-hour programme, the nuclear missiles housed in the area suddenly take flight. Characters look on in horror in numerous intercut vignettes. Within the montage, the film depicts military personnel launching nuclear missiles and preparing bombers for take-off. Several minutes later, an orange explosion occurs over Kansas City, and another quickly follows. Images of pluming mushroom clouds are intercut with special effects shots showing multitudes of people being vaporised in the nuclear fire. Following this 'launch-and-explosion' sequence, the second hour of the programme tracks the surviving characters in the devastated and irradiated world. Everyone suffers from radiation poisoning and social unrest leads to mass confusion and violence; all the main characters eventually succumb and die. The last image depicts a mass of people in a makeshift infirmary dying of sickness, and the programme implies that none of them will live much longer. Finally, text appears on-screen stating that the events represented in the film are *less* severe than would occur in an actual nuclear exchange.

The Day After thus situates nuclear warfare within the terms of total global destruction, as it depicts absolutely no possibility for survival. To a great extent, the programme's narrative structure allows for this fatalism. As Laurie Shulze notes, made-for-TV movies typically feature melodramatic narratives about timely and provocative social issues (1994: 167). Thus, in 1983, Ronald Reagan's public rhetoric and defence policies aggravated tensions about nuclear weapons, as he promoted the 'star wars' Strategic Defence Initiative (SDI), referred to the Soviet Union as 'the Evil Empire', and dramatically increased military spending. However, the 'nuclear freeze' movement also gained popular and political strength during the early 1980s, and such resistance to nuclear proliferation demonstrates the heterogeneous social forces that made *The Day After* relevant at the time (Perrine 1998: 162). Most importantly, however, Shulze states that because made-for-TV movies appear on the air only once and have a limited duration, they regularly push the limits of acceptability in their representation of controversial issues (1994: 166). The singular nature of the made-for-television movie format allows *The Day After* to portray nuclear warfare as bleakly as it does, representing the end of civilisation graphically and conclusively. As a one-time television event, the programme has no obligation to create possibilities for future narratives. It ends it all, once and for all.

Or does it? In the autumn of 2002, nearly twenty years after the broadcast of *The Day After*, the second season of the programme *24* went on the air – and also depicts a nuclear explosion. During the first half of the season, Bauer locates and takes possession of a nuclear bomb from the terrorists who intended to detonate it. However, when he is unable to diffuse it, President Palmer and other officials decide someone must take the bomb to the Mojave Desert to minimise the damage of the inevitable explosion. In 2.15, George Mason (Xander Berkeley), another CTU agent, flies with Bauer into the desert in a small biplane. At the last minute before the detonation, Bauer jumps from the plane and parachutes to 'safety', hiding behind a rock as the bomb goes off. Mason, who was already dying from radiation poisoning following an earlier accident, is the only casualty of the explosion.

In constructing this narrative, *24* resembles *The Day After* and other television melodramas inasmuch as it defers social crises to the domestic sphere, features moments of excessive emotion, and sustained multiple, simultaneous plotlines. However, *24* masculinises the genre of television melodrama in particular ways. As Ina Rae Hark notes, the show's first season situates its plots of espionage, terrorism, and political subterfuge within a melodrama of troubled fatherhood (2004: 130). As Bauer and Palmer deal with labyrinthine terrorist plots, the men similarly cope with threats to (or from) female members of their family. At the first season's conclusion, Bauer and CTU thwart the attempt on Palmer's life within the twenty-four hour period of the narrative, yet not before the terrorists kill Jack's wife (1.24). His success as a super-spy results in his failure as a husband.

The second season similarly fuses the social and the familial. It begins with Bauer estranged from his daughter, Kim, as she blames him for the death of her mother. In 2.1, she refuses to speak to him when he arrives unannounced at her job as a nanny, which visibly causes him emotional stress. By the end of the season, however, and after surmounting innumerable deadly obstacles, Bauer and Kim reunite happily to re-formulate their family (2.24). Similarly, Mason reconciles with his estranged son after it becomes apparent that he will die soon from radiation poisoning (2.7). Finally, after Palmer separates from his wife, Sherry, in the first season, she continually attempts to get back in his good graces during the second. Her efforts to gain government security clearances and attend high-level policy meetings function in tandem with her attempts to rekindle a romance with her ex-husband. However, this political/romantic reconciliation disintegrates when it becomes apparent that she worked with the terrorists behind the nuclear attack. In all these cases, the male protagonists struggle to maintain the unity of the family in the face of political and military threats.

This masculinised melodramatic structure bears heavily upon the representation of the nuclear explosion, as government agents try to prevent, contain, and react to the detonation; that is, the primary narrative agents in *24* are male government agents. Whereas *The Day After* portrayed ordinary citizens and denied these characters agency in dealing with their fates, *24* selectively provides its protagonists with access to and control of nuclear weaponry. In this way, *24* recalls older nuclear narratives such as *Fail Safe* (Sidney Lumet, 1964), as it places nuclear weaponry in the hands of the 'proper', primarily male, authorities (Evans 1998: 159).

Even so, *24* retains the excessive emotionality typical of melodrama. Bauer succeeds in removing the bomb from Los Angeles, but not before he has a final, emotionally charged telephone conversation with his daughter. When Palmer views the glow of the explosion on the horizon from Air Force One, he looks down in a sombre moment of reflection. Notably, Kim also witnesses the explosion from behind a mountain ridge. Within the context of the narrative, however, the grief on her face derives from her belief that her father just died in the blast, and not from any concerns about fallout or other consequences of a nuclear explosion (2.15).

Although *The Day After* and *24* share many stylistic conventions of melodrama, *24* structurally resembles a different television format, the soap opera. As such, the programme continually delays narrative closure and this serial structure radically circumscribes its depiction of the nuclear blast. As a serial narrative airing over many weeks, *24* must allow for future episodes and even seasons. Indeed, after the explosion, the remainder of the season dramatises Palmer's reaction to civil unrest provoked by the nuclear explosion, Bauer's efforts to prove the bomb was not the work of a fictionalised Middle Eastern nation, and Palmer's resistance to those who would attack that country in a rash act of retaliation. Although these plots are rife with danger and intrigue, the fact remains that the narrative continues intact, whereas the plot of *The Day After* negates any future narratives. Because of its format, *24* cannot examine global nuclear warfare, but rather the programme depicts a single nuclear device and thereby limits the extent of possible narrative consequences of the explosion. Most remarkably, the nuclear explosion in *24* kills only one person and radioactive fallout presents almost no danger whatsoever. This indicates a significant shift in the nuclear narrative as it exists on television. For all that *24* demonstrates the continued awareness of nuclear weapons as a threat to public safety, the programme connotes that this threat is containable and limited.[1]

In addition to these differences in narrative structure, *24* and *The Day After* use strikingly different aesthetic strategies, and these differences also shape the programmes' characterisations of nuclear weapons. Primarily, *The Day After* uses the conventions of glossy, high-end television productions. However, several sequences utilise hand-held images of high-grain film stock, replicating the look of *cinéma vérité* documentaries (Perrine 1998: 164). During the nuclear attack, this technique is used to show military men confirming the launch codes in a bomber and, in its depiction of the nuclear explosions, the programme intercuts between the special effects shots and documentary images of real-world nuclear tests. Mobilising a set of aesthetic strategies that John Caldwell calls the 'docu-real', *The Day After* grounds its moments of high style in historical reality (Caldwell 2002: 259). The 'docu-real' refers to the overt use of documentary strategies as a way of critiquing the existing aesthetic norms of a programme (Caldwell 2002: 259-60). The docu-real aesthetics used in *The Day After* displace the heightened emotionality of its melodramatic moments with senses of immediacy, realism, and 'liveness'.

The sense of liveness in *The Day After* reinforces the impact of nuclear weapons by representing nuclear war as televisual catastrophe. Jane Feuer argues that television's 'liveness' allows programmes to make claims of immediacy and presence, even though television is comprised of a collage of sources with disparate time-space relations (1983: 16). As an ideology, 'liveness' acts as a conduit between these discontinuous elements, and in this way television works to legitimise its discourse. The liveness registered by *The Day After* reveals the programme's ambition to depict the 'reality' of nuclear warfare, and specifically situates this depiction as monumental televisual 'catastrophe', in the sense indicated by Mary Ann Doane. Doane theorises three modes of television: information, crisis, and catastrophe. Information is based on immediacy and continuity and constitutes the most regular function of television (1990: 223-8). Crisis, on the other hand, is comprised of those events that provoke televisual interruptions that occur and resolve over a finite period of time (1990: 223, 237). Catastrophe is distinguishable by a radical interruption in the normal flow of time, one that is massive in scale, threatens death, and indicates a failure of technology (1990: 228-38). Notably, Doane states that nuclear disaster constitutes the height of potential catastrophe, as does Patricia Mellencamp in her respective discussion of televisual catastrophe (Doane 1990: 231; Mellencamp 1990: 260).

Like several other nuclear narratives from the period, *The Day After* conveys liveness by aligning itself with crisis news coverage. For instance, the television movie *Special Bulletin* (National Broadcast Company, 1983) overtly emulates a live news report. Similarly, in his analysis of *The Day After*, Gregory Waller notes that the HBO production *Countdown to Looking Glass* (1984) seeks to convey immediacy by imitating a news broadcast and 'crisis telejournalism' (Waller 1987: 13). Likewise, *The Day After* conveys most of the narrative information regarding the crisis between the USA and the USSR as characters view 'live' television news broadcasts within the diegesis. These broadcasts mimic the news bulletins that might really interrupt normal broadcasting in such a situation or any real-world crisis. This implicates how *The Day After* self-reflexively aims for immediacy. In the manner of televisual crisis coverage of the early 1980s, the narrative depicts an ongoing, temporally synchronous, and unresolved crisis in the world.

However, when the missiles take flight, no warning is given. *The Day After* takes all responsibility to depict this massive televisual interruption. Remarkably, the visually spectacular and emotionally harrowing launch-and-explosion sequence lasts twelve minutes. Given its sudden occurrence and extended length, the sequence radically interrupts the progression of the narrative in a gesture toward a catastrophe of the highest order. The intermittent use of *vérité* aesthetics maintains the sense of immediacy and liveness throughout this montage. Notably, the original broadcast of *The Day After* featured no advertisements following the launch-and-explosion sequence. Although the lack of commercials resulted from caution on the part of advertisers, it textually connoted that the greatest interruption had already occurred and that no other was possible. The programme provided images for and commentary upon the ultimate televisual catastrophe, ultimate in that its reality would wholly negate televisual imaging and commentary altogether.

24 also aims at televisual immediacy and liveness in order to render the devastating effects of nuclear weapons. However, *24* conforms to broad changes in television aesthetics since the 1980s that reconfigured the aesthetics of liveness. The programme gained much initial press for its real-time narrative chronology, wherein the story and the narrative occur synchronously over twenty-four hours (Genette 1980: 27). The programme reinforces this narrative conceit with a distinctive visual motif: an on-screen 'real-time clock' that displays the time within the diegesis. Although the clock occasionally appears during the narrative, it appears uniformly as the 'bumper' between commercial segments as well as at the end of episodes. In this respect, the clock effaces discontinuities between 'segmentation and flow' and visually illustrates the synchronicity between the time of viewing and the narrative chronology (Feuer 1983: 15–16). Further, *24* consistently uses split-screens to depict separate events in different 'windows' within the television frame. In some cases the screens reveal different perspectives on the same scene. In many other cases, however, the split-screens depict geographically separate but temporally synchronous events. For example, in 2.15, one screen shows Kim wandering on a rural highway, another shows agent Tony Almeida at CTU headquarters, while a third depicts government agents moving the nuclear bomb, and finally a fourth screen shows Bauer at an airfield.

The 'real-time clock' and split-screen effects conform to John Caldwell's description of the 'videographic' tendency of 'televisuality,' or the excessive style in television begun in the 1980s (1995: 5–6, 12–13). In this respect, 24 resembles the look of twenty-four hour cable news channels, such as the Cable News Network (CNN), and the multi-tasking 'windows' of a computer connected to the Internet. Of course, since the 1980s, both CNN and graphical-interface computer software became commonplace and, moreover, both became strongly associated with notions of multiplicity and simultaneity. Following these new aesthetic tropes of 'liveness', the multiple screens and videographic flourishes of 24 gesture towards the discontinuous elements that comprise televisual flow. However, rather than causing significant narrative or aesthetic disruptions, the deft use of split-screens makes these elements all the more coherent. By fragmenting various scenes into multiple windows and yet also placing them in the same visual field, 24 displays the chronological simultaneity of its multiple narrative threads. As the on-screen clock connects this chronology to the temporal conditions of viewing, 24 renders liveness precisely *through* its visual fragmentation and videographic flourishes.

Although these strategies register liveness for a new televisual context, the programme reconditions nuclear weaponry from catastrophe to crisis. Within the narrative, Palmer illegally imprisons a reporter who knows about the nuclear threat in order to suppress news of the bomb from going public before it explodes; the programme insinuates that mass panic among citizens outweighs the threat of their annihilation (2.2). In this way, the programme refrains from dramatising crisis coverage within the diegesis. However, 24 emulates the crisis coverage that it suppresses within its own narrative. Through the real-time and spatially fragmented visual structure, illustrated by the on-screen clock and multiple split-screens, the crises in the programme mimic the continuous, synchronous, and unresolved aesthetics of crisis news coverage. Unlike the moment of the early 1980s, however, when social crises would prompt the interruption of normal television broadcasts on the major networks, 24 renders crisis for the post-CNN era of continuous, visually fragmented news reportage. As on CNN, crisis structures the visual excess and continual temporality of the programme.

When the nuclear explosion occurs, it does not interrupt the progression of the narrative. Instead, it provides a moment of visual intensity, among the many gunfights, car chases, and 'videographic' flourishes that regularly appear on 24. Rather than interrupting the narrative, in fact, the detonation is itself interrupted by the end of the episode. When 2.16 begins, the detonation is recounted in the 'last time on 24 ... ' lead-in, and the explosion appears again at CTU headquarters via satellite imagery. The government agents watch in awe as the mushroom cloud ascends on multiple video screens. By rendering the explosion a visual spectacle for the programme's characters to behold, rather than as an experience of physical annihilation, 24 mitigates the catastrophic impact of the nuclear bomb. Soon after the blast, Almeida rallies the agents with a rousing speech while images of the explosion play and replay behind him, much like CNN continually replays spectacular images of various disasters. Quickly enough, the agents resume their jobs and the narrative proceeds to new problems and new crises. In this respect, 24 integrates the image of the nuclear explosion within a regularised visual scheme, and thereby construes the explosion as a crisis rather than a catastrophe.

In these ways, 24 participates with the historically durable nuclear narrative genre, yet alters the narrative and aesthetic framings of nuclear weaponry for the post-9/11 American context. Starkly contrasting with the cold war totality seen in The Day After, 24 depicts nuclear bombs as just one of a number of threats from 'weapons of mass destruction', the devastating powers of which, although massive and/or visually spectacular, are confined to limited spaces, times, and human casualties.

Yet, as a cultural manifestation of social issues, 24 does not function simplistically as a mirror. Indeed, nothing demonstrates the terrifying relevance of 24 more than the following: the first episode of the second season aired in late October 2002, just after the US Congress authorised war with Iraq if it did not give up its 'weapons of mass destruction'. As Bauer sought out a rogue nuclear device on 24, rhetoric about Iraqi WMD and specifically *nuclear* weapons flooded from the White House through 2002 and into 2003. Despite numerous anti-war peace rallies held across the United States, war appeared inevitable as television news programmes promulgated the discussion of Iraq's threat to the USA and the world. On

4 March 2003, *24* depicted a nuclear bomb exploding within the USA, dramatising many Americans' worst fears about terrorism, and the next episode depicted the second half of the explosion on 25 March. Between these episodes, 'interrupting' *24*'s narrative and its visualisation of a nuclear explosion, the United States invaded Iraq. On 21 March 2003, live news coverage showed the air-bombings that rendered 'shock and awe' in Baghdad with massive explosions. Here was the inverse of *24* but following the same logic: a live, immediate, and televisually spectacular display of weapons of mass destruction. But no nuclear arms or any other WMD were found in Iraq. In fact, in a speech delivered on 14 December 2005, George W Bush admitted that 'much of the intelligence turned out to be wrong' regarding Iraqi WMD, conceding that the stated reasons for the invasion of Iraq were based on misconceptions and untruths (quoted in McKinnon and Dreazen 2005: A.1).[2] Living after *The Day After*, can we take solace that the nuclear narrative remains confined to fictions?

NOTES

1. The television movie *Special Bulletin* (National Broadcast Company, 1983) presents an exception to this historical trend. In this 'loose nuke' scenario, a single nuclear device explodes in Charleston, South Carolina, and renders only localised damage. Nevertheless, this narrative is firmly situated within the larger nuclear stand-off between the USA and the USSR. Moreover, many more 'loose nuke' theatrical films were made after the fall of the Berlin Wall, such as *True Lies* (James Cameron, 1994), *Broken Arrow* (John Woo, 1996), and *The Sum of All Fears* (Phil Alden Robinson, 2002), which, like *24*, reflect a newly configured anxiety about the unmonitored traffic and detonation of single warheads within the United States.

2. McKinnon and Dreazens's article covers a speech President George W Bush delivered on 14 December 2005 at the Woodrow Wilson Center in Washington DC. A full transcript of this speech is available as a press release on the White House website, at www.whitehouse.gov/news/releases/2005/12/20051214-1.html.

00.08

24 AFTER 9/11

THE AMERICAN
STATE OF EXCEPTION

ANNE CALDWELL
AND SAMUEL A CHAMBERS

In December 2005, the *New York Times* revealed to Americans and to the rest of the world that President George W Bush had authorised domestic spying by the NSA, circumventing the 1978 Foreign Intelligence Surveillance Act designed specifically to deal with this issue, and going beyond even the loose and already controversial boundaries of the 2001 Patriot Act (Baker 2005; see also Cole 2005). Despite being legally authorised to wield perhaps the greatest powers in history to encroach on Americans' civil liberties, President Bush secretly went beyond those laws. In doing so, he justified the exceptional status of his and the NSA's actions by explicit and implicit reference to the changes wrought by 9/11 (and concomitantly to legal opinions on the scope of presidential authority, and the Congressional 'Use of Force' Resolution of 14 September 2001).

While the entirety of the first season of *24* aired after 9/11 – the series premiere aired on 6 November 2001 – the show was conceived and created, the episodes written and directed well before the terrorist attacks on New York and Washington. Thus, the second season of *24* marks the first post-9/11 representation of counter-terrorism on the show (and also, in a sense, *to* American audiences). More important than the timing, this season of *24* communicates to its viewers the very sense that American politicians, and particularly the Bush administration, have been insisting upon and repeating ceaselessly since 9/12: '9/11 changed everything'. Season Two of *24* thus offers viewers a representation of the 'new world' that is, putatively, post-9/11 America and its 'war on terror'.

This chapter will analyse the politics of *24*'s second season through the concept of 'the state of exception'. Drawing particularly from the writings of Giorgio Agamben, we will offer a reading of the second season of *24* guided by Agamben's understanding of the state of exception. Not only does the theory of the state of exception help to elucidate the political stakes of the show, but the logic of *24* draws to light the significance of the theory of exception for our understanding of democratic and liberal politics in the twenty-first century. Read together, *24* and the theory of exception show us how American domestic politics and foreign policy function in a post-9/11 world.

The second season of *24* illustrates politically and theoretically significant facets of the 'state of exception'. First, the transition from the exception as just that – a rare and exceptional event that only occasionally interrupts the standard order – to the exception as the norm, occurs much more subtly, easily, and quickly than we might at first presume. Second, once the exception becomes regularised, all exceptional acts hold the same surface plausibility. One can map out differences in the exception, as we will here, but the effort to draw up criteria to distinguish some exceptional acts from others proves highly contingent and never ultimately tenable. Consequently, any theory of the 'state of exception' will demonstrate the futility of distinguishing between legitimate and illegitimate exceptional acts. The exception is precisely that which calls into question our criteria for legitimacy. The zone of the exception proves to be a liminal realm in which the clear lines of legitimacy blur. *24* attempts to draw those lines, and, in so doing, demonstrates their fuzziness, along the way shedding important light on America's own 'state of exception' since 9/11.

THE STATE OF EXCEPTION

The state of exception is a highly ambiguous and always politically fraught concept; one can locate little consensus among scholars on its exact meaning. While the roots of the exception can be traced back to the mechanism for instituting dictatorship found within Roman law, today, in general, 'state of exception' refers to a situation of crisis or emergency, wherein normal law is suspended. Distinct political traditions exist for dealing with the exception: some place the exception *within* the rule of law (as with the Roman example), while others do not. For example, France regulates the use of the exception by law, under the heading of a state of siege. Great Britain does not, and instead refers to martial law. The United States similarly has no legal provisions for the exception: the constitutional basis for addressing emergencies remains thoroughly ambiguous. As is well known, Article 1 of the US Constitution permits the suspension of habeas corpus when required by public safety. War powers, additionally, are uneasily shared by a Congress which declares law and war, and a President who executes the law and commands the military.

The gradual expansion of exceptional practices over the course of the twentieth century intensifies the liminal nature of the exception, generating an overlay of democratic and absolutist forms, of legal and extra-legal events. The Nazi regime's legal seizure of power is a familiar instance of a state of exception. As Agamben, one of the foremost political theorists of the exception, states: immediately after coming to power, Hitler 'proclaimed the Decree for the Protection of the People and the State, which suspended the articles of the Weimar Constitution concerning individual liberties. The decree was never repealed, so that from a juridical standpoint the entire Third Reich can be considered a state of exception that lasted twelve years' (2005: 2). The first clear example of the modern state of exception, however, occurred during the French Revolution. Agamben emphasises this origin, lest we 'forget that the modern state of exception is a creation of the democratic-revolutionary tradition and not the absolutist one' (2005: 5). In the United States, the first widely cited use of exceptional powers was accomplished by Lincoln to address the Civil War (Fisher 2004). Beginning with the First World War, the state of exception and its techniques have been regularly, if ambiguously (and sometimes secretly), used by western democracies.

A state of exception can be 'declared' in different ways, and once declared it may be implemented through varied and disparate practices. In countries where the exception is constitutionally regulated, a legal state of siege can be declared. Even in countries which do not legally regulate the exception, similar declarations are possible. In the United States, a limited emergency was declared in 1939, and an unlimited one in 1941 (Agamben 2005: 22). Nor is the state of exception limited to war. President Roosevelt treated the Great Depression as a national emergency, and was granted by the 1933 Congressional National Recovery Act 'an unlimited power to regulate and control every aspect of the economic life of the country' (ibid). Techniques of exceptional rule include the extension of military powers into the civil sphere, the suspension of the constitution (or parts of), legislative delegation of extensive powers to the President, a presidential assertion of such powers, and the power of the executive to issue decrees with the force of law.

These examples demonstrate Agamben's central point about the exception: the consistent ambiguity of its status as either a juridical event or a political one. As a juridical act, the exception *suspends the law*. This presents a unique dilemma: how can a legal act suspend its own order? As a political event, the exception *has no legal form* – it follows from necessity and proves *indifferent* to law. This presents a different dilemma: if the rule of law can be suspended by that which lies outside of it, then hasn't rule of law itself been thoroughly subverted?

Such dilemmas illustrate the exception as a 'limit concept'. Because the exception 'is a suspension of the juridical order itself, it defines law's threshold or limit concept' (2005: 4). Even the effort to define the exception based on its evident grounds participates in this uncertainty. If one treats the exception as a political event grounded in necessity and a state's right to its own preservation, then the apparent 'facts' of the situation and its 'necessity' require a determination as to what the facts are, what they mean, and whether necessity exists (2005: 23, 29–30). The liminal nature of the exception now emerges clearly: 'in truth, the state of exception is neither external nor internal to the juridical order, and the problem of defining it concerns precisely a threshold, or a zone of indifference, where inside and outside do not exclude each other but rather blur with each other' (2005: 23). It is precisely in working through and dealing in this liminal realm that the second season of *24* can shed light on the state of exception in general, and on the particular case of American foreign and domestic policy after 9/11.

Whether classified as political fact or legal decision, the exception's original existence is based on its evident necessity and its temporary nature. This nature, Agamben stresses, significantly changes in the twentieth century, such that the exception becomes the norm. The transformation proves especially clear in the expanded powers of the US President. Once temporary, the exception has now become 'the dominant paradigm of government in contemporary politics' (2005: 2). These transformations have profound significance for constitutional democratic regimes: if the exception becomes the rule, we may lose the ability to make stark distinctions between democracy and dictatorship. Agamben draws this logic out: 'this transformation of a provisional and exceptional measure into a technique of government threatens radically to alter – in fact, has already palpably altered the structure and meaning of the traditional distinction between constitutional forms. Indeed, from this perspective, the state of exception appears as a threshold of indeterminacy between democracy and absolutism' (2005: 2–3).

In addition to the expansion of its temporary nature, the necessity of a state of exception has been changed by its regular use. Agamben points out that since the Second World War, a willed or '*voluntary* creation of a permanent state of emergency ... has become one of the essential practices of contemporary states, including so-called democratic ones' (2005: 2, emphasis added). This discretionary element of the late twentieth century state of exception offers a useful lens to analyse the American response to the events of 11 September 2001. As domestic critics of the President's quick assertion of a war footing argued, Osama bin Laden and al Qaeda could be treated as criminals, a category that both American domestic law and international law were capable of handling. Yet President Bush resolutely insisted on treating the attacks on Washington and New York not as criminal acts but as acts of war – *exceptional acts* requiring for their response *exceptional measures*:

> President Bush's decision to refer to himself constantly as the 'Commander in Chief of the Army' [sic] after September 11, 2001 must be considered in the context of this presidential claim to sovereign powers in emergency situations ... Bush is attempting to produce a situation in which the emergency becomes the rule, and the very distinction between peace and war (and between foreign and civil war) becomes impossible. [Agamben 2005: 22]

24 AND THE INCESSANT EXCEPTION

Season Two of *24* opens directly onto some of the most graphic and direct scenes of torture ever aired on American network television. Shows such as *Alias* frequently *imply* brutal torture (e.g. through pre-torture 'discussions' between a captive and his or her captor, surrounded by gruesome instruments of torture) and occasionally they show glimpses of serious physical abuse, but *24* provides viewers with a series of truly ghastly images (2.1). The setting is Seoul, South Korea; the programme places emphasis on the fact that the featured torturers are all native Koreans (and thereby non-US citizens). Yet it remains just as clear that the men sitting in the shadows of the room nearby, who hear the information extracted from the torture victim, are undoubtedly covert US government operatives.

The season thus begins in a state of exception – outside US soil, engaged in illegal and unauthorised acts of torture. And this occurs even before the information produced through that scene (information described later as having 'extremely high credibility') will produce the conditions for the state of exception in which the entirety of the season operates. The torture victim finally talks, claiming that a nuclear weapon lies in terrorist hands, somewhere in Los Angeles. And it will be detonated 'today'. To heighten this sense, the next scene cuts to President Palmer fishing with his son. Here we find Palmer out of his suit, outside Washington, literally 'off the shore' sitting on a boat. Palmer, who quickly learns of the terrorist threat, will spend the entirety of the season acting from his base in Oregon – literally as far from the seat of government in Washington, DC as one can go within the contiguous United States.

The opening episode quickly increases the emphasis on exceptional status. As if the viewers might not grasp the extreme nature of the terrorist nuclear threat on US soil, Palmer's adviser says starkly: 'to my knowledge no president has been re-routed by the NSA on a morning off' (2.1). And as if the torture and the nuclear threat did not sharply define the potential position outside or beyond the law, Palmer's first action in response to the crisis is to call on the aid of a non-active, unstable agent, Jack Bauer. Once more, the dialogue reiterates precisely that which the images and plot are screaming, as Palmer tells Bauer: 'this is not a routine request'. Thus, within the first 15 minutes of Season Two's 24 hours, the show has made dramatic alterations to the narrative fabric it produced in Season One. Without a doubt, 'the world has changed'. These words echoed in the US public sphere after 9/11, and here they clearly apply to and shape the fictional world constructed by 24. The season operates under the conditions of the state of exception, a point brought forcefully home by the climax of 2.1.

Following Palmer's orders, George Mason (Xander Berkeley), the head of the Counter Terrorism Unit (CTU), convinces Bauer to go undercover to make contact with criminal Joseph Wald (Jon Gries) who may know something about the terrorist plot. Bauer immediately demands to see

Federal prisoner Marshall Goren (Carl Ciarfalio) scheduled to testify against Wald. Assuming Bauer plans to interrogate Goren about Wald's whereabouts, Mason pulls a number of strings to deliver Goren to CTU, where he meets with Bauer in the conference room. Bauer asks Goren only one question – 'you are Marshall Goren?' – before, after a dramatic pause, pulling a gun and shooting him in the chest. Mason immediately explodes, 'are you out of your mind?!' Bauer responds with the same urgency, in an exchange that punctuates the emphasis on state of exception: 'You want to find this bomb? This is what it's going to take'. Mason protests about killing a witness and Bauer merely continues: 'that's the problem with people like you, George. You want results but you never want to get your hands dirty. I'd start rolling up your sleeves'. Bauer then goes on to literally get blood on his hands before telling Mason that he's 'going to need a hacksaw' so that he can remove the head from the body. Nothing, this scene tells us, is unacceptable today; anything goes.

Yet 24 fascinates precisely because 'everything' does not exactly go. 24 highlights the liminal status of the exception, revealing the extent to which a decision is always necessary as to what constitutes exceptional measures and when they are appropriate. In the process, the show reveals both the genuine need for the exception and the space opened up for distorting and abusing the exception. The legitimacy of even the most evident exceptions has no clear criteria. However, in the show, unlike regular life, it is much easier to recognise putatively legitimate exceptional practices since the audience receives clearer information than everyday citizens. In any event, the pervasive awareness of an exceptional situation portrayed in the opening episode never disappears. 24 offers viewers the exception incessantly. In this respect 24 conveys the sense of twenty-first century politics that Agamben notes: the exception has become the norm, its techniques transformed into a regular tactic of politics. The regularisation of the exception in this sense corresponds to the twentieth century's fascination with war (Patocka 1996; Hedges 2003).

Thus, the opening scenes of 2.1 are in no way unique, as every 'side' involved in the complex political situation makes use of torture. Members of Second Wave, the terrorist group responsible for the bombing, torture both Kate Warner (Sarah Wynter) and Bauer. Later, to extract information from the head of Second Wave Syed Ali (Francesco Quinn), Bauer ups the ante by establishing a live feed to Ali's home country, showing Ali's family held by security forces. Bauer orders the forces to shoot Ali's son, and after they do so he threatens to kill Ali's second son. Ali talks (2.11). This scene, however, turns out to be faked, a fact Bauer later uses to get Ali to tell him the evident truth: the recording of a meeting in Cyprus among three Middle Eastern countries, conspiring to detonate a bomb on US soil, is itself a fake (2.15).

Less graphic but more disturbing is Palmer's authorisation of the torture of Roger Stanton (Harris Yulin), the head of the National Security Agency, based on a suspicion that Stanton has knowledge of the bomb's location (2.10). Palmer calls aside a Secret Service member with CIA training, saying 'What I'm about to ask you to do falls outside the parameters of your charge at SS.' Asked how far the agent can go, Palmer says, 'Whatever you need to do.' The presidential order to torture a government official is precipitated by the determination that existing evidence does not warrant the arrest of Stanton. Mike Novick (Jude Ciccolella), the Chief of Staff, suggests the President remove Stanton and 'deal with the legal ramifications tomorrow'. He adds that the President 'may need to expand the limits of how far you've been willing to go in the past'.

Acting outside 'normal parameters' is a regular practice among 24's CTU agents. Continuing his participation in these practices, Bauer fires his gun near the head of a witness, and then drugs a CTU agent (2.5). A later exchange between Bauer and acting CTU director, Tony Almeida, reinforces the regular status of the state of exception for Bauer. He insists that Almeida has a responsibility to tell Palmer that the Cyprus recording may be a fake (2.15). Almeida responds, 'You're going to lecture me on responsibility? ... We both know how you work. You consider going against the grain some kind of a virtue.' Confirming Almeida's description of him, Bauer then calls Palmer himself – another operation outside the normal protocols. While Almeida appears here as a critic of the exception, he later drugs his superior so that he can continue to help Bauer (2.22). At CTU, exceptional actions not only become regularised, but also are continually made to appear legitimate: the agents pursue leads that routinely turn out to be true. And the agents always appear to be working for the good of the country, to stop an indisputably imminent threat (i.e. to be doing exactly what President Bush claims he was doing in authorising domestic spying).

At the same time, but in crucial contrast with the actions of CTU agents, members of the executive branch also operate outside normal protocols. The very crisis in question has been produced in part through such actions:

the NSA let the nuclear bomb into the country in order to catch Second Wave (2.12). A secret special operations team, whose normal business is the exceptional, was to prevent the detonation. Yet the team is taken out, leaving the weapon under Second Wave's control. Once the bomb is safely detonated, Palmer delays final authorisation for a retaliatory attack until he can confirm the Cyprus recording is not fake (2.16). Cabinet members, long worried that Palmer's defence policy is too weak, fret at his delay. Novick conspires with Vice-President Jim Prescott (Alan Dale) to hold a cabinet vote on removing Palmer from office (2.16). Prescott showcases the tortured Stanton to demonstrate that Palmer can no longer 'discharge' his duties, unaware of the irony of suggesting Palmer has gone too far in the midst of a cabinet coup. The exceptional effort to unseat a sitting President appears an illegitimate exception (2.21). Not only is it an unprecedented measure, invoking the 25th Amendment for purposes beyond its conceived intent; it is, as viewers can gather, without foundation. The recording is a fake.

24 rehearses a large set of exceptional practices, showing both the need for and danger of those responses. Once exceptional measures are regularly taken, all exceptional measures appear equally plausible. They culminate, in 24, in a 'legal' act, invoking the Constitution to remove the President. In doing so, democratic rule is compromised, as the man elected to govern the country is removed from office by lower level officials.

THE STATE OF EXCEPTION AND THE RULE OF LAW: AMERICA AFTER 9/11

American policy since 9/11 has appealed to a variety of justifications for exceptional measures, and continues to make use of varied exceptional techniques – some of which, until quite recently, have been neither public, nor general Congressional knowledge. The White House regularly justifies the President's sweeping measures against terrorism as part of the powers vested in the President as both the executive and the Commander in Chief. In addition to, and perhaps also in conflict with, this argument, the White House also makes the case that in granting to the President the power to use 'all necessary and appropriate force' to combat terrorism, Congress has provided legislative sanction to the President's actions. Here, the exception is treated as a legal event. Its legality, however, largely depends on one man: the Act states that force may be used 'against those nations, organisations, or persons *he determines* planned, authorised, committed, or aided' (emphasis added) in 9/11.

American policy, however, has also treated the exception as a political fact. The President's rhetoric, echoed by Republicans in Congress and parts of the public, suggests that a state of war is self-evident, and that this empowers the President to undertake all necessary actions to protect the American people. The sense that 'the constitution is not a suicide pact' reflects a general sensibility that 'a state of exception' is justified ultimately by national self-preservation, indifferent to questions of legality. At the same time, the factor of time has clearly influenced Congressional and public sentiment about the exception. Five years of national crisis indicate both the tendency of the 'temporary' to become 'regular' and the way agreement on exceptions deteriorates over time.

The different justifications the White House has offered in defence of its actions highlight the complexity of the exception. While those who invoke the exception as a form of rule do so as if the need and practice were self evident, Agamben insists that the exception complicates the very meaning of legal juridical orders. The Bush administration rehearses all the varied ways that the exception can be justified: exceptional measures are necessary for the protection of the American people and state, regardless of their legal standing; exceptional measures are, nonetheless, legal; either they have been authorised by Congress, or they belong to the constitutional purview of the President; they belong to the President either in light of his executive position, his representation of the general public, or his military position.

It is in this context that we can return to 24's portrayal of the state of exception. A whole host of questions immediately arise: What does 24's construction of the state of exception tell us about contemporary US and international politics? Is it participating in that politics, merely reflecting it, or commenting upon it critically? (see Grossberg 1992). What is the legal and political status of the rule of law in 24's second season, and how does it speak to the status of the rule of law in the US today? One plausible approach to 24's depiction of the state of exception would be to seek a set of criteria that can help us to adjudicate between legitimate invocations of the state of exception and illegitimate ones. Such criteria could draw from differences in levels of power (national, state, local) or positions of actors (those authorised to undertake exceptional acts and those not). We would suggest that the most likely factor lies in a distinction between broad-based exceptions that apply at the general level of public policy, and specific, focused actions that apply only to a particular threat. Thus, to play out this example, the measures Bauer and the other CTU agents take have very specific and concrete aims: to stop a bomb from going off, and to give the President all accurate evidence for him to use in making a decision on war. In stark contrast, the aims of the cabinet prove quite broad: they always wanted a stronger defence policy, and they attempt to invoke a state of exception so as to achieve that goal – a goal distinct from the particular terrorist threat that the nation faces. Those members of the cabinet opposed to Palmer have already decided a course of action; unlike Palmer, they are interested only in finding or manufacturing evidence to support that decision.

This example proves how easy it is to construct criteria that would seek to distinguish between the legitimate exception and the illegitimate one and, no doubt, there are significant differences. However, when it comes to the state of exception, such distinctions cannot ultimately hold. We have tried to make the case, above, for Palmer as a 'good guy', and in the narrative of the show it is hard not to view him that way. Yet we cannot forget that Palmer *authorises the torture* of a government official. The criteria prove untenable because the 'state of exception' operates in precisely that liminal realm in which *legitimacy cannot be clearly or easily maintained* (Derrida 1992). The problem, but also therein the very importance, of both the theory and exercise of the state of exception hinges on the fact that within a state of exception no criteria of legitimacy can ever be firmly grounded. This logic holds because the invocation of exceptional status removes the very grounds in which one might attempt to fix such criteria (Norris 2000: 46–7). As a result, anyone might claim exceptional circumstances to justify their actions. As Agamben puts it, 'The state of exception is an anomic space in which what is at stake is a force of law without law' (2005: 39).

This means that the question concerning the state of exception can never be a question of legitimacy. We must ask, instead, much more complicated, demanding, and problematic questions – questions about how the state of exception is justified rhetorically and politically, about how it functions in terms of the political order and the rights that order bestows upon citizens, and most importantly about when the state of exception can end. When can the rule of law be restored and the state of exception brought to a close? How can the function and purpose of the state of exception be limited so that it does not merely become the norm? If the state of exception is to maintain a genuine relationship to the rule of law, then it cannot do so by claiming that the rule of law justifies the exception. It can only do so through upholding the rule of law, through circumscribing the state of exception.

This line of analysis might also imply, in the case of current American foreign and domestic policy (with the state of exception the two are always inextricably intertwined) that one cannot merely respond, as President Bush has, by claiming that the exception is warranted by law (see Chambers and Williford 2004). Indeed, the exception is always an exception *to* the law. If it were truly warranted, if it were simply, legally legitimate, then there would be no need for the exception. The politically responsible response to finding oneself within a state of exception – to discovering the presidential authorisation of domestic spying – must include the posing of difficult questions concerning the invocation of the state of exception. To respond, instead, and as President Bush has, with a simultaneous defence of his actions as legitimate and an attack on those who leaked the story as the ones who defied the law, is to turn the state of exception into the norm. It is, therefore, and as other commentators have already suggested, to suspend the rule of law and to blur the distinction between democracy and dictatorship. The very point of the rule of law, as emphasised from Locke to the Federalist Papers, is to limit the passions, partiality and discretion of rule by an individual – not to expand them. In working out and working through an exceptional, if fictitious, scenario, 24 expands the democratic imagination in ways that can enable a more appropriate response to the challenges that US leaders, US citizens, and citizens globally face in a post-9/11 world.

00.09
JUST-IN-TIME
SECURITY
PERMANENT EXCEPTIONS AND NEOLIBERAL ORDERS

TORIN MONAHAN

The television series *24* depicts a world in a state of constant crisis and flux. It is a uniquely globalised world that demands skills of rapid assessment, adaptation, and technological acumen. Because nothing less than the survival of entire cities or nations is at stake in each moment of conflict, every interaction is one of heightened tension and instability, both for the characters and the viewers. The world of *24* is also incredibly brutal because it demands the blurring of individual identities, social relations, and state legalities. This constant crisis of identity and of 'truth' takes its toll on the characters who not only subject themselves to grave physical harm and push themselves into psychological disorders or substance abuse, but must also harm and even kill their friends and colleagues (i.e., those 'on their side') for the ever-elusive promise of achieving security.

In many ways, *24* functions as a metaphor for modernity. It presents, in highly crystallised form, the emerging social orders and contradictions of globalisation. Global flows of people and goods are perceived as necessary for national economies and for democratic ways of life, yet these flows also catalyse vulnerabilities: terrorism, military intervention, and economic instability, to name a few. The neoliberal state heightens its security apparatuses while dismantling its social programmes. Whereas neoliberalism is typically understood to indicate the privatisation of public services or resources, it now takes on an added disciplinary dimension with the simultaneous augmentation of security forces throughout societies. Thus, the state-run 'Counter Terrorism Unit' (CTU) in 24 is well-funded and stocked with the latest high-tech surveillance systems, but some of the show's characters must contend with conditions of pressing poverty and insufficient child support, for instance. There is some evidence, in fact, that the unwitting 'bad guys' in the show are driven into collusion with 'real' terrorists because of their economic insecurity. The window that viewers are given to state agencies, such as CTU, paints them as bureaucracies burdened by unnecessarily strict rules, procedures, and chains of command. These agencies function, it seems, in spite of themselves, due in large part to flexible individuals who can work between agencies and in the margins of acceptable behaviour. In this way the show echoes and reinforces dominant neoliberal sentiments expressed by the media and others in the current political environment. Finally, the structure of the show as a real-time, twenty-four-hour day effectively symbolises the non-stop, just-in-time production models of economic globalisation, but with an added emphasis on the need for constant, self-sacrificing labour and responsibility. The future of the world depends on it.

This chapter interrogates the dominant political messages of 24. It perceives the show simultaneously as a form of captivating entertainment and as a profound representation of the pressing contemporary problems of modernity. First, it demonstrates how security threats are constantly mobilised in absolute terms, such that they seemingly necessitate the suspension of the law, direct masculine action, and the reduction of people to mere bodies that can be manipulated by the state. Second, it analyses the social crises engendered by the prioritisation of security operations over the everyday needs of people. The scaling-up of surveillance and security apparatuses and the dismantling of the welfare state are two intertwined expressions of neoliberalism that are increasingly normalised by entertainment programmes such as 24.

ABSOLUTE INSECURITIES

Absolute and ubiquitous threats characterise the world of 24. Questions of scale and scope implode as all dangers take on the significance of finality.

Thus, the plot is driven by assassination attempts upon the President (Season One), nuclear attacks upon major US cities (Season Two), bio-terrorist releases of deadly viruses into the population at large (Season Three), the meltdown of nuclear reactors across the US (Season Four), and the dispersal of nerve gas in public and military zones (Season Five). Each threat gives way to another, just when the characters and viewers long for – and expect – resolution and safety; the best that can be hoped for is temporary management, containment, or postponement of the indiscriminate annihilation of civilian populations. Even individualised threats and sacrifices symbolise absolute ones because any loss of positional advantage could destabilise the tenuous state of security.

The initial threat is upon the sovereign himself, who is cast here as the first African-American President of the United States: David Palmer. The sovereign, in this instance, is the one with the power to declare a state of emergency and exception, whereby the law is suspended for the protection of the common good (Diken and Laustsen 2002). More than being just a man caught within the constraints and contradictions of his office, Palmer is the symbolic head of state, the embodiment of democratic and meritocratic ideals. Agents of the state, such as the primary protagonist Jack Bauer, implicitly recognise their role within this disintegrating functionalist paradigm as shielding the President from any attack, physical or symbolic, and thereby ensuring the stability of the nation for just a few minutes longer. While assassination attempts upon Palmer's life are always present, his involvement in and approval of ethically questionable security interventions could also have ramifications for him (and his career), with similar deadly potency. The sovereign, in essence, must be protected from himself, from the self-defiling orders that his office demands he give, from the moral abyss upon whose rim he teeters.

Examples of such unsavoury and morally damning involvements proliferate throughout 24. They include Season One's background story of Palmer's authorisation of covert operations in Kosovo, in which Bauer led a team of agents on an extra-legal assassination attempt of a war-crimes suspect – an operation that took innocent lives, failed in its mission, and triggered a revenge plot. Routine interrogation and torture of suspects also figure prominently here as tacitly condoned methods, especially when immediate information extraction is necessary to ensure public safety, which is always the case. Other sanctioned actions include things like jailbreaks of criminals in order to prevent biological attacks (in the form of a deadly virus); in this case, as with many of these, Bauer presents the scenario to the President and interprets his lack of objection as support: 'If you don't say anything, Mr. President, I will accept that as a go for this mission.' The President answers with his silence (3.4). Finally, in what might be the most extreme of circumstances (in Season Three of the show), the President provides an off-the-record order for Bauer to kill his supervisor, Ryan Chappelle (Paul Schulze), with the aim of preventing the same biological attack upon civilian populations. Bauer complies, with some remorse but no hesitation, by shooting his boss point-blank in the head (3.18).

These extreme actions are necessitated by circumstance because threats to the sovereign are interlinked with absolute threats to society, such as nuclear or biological attacks on American soil. In the face of catastrophic events of this nature, which are ever-present modalities of modernity, the future itself depends upon radical intervention and individual sacrifice, or so the logic goes. The characters respond by creating what Giorgio Agamben would call 'states of exception,' which quickly propagate, becoming the rule. Agamben writes: 'The state of exception is not a special kind of law (like the law of war); rather, insofar as it is a suspension of the juridical order itself, it defines law's threshold or limit concept' (2005: 4). In other words, while it may not be legal to suspend the law, the preservation of a functioning legal society may depend upon it, or so it appears in the context of the show. By suspending the law for the purposes of security, however, legal structures and principles are eviscerated, losing their importance and force as mechanisms for maintaining social order.

Any actions can be justifiable when they occur by means of the suspension of the very rule of law, facilitating – in turn – the subjection of humans to fundamental operations of power or 'bare life,' stripping them of identities, citizenship, and value within emerging 'zones of indistinction' (Agamben 1998). By reducing people to instrumental objects, which are seen either as pawns to be manipulated or as receptacles of information that must be extracted, humanity is excised from the object *and* the subject, the interrogated and the interrogator. Paradoxically, such practices are done in the name of preserving their opposite: civil society, human rights, political accountability and democratic processes.

Individual choices in this arena are always false choices. The stakes are simply too high for characters to resist – for too long – the injunction to prioritise the demands of political structures and the survival of nations. Even terrorists and their accomplices seem tightly bound to structural logics and clan biographies that strip their autonomy, predisposing them to plot against the state, sometimes in spite of their personal interests and vendettas. In 'states of exception', individuals must make personal sacrifices. Thus, Bauer's wife, Teri, is murdered in Season One, while he is preoccupied with matters of national security: eliminating those who made an attempt upon the President's life (1.24). In Season Three, we find that Bauer has developed a heroin addiction, which he 'needed' to do in order to go under cover and infiltrate a drug ring (3.3). Bauer's partner, Chase Edmunds (James Badge Dale), is also brutally tortured in Season Three, while Bauer refrains from interfering directly, lest he blow his own cover (3.9); Bauer even puts a gun to Edmunds' head and pulls the trigger, unaware that the gun was not loaded, to prove that he had totally rejected his former identity as a morally incorruptible agent (3.8). In the same season, Tony Almeida and Michelle Dessler, characters who are married and both work at CTU, must each refrain from rushing to the other's aid when Almeida is shot in the neck (3.4) and Michelle is trapped in a virus-infected hotel (3.17); they are needed on the job, and they submit – at least in the short term – for the 'greater good.' In Season Four, Bauer forces a surgeon at gunpoint to save the life of an informant while the estranged husband of Bauer's love interest dies on a nearby operating table (4.20). Of course, there are gender stereotypes at work here too, where those who cannot sufficiently sacrifice are emasculated by the discursive practices of others, implying that if they cannot 'cut it' then they should leave and go and join the uninformed, hapless public.

While personal sacrifices abound, the law need not be preserved, so opportunities for revenge are taken, which then serve to reify the ongoing states of exception that govern this world. From this standpoint, Bauer does kill freely and consciously, sometimes without an immediate need for doing so, because terrorists and traitors, once loose, may return to kill again. Bauer learned this lesson the hard way in the case of Nina Myers, who killed his wife in Season One and then returned to insinuate herself into the next two seasons before he unceremoniously blew her away (3.14). This is the nature of responses to dilemmas constructed in absolute terms: 'There is always something indefinite about the world: it is laden with contingencies and surprises; it is a vital context which is never mastered once and for all; for this reason, it is a source of permanent insecurity. While relative dangers have a 'first and last name,' absolute dangerousness has no exact face and no unambiguous context' (Virno 2004: 32). 24 confounds this interpretation, however, in the sense that few dangers are 'relative' in nature, and even those that may seem purely personal imbricate with large-scale, complex systems to eclipse relative relations altogether in the final analysis. The relative has become the absolute; the absolute has become the dominant; the state of exception has become the rule.

Furthermore, gender roles and gendered actions take on added significance in the land of absolute, twenty-four-hour danger. Women are expected to pick up the social slack of taking care of children and adults; male administrators predominate; and female characters, more often than not, jeopardise missions of critical importance through their relative emotional and physical weakness – seen clearly in Kim Bauer's penchant for getting kidnapped – or through their meddling – seen with Palmer's (ex-)wife's constant plotting. Even when Edmunds, Bauer's partner and arguably the toughest male character in the show, has a romantic relationship with Kim, he is advised to resign as a 'field agent,' demonstrating that the relationship has a feminising effect upon him, rendering him unfit for dangerous work.

Beyond sexist stereotypes, 24 exudes hyper-masculinity through its constant valorisation of direct action. Decisiveness is valued, not reflection. The temporal pressures of second-by-second insecurities mandate and naturalise frontier mentalities of shooting first and asking questions later. In this light, governmental agencies and (inter)national laws are feminised bureaucracies and conventions, respectively, out of touch with the field and as such insufficiently adapted for the rapid responses necessitated by absolute dangers. Entrepreneurial agents, especially rogue ones who create and operate within zones of indistinction, are the only ones that can act sufficiently. The underlying implication is that the protagonists would certainly prefer to think things through, follow rules, and obey the law, but that the circumstances of modern risk societies foreclose such time-consuming endeavours. Thus imperatives for speed and decisive action become social facts and everything else anachronism.

24's projection of constant, dire security threats invokes states of permanent exception. These exceptional conditions repeatedly exceed the institutions and legal apparatuses established for dealing with them. In turn, individuals, whether characters or viewers, are told that they are now – and forever will be – vulnerable to external and internal threats to their well-being, and that external/internal distinctions have all but collapsed. Individuals should distrust the capabilities of the state for meeting the needs of people and should take matters into their own hands, by whatever means necessary. At the very least, individuals need to forgive the human and legal violations of rogue agents (or politicians) who seemingly have no choice but to bend or break, exceed or suspend, the rules to ensure the safety of the populace. The irony of this message, which is a message of 24 as a whole, is that 'common people' may never know the rationales behind legal infractions or major catastrophic events; in fact, they *must not know*, because that would engender even greater fear, insecurity, and social instability.

NEOLIBERAL CRISES

Behind 24's terrorist plots and security (re)actions loom social crises of growing magnitude. Parenting is one of the first observable casualties in this battle against absolute threats. In Season One, for instance, Bauer's wife calls him to say that she found marijuana joints in their daughter's desk (1.1); his response is an apology for not being there, but given his job expectations, the viewers are made to understand that he simply cannot (ever meaningfully) be there. This theme recurs throughout all seasons of 24 as a more general sacrifice required of counter-terrorism agents, no matter what their rank or standing. This could not be more apparent than in Season Four, where the theme of sacrificing children and parenting is amplified to dramatic proportions. In this case, the daughter of CTU head Erin Driscoll (Alberta Walsh) commits suicide in the building's medical facility while her conflicted mother attends to pressing security threats instead of her daughter's needs (4.11). A variation on this theme also emerges in Season Two. When special agent George Mason (Xander Berkeley) discovers that he has been exposed to a lethal dose of radiation and will shortly die, he has the police bring his neglected son to him by force, attempts to apologise for his absence and coldness (2.7), and soon thereafter gives what remains of his wasting body to the state by knowingly piloting a plane with a nuclear device on board to its (and his) fiery conclusion (2.15).

Other social devolutions reveal stark contrasts between CTU's technologically scaled-up world of just-in-time security and the character's lack of basic human necessities. The state invests heavily in the former and not at all in the latter. The plot in the first half of Season Three, for example, is driven by the terrifying prospect that a teenaged boy may have brought back from Mexico a deadly virus capable of killing millions of people – all because he was trying to help his struggling family pay the rent on their low-income apartment. Viewers are led to sympathise with this character, who is, after all, a white kid trying to do the right thing and is even willing to take his own life when he discovers that he may be a vector for this deadly pandemic.

In another less critical example, various female characters are charged with caring for and hiding Edmunds' baby throughout Season Three when he is off in the field helping to save the nation. While clearly a subplot designed to create tensions among characters, the subtext is profound given the vast resources obviously poured into CTU (the temporary holding facility for the child). Childcare is simply not available in this story, so one must rely upon other individuals, all of whom happen to be women, and some totally unreliable. The constant work hours demanded of employees at CTU, at least in periods of twenty-four-hour crisis, communicate the irresponsibility of having children or families to begin with. When agents are distracted by these external obligations, whether they are the parents or not, then entire missions may fail, elevating all personal distractions or relationships to the level of potential catastrophe for everyone. This, in fact, is a major plot device of Season One where Bauer is given a choice between saving either his family or the President – he has the cold determination to choose the latter.

Although intentionally blurred in the show, it is productive to draw a distinction here between 'human security' and 'national security,' the former indicating freedom from fear or want and the latter insulation of nation states from attack (Monahan 2006). One might expect calls for social intervention into some of the root causes of human insecurity that facilitate (and probably fuel) terrorist activities; instead, the responses are technological fixes in the form of CTU surveillance and rapid response to contain threats, not cure their causes. As with the discussion of gendered action above, attention to social problems and root causes of human insecurity are too soft in their approach, too systemic in their demands, and too time-intensive to even warrant mention. High-tech containment is possible because it is finite, immediate, and largely individualised; anything else is understood to be implausible in the context of national security crises. In this way, human security is simultaneously delegitimised as a worthwhile endeavour and subordinated, financially and symbolically, to the growing national security apparatus.

In conclusion, the show *24* neatly refracts the key instabilities of modernity. The economic vulnerabilities of post-Fordist, transnational, information-dense systems of capitalist production merge with national and political insecurities brought about by terrorist attacks. In the enfolded representational space of the show and real life, both of these forces are mobilised by political actors and the media to mandate the evacuation of public resources, democratic process, and (inter)national laws. Speed is the imperative of the contemporary political and economic landscape (Virilio 2005, 1986). The actively constructed social fact of rapid response as an ethical obligation forecloses alternative possibilities and legitimates the status quo of neoliberal security and individualised public sacrifice *for* the public good. This imperative for immediate action further catalyses the creation of zones of indistinction and states of permanent legal exception whereby the torture and consumption of human bodies appears to be merely collateral damage in the war for national security. In fact, spatial distinctions start to disappear so that these 'external' practices communicate the very 'internal' operating logic of governance regimes in our time. As Avital Ronell wonderfully articulates, 'The worst moment in the history of technology [which is 'the concentration camp'] may not have an off switch, but only a modality of being on' (1989: 16). The mitigation of that modality is itself an ethical demand for action. Time, as *24* reminds us, is running out.

00.10

'TELL ME WHERE THE BOMB IS, OR I WILL KILL YOUR SON'

SITUATIONAL MORALITY ON 24

SHARON SUTHERLAND AND SARAH SWAN

Premiering in the wake of 11 September 2001, *24* and its plot of terrorism in America was eerily timely. The show presents a country, and a man, using desperate measures in increasingly desperate times. Virtually every episode features Jack Bauer in a life-and-death situation, where he must act to save his family members, his colleagues, the President of the United States, or the entire country from the impending threat of terrorist attack. The dire realities of the situation demand that Bauer act quickly and decisively, and he does. Fortunately, his actions are nearly always effective. Unfortunately, they are also frequently illegal and perhaps necessarily of questionable morality given their illegality. As legal scholars, we have become increasingly fascinated with *24*'s treatment of the interaction between legal rules and moral decision-making. Generally, legal rules are deeply connected to a society's moral sense; morality informs and structures the law and the law reflects and influences morality. As a consequence of this relationship, scenes in which a protagonist continuously breaks a society's laws might be expected to elicit a moral disquiet from the observing audience. Yet *24* presents us with a study of characters, most especially Bauer, who under intense and unrelenting pressure increasingly choose illegal courses of action to meet their goals, and asks us to accept the choices made as necessary ones. We are interested in examining the justifications offered for these choices against the backdrop of our criminal justice system.

In this chapter, we have chosen to focus on the many killings committed by 'good' characters, and to examine these killings against existing legal excuses and justifications. Tellingly, it is a challenge in the world of 24, where so many of the characters' motivations are seen in shades of grey, to readily define 'good' characters. Certainly the understanding of 'good' presented by the show is that characters are morally good if they follow Bauer's lead and seek the same results as he does. Others, even when motivated by a desire to save the country from terrorists, can be 'bad'. For example, in Season Five, Walt Cummings (John Allen Nelson) is one of the 'bad' guys because he has colluded with terrorists (5.2–5.5). This is despite the fact that his motivations were wholly patriotic. Bauer, of course, has also worked with terrorists, and has even murdered innocent people in the employ of terrorists. 24, however, has shown us that Bauer's choices are 'right': they balance the competing interests appropriately. We know this because we have seen over time that his choices are inevitably justified by the results. Cummings' choices, on the other hand, are viewed as having been 'bad'. It is not simply that he conspired in the murder of a former President (5.1–5.3), it is that he did not adequately weigh the potential consequences of his actions, and set in motion a likely terrorist attack on the United States and its citizens. For the purposes of this paper, therefore, we consider the justifications offered and implied for the killings committed by the 'good' characters – the characters who support Bauer. Our goal is to examine the situational morality of 24 and its reflection on justified homicide in the post-9/11 world.

LEGAL DEFENCES TO MURDER

Murder is sometimes defensible: the criminal law provides a limited number of justifications or excuses to the charge of murder. In the common law, 'justifications' are often distinguished from 'excuses': a justification, if proven, negates the wrongness of the criminal act, while an excuse negates only the culpability of the person committing the act. To illustrate, a person killing in defence of himself, or killing in defence of his child, is considered justified in his actions. In other special circumstances, where a person is provoked or suffers from a mental disorder, it is thought to be unfair to blame that person for her violation, so she is excused. Excuses and justifications are manifestations of societal morality: we impose sanctions on acts that we consider morally wrong, while we forgive killing as morally acceptable when it fits into one of the traditional categories of justification. In the following sections we examine a sample of 24's homicides which are clearly within the traditional defences for murder, especially self-defence and defence of others. We will then consider the more morally ambiguous homicides which do not fall cleanly within these categories, and consider the degree to which they either reflect existing defences or instead demonstrate a new shift in our morality.

SELF-DEFENCE

Perhaps the least controversial of all defences to murder is self-defence. Under this defence, anyone may lawfully use force to defend themselves against imminent harm. The amount of force generally has to be proportional to the harm posed, in the sense that beating someone to death is not an appropriate response to a small slap, but when it meets the requisite criteria, self-defence is a wholly acceptable justification for homicide.

Unsurprisingly then, the hundreds of self-defence homicides committed by Bauer and others at CTU are largely unremarkable. For the most part, the characters involved in these incidents continue with their duties with no evident reflection on the act itself. This is simply part of the life of a CTU agent. Three instances of self-defence, however, remind us of the moral magnitude of killing, even in self-defence, and provide a counterpoint to the seeming presumption that killing is an expedient and appropriate form of self-defence. Interestingly, all three of the instances involve women who are forced to kill for the first time.

In Season One, Teri Bauer shoots and kills the man holding her and her daughter Kim prisoner. She describes the cause and effect of her act to her daughter: 'Kimberly, I had no choice, he was going to kill us. Taking a person's life ... believe me I feel sick ... ' (1.12). Teri's response is normal: the taking of another's life, even in these extreme circumstances is distressing. Kim has a different reaction to their captor's death, telling her mother, 'That's just it, Mom. I don't feel bad at all. I don't feel anything except happy he's dead.' Kim's reaction more closely mirrors the audience's likely response: relieved to see these good characters escape, with little empathy for the deceased kidnapper. The audience does not share Teri's struggle: we know that the victim fully intended to kill both Teri and Kim, and we do not mourn the loss.

In Season Two, it is Kim who must kill to defend herself (2.12). Caught in a house with the murderous Gary Matheson (Billy Burke), Kim manages to knock him unconscious and call her father, Jack. When Matheson starts to regain consciousness, Bauer, in a somewhat unusual 'father knows best' example, orders Kim to shoot him. Obeying his command, Kim shoots her former employer twice. The incident is obviously traumatic for her: she shakes, sweats, and cries, showing that when she is forced to kill, the experience does not leave her unmoved. Part of the reason for Kim's response may be the nature of Matheson's death. In many jurisdictions, the fact that Kim shot Matheson when he was barely conscious would have demonstrated that the threat to her life was no longer imminent. It could be argued that Kim had a duty to retreat in these circumstances. Thus, her distress suggests an appropriate moral reaction to the event. The audience is sympathetic to her conflict, and indeed relieved to see this often weak character show a tendency toward self-preservation.

Like Kim, Chloe O'Brian, a CTU computer specialist, also learns what it feels like to kill someone. When a terrorist shoots at the car she and an informant are hiding in, CTU agents guide her through the process of getting a shotgun from the back seat, and shooting the assailant (4.20). Her emotional experience of the event mirrors Kim's reaction when her mother kills someone, though Chloe takes it one step further and questions her own morality at feeling nothing:

> When I shot that guy, I thought that I would go all fetal position, but the truth is I didn't feel anything. At all. I hope I'm not some kind of psychopath.

Although Chloe certainly has some personality quirks, the very fact that she is able to recognise the significance of her action, and the significance of her reaction to it, should persuade her that 'psychopath' is an unlikely diagnosis. Rather, she is simply someone who recognises that although death might be justified, it gravely impacts upon the person inflicting the sentence. The internal wrestling between the knowledge that the act was necessary for survival and the knowledge that said survival came at the price of another's life should indeed give pause. Chloe's act, combined with Kim and Teri's, remind the audience of the significance of killing, and serve as touchstones for the many other homicides with more ambiguous justifications.

DEFENCE OF OTHERS AND DURESS

Another defence explored on *24* is the defence of others. Killing a person in defence of another is dramatically effective, and also emotionally acceptable to most audience members. We can readily imagine killing to save a family member or loved one. On *24*, though, family members are not normally in imminent danger such that defence of others arises: instead their deaths are threatened by both the good guys and the bad guys in order to coerce cooperation from agents and terrorists who are otherwise too committed to their task to 'break'. The result is that, in *24*, family members are almost always in peril.

This threat of harm allows for an alternative defence – duress. According to the concise definition offered by wikipedia.com, duress arises where the threats made 'actually overwhelmed the defendant's will and would also have overwhelmed the will of a person of ordinary courage ... so that his or her entire behaviour was involuntary.' In general, the defence of duress relies upon a showing of proportionality: the actions committed under duress must not be greater than the harm threatened. It is not, however, clear that the defence of duress would be available to those accused of murder. The vast majority of states categorically reject the defence in those circumstances, but perhaps some of Bauer's actions – short of intentional killing – might be excused as occurring under this defence.

In Season One, Ira Gaines (Michael Massee) seeks to control Bauer by kidnapping his wife and daughter. Gaines telephones Bauer and warns, 'Do what I tell you, Jack, and you might see your daughter again' (1.6). Bauer responds unequivocally: 'If you hurt my daughter, I will kill you', and 'If you hurt my wife or my daughter, I will kill you, you son of a bitch.' Bauer does, however, do as he is told in order to protect his family. When Gaines orders him to shred a note telling CTU that it is being watched, Bauer obeys (1.6).

In 1.7, Bauer appears to take a much graver step in following orders from his family's kidnappers: on instructions from Gaines, Bauer apparently shoots his colleague, Nina Myers. In this instance we are relieved to see Nina get up from the bank which she has fallen down, and to discover that Bauer did not really make the choice to shoot an (apparently) innocent person to save his daughter. While we might very easily understand Bauer choosing Kim over Nina, we would not be prepared to treat the choice as morally right. As the law reflects, we are not comfortable with applying the defence of duress to intentional killing.

While Bauer is forgiven for his actions in Season One, when placed in a similar situation, Tony Almeida is not forgiven. After Stephen Saunders (Paul Blackthorne) kidnaps Michelle Dessler, Almeida follows Saunders' orders in a desperate attempt to keep her alive. Even though Michelle tells him not to give in to Saunders, Almeida subverts the ongoing investigation and brings Saunders his daughter – ironically the only leverage that CTU had against Saunders (3.20). Although we understand and sympathise with Almeida, his actions are viewed as indefensible. Almeida committed treason by placing Michelle's life above his duty to his country, and we accept that he should be punished for such behaviour.

It appears that Almeida's actions are not greatly different than Bauer's: neither committed an intentional homicide under duress; rather, both sabotaged an ongoing investigation. There are, however, two important differences between Bauer's actions and Almeida's. Firstly, Bauer's transgressions were arguably more proportionate to the threat: he failed to pass on important information and pretended to kill a colleague, but the threat to Kim was imminent, while the threat to the country was not clear. Almeida's actions had much more horrifying potential consequences which were very clear to him as he subverted the operation. As he's told (3.23):

> You facilitated the escape of a man who was responsible for the death
> of Ryan Chappelle and almost a thousand civilians, and who was
> contemplating killing millions of others. Then you tried to neutralise
> the only leverage we had against him by giving him back his daughter.

Secondly, Bauer is able to rely upon television's 'hero defence'. In addition to the standard legal defences, we cannot forget that Bauer is one of a long line of popular-culture heroes to whom different rules often apply. After all, audiences love a hero, and expect him to act differently than the average man. As such, we grant them licence to do what they need to do in order to catch the 'bad guy'. We recognise that, sometimes, people do what they have to do to get the bad guy, and we accept these actions as necessary and justified. We cheer for crime-fighters who carry out their mission of fighting crime and evil with a no-holds-barred approach, unbending to bureaucracy and arbitrary rules. In short, Bauer is forgiven for his transgressions because we know that, as the hero, his choices will be proven to be right in the end. Almeida does not have the same pop-culture infallibility, and is arrested for his crime.

It is important to note that Bauer increasingly adopts the techniques used by terrorists: like the villains, Bauer has no qualms about threatening the innocent family members of his enemies. In Season Three, Bauer uses Saunders' love for his daughter against him: he threatens to send her into the hotel where a weapons-grade virus is raging, an act which is tantamount to a fast but excruciatingly painful death sentence. Bauer says mercilessly to Saunders, 'When she is infected, I'm going to make you watch her die' (3.23). Saunders fortunately gives in before his innocent daughter is sacrificed, but Bauer's ploy only works because Saunders, and the audience, believes that Bauer will subject Saunders' daughter to a cruel death unless Saunders gives him the information he wants. Although Bauer's motivation is to save the world, whereas Saunders' is to destroy it, Bauer's use of the terrorist's technique is highly problematic. These techniques and many of the homicides Bauer commits must be justified, if they can be, under some less morally certain defence.

NECESSITY: THE SACRIFICE OF ONE FOR MANY

In 24, the defence of necessity gains prominence, as the show continually asks whether we are willing to sacrifice one innocent person to save millions. The defence of necessity in Anglo-American law is always treated with extreme caution, and is rarely successful. The defence is almost certainly excluded by international convention where the action sought to be excused is murder. The United States is a signatory to the *Convention against Torture and Other Cruel, Inhuman or Degrading Treatment or Punishment* which unequivocally declares that no public emergency which threatens the life of the nation can justify torture. It follows that there is no circumstance – outside legal acts of war – in which international law would permit the possibility of killing an innocent person to save many. American law independently reaches similar conclusions: although more than twenty states have adopted the 'Choice of Evils defense' which justifies necessary conduct to avoid harm, some states have expressly excluded the defence in cases of intentional homicide, while others restrict its use to 'technically criminal behaviour which virtually no one would consider improper', a standard which clearly cannot apply to intentional homicide (Christie 1999: 1027).

Generally, 24 holds that, in desperate times, it is permissible to take an innocent life in the hope that it will save others. In this way, the show tends towards the utilitarian view that the death of a few to serve the greater good is justified. And it most certainly presents us with situations where our fears are most likely to drive our support for these difficult choices. Bauer's threat to expose Jane Saunders (Alexandra Lydon) to the deadly virus is dreadful, but the entire country – and possibly most of the world – is at risk. Similarly, in Season Two, George Mason (Xander Berkeley) refuses proper medical aid for Paula Schaeffer (Sara Gilbert), because she is the only person with information about how to decrypt data crucial to stopping a terrorist attack. Although he knows it will kill her, he orders her to be kept coherent long enough for her to give him the necessary information (2.5).

The same issue is raised when President David Palmer (Dennis Haysbert) and his aide debate the morality of killing Syed Ali's family in order to save millions of lives in Los Angeles (2.12). In one of the rare instances where the show suggests such a trade is immoral, Palmer refuses to authorise the executions. Luckily, Bauer is able to deceive both the audience and Syed Ali (Francesco Quinn) into believing that Palmer has ordered the death of Syed's son, but the audience is left to grapple with its relief that a solution was found that forced Syed to speak. The episode clearly suggests the morally complicated truth that Syed only begins to talk after he believes one son is dead and that Bauer will kill more of them, and that he would not have talked under any other circumstances. If deception were impossible, viewers know that the expedient and effective action would be literally killing Syed's children. Palmer will not permit that step, but the question lingers whether viewers would consider it to be morally justified in the circumstances.

Another instance of the life of one man balanced against the life of many occurs when Saunders demands that Palmer order the death of CTU agent Ryan Chappelle (Paul Schulze). If Palmer does not deliver the body of Chappelle to him, Saunders will release a deadly virus. In one of the most poignant scenes from the entire series, Bauer takes Chappelle out to the train tracks, and shoots him in the head (3.18). Bauer kills Chappelle as a necessary sacrifice, but his regret is palpable. Chappelle, however, is an agent of the state who has accepted the risk of death in the service of his country. While he is clearly not ready to die, the audience can view this death as falling within a different category of necessary action than the murder of a civilian would: arguably Chappelle's death is more analogous to the death of a soldier in wartime.

In this instance, someone else has made the decision, and Bauer is merely following orders. In most circumstances, Bauer is not acting under authority and cannot try to argue that he is following a lawful order. However, even in this circumstance, Bauer's actions are highly controversial: the Nuremberg Defence – 'only following orders' – is excluded in the United States by the Uniform Code of Military Justice. An American soldier can, and arguably must, refuse an unlawful order. In this case, Chappelle's murder could be illegal under international law, and even Palmer cannot legally order Bauer to carry out the task.

In Season Four, however, we see Bauer make the same decision himself, when he must weigh one life against another. When he bursts into the CTU hospital where the one man who can possibly prevent a missile from hitting Los Angeles is in critical condition, Bauer forces the doctor away from the dying patient he is attending in order to save the villain with critical information instead (4.20). Although the audience is asked to side with Bauer, the grief of the dead patient's wife and Bauer's lover, Audrey Raines (Kim Raver), is heartbreaking. Her rants against Bauer that he killed her husband ring true, yet we are asked to accept Bauer's choice as sad, but necessary.

GETTING IN WITH THE BAD GUYS

Another set of Bauer's choices which become increasingly difficult to justify comprises those crimes committed to accomplish the aim of infiltrating criminal organisations. These actions can only be justified if we accept an 'ends justifies the means' defence; they are not captured by self-defence, duress, necessity or any of the defences we have discussed. Nor are they justified by the very limited exceptions in which agents of the state (soldiers, prison officials, etc.) may kill an individual (war or state-ordered execution). They are simply utilitarian acts aimed at an indeterminate future benefit for society.

In order to successfully infiltrate the bad guys, and make them believe he is one of them, Bauer hurts other people, and himself. In a painfully obvious example of self-harm, Bauer stabs himself to make it look like he was injured in an attack (4.14). In a more insidious example, Bauer becomes a heroin addict. Whether or not Bauer actually needed to become a heroin addict to maintain his cover is unclear but, in any event, Bauer's self-harm is not contentious. It is presumed that he can make the informed choice to take these actions to further his goals even if the criminal leader, Hector Salazar (Vincent Laresca), suggests that Bauer's actions will inevitably corrupt him (3.1):

> I'm concerned about you, Jack. The things you did to get me here I wouldn't wish on anyone. Let's face it, you'll never be the same.

Much more questionably, Bauer's efforts to show his loyalty to the bad guys extend to taking the life of others. In 2.1, Bauer kills a man who was set to testify against a terrorist. He bluntly informs his CTU boss: 'You wanna find this bomb, this is what it is going to take ... I'd start rolling up your sleeves – I'm gonna need a hacksaw.' Later, Bauer presents the man's head as an offering to the terrorist. Tellingly, Bauer kills him in what looks suspiciously like an act of vigilante justice: after reading through the man's crimes, which include eight counts of kidnapping a minor, two counts of child pornography and one count of first-degree murder, the man tells Bauer that his deal with the government means he 'will walk' away, and serve no time for anything. It is at this point that Bauer suddenly pulls out his gun and shoots him in the chest. The victim's history is intended to reassure the audience that the man deserved to die, so Bauer's action is somehow still justifiable despite the clear and consistent message of the law that vigilante acts are never justified.

Bauer makes another horrifying move to be accepted by the gang: he stands by while they kill an innocent man from the phone company (2.1). When the dead man's friend finds out Bauer's true identity, he is disgusted that Bauer, a federal agent, would let such an innocent man die and do nothing to stop it. His 'average man' status suggests that his disgust must be shared by many members of the audience. How then can Bauer remain a 'hero' figure? Again, we must come to the conclusion that Bauer is excused purely because he *is* the hero. Simon posits that the hero must be allowed to operate in a different moral sphere from others:

> The hero would be foolish to respond to danger in the morally conventional manner. The morally conventional manner is to remain passive and law-abiding, and to rely on the government for protection from the lawless violence ... for the most part, however, the government is neither willing nor able to provide this protection

... they are at a tremendous disadvantage vis-à-vis the menace. They have to play by the rules, while the mob and its analogues do not. The mob can shoot people in the back, torture, and bribe; the government generally cannot. [2001: 421]

Bauer does not confine himself to the rules of the government; instead, he adopts the warfare tactics of the terrorists. He interrogates and tortures, he threatens family members, and he kills innocent people. There is no question that these tactics are effective, but could we view them as morally justified if Bauer wasn't protected by the identity of hero? Certainly the law does not recognise this defence.

VENGEANCE

Some of Bauer's actions cross even further into the morally suspect, particularly where his motivation is arguably revenge. In this area, however, we are influenced, as an audience, by a long history of revenge drama in which the protagonist sets out to avenge a heinous act – usually the murder or rape of a close family member. While the heroes of such tragedies are often punished for their acts – and frequently die themselves having carried out their vengeance – the sheer number of revenge tragedies in our cultural history evidences our empathy with the vigilante murder of specific individuals who 'deserve' to be punished for their own criminal acts. The criminal law itself is premised upon our need for retribution at least as much as on goals of restoration and transformation. A desire for revenge is normalised by our criminal justice system, if not justified by it.

Season One begins 24's fascination with revenge. Bauer and his CTU cohorts are unaware of it, but the Drazens, the season's villains, are out for revenge on Bauer and everyone involved with killing the wife and daughter of Victor Drazen (Dennis Hopper). Although Bauer denies knowing that Drazen's wife and daughter were inside the building that he bombed, and blames the deaths on faulty intelligence and on Drazen himself, the Drazens want revenge for their family member's deaths. Drazen tells Bauer: 'when a man goes halfway around the world to set off a bomb, he's responsible for any accidents that result' (1.23). Certainly if Bauer were a private citizen and his act was not an act of war, the criminal law system would agree with Drazen. In this case though, Bauer's actions are shown as clearly appropriate because they were aimed at stopping genocide, whereas generally, when someone commits a dangerous act, he is criminally responsible for any harm connected with that act. The audience is asked to excuse Bauer because he did not intend to harm any innocent people and he performed his duties in the name of combating terrorism, but Drazen's accusation requires that we consider the level of Bauer's culpability before exonerating him.

While Bauer seems genuinely surprised and saddened to learn that he placed the bomb which killed Drazen's wife and daughter, he of course rejects Drazen's retributive and literal eye-for-an-eye justice. When Drazen says to Bauer, 'You think I am a monster because I want revenge on your wife and daughter as well as on you,' Bauer informs him, 'You were a monster long before you ever heard of me' (1.23). While we as the audience also reject Drazen's proposed form of revenge, in a shocking reversal we see Bauer don the same cloak of vengeance later that same day. When he believes that the Drazens have killed his daughter, Bauer shoots and kills an apparently defenceless Victor Drazen, having already killed his brother in an exchange of gunfire (1.23). Nor is this the only time Bauer acts in vengeance: in 3.15, he kills Nina, firing three shots into the woman who killed his wife. When Michelle is told of Nina's death at Bauer's hand, her first response is to question whether it was justified. Almeida assures her that it was, and that Bauer 'wouldn't risk this operation just to get vengeance'. Michelle, still unconvinced, echoes our own doubts: 'Are you sure about that?' (3.15).

We are not sure. After all, we witnessed the event:

> Bauer: You don't have any more information, do you, Nina?
>
> Nina [weakly]: Yes, I do.
>
> Bauer [observing her inching towards her gun]: No, you don't.
>
> [Bauer shoots her]

Even without observing the incident, Bauer's boss, Chappelle, suspects Bauer of exacting vengeance. When he asks Bauer what happened, Bauer claims that Nina tried to escape, so he shot her in self-defence. Together, they review the security tapes. Since Bauer's body blocks the camera's view, it is difficult to see what happened. Bauer insists that Nina was going for her gun, which we know is technically true, but not an accurate presentation of the danger level, and Chappelle does not believe him. Chappelle knows that Bauer was aware of precisely where the cameras in those rooms were and starts lecturing him on due process and the law. Bauer snaps:

> Don't you tell me about the law! Nina Myers killed my wife and they
> let her go. And she would have killed my daughter if I hadn't gotten
> there when I did.

Clearly Bauer is not above vigilante justice, and the audience is asked to
accept it in him, while at the same time condemning it in others.

Even Bauer's own daughter, who has as much reason as him to want
Nina dead, seeks some assurance that he did not simply act in vengeance.
Bauer tells Kim, 'I said I wasn't sorry that Nina was dead. I wasn't sorry that
I shot her ... she posed an immediate threat to you, to me and to thousands
of innocent people.' Yet Kim still asks, 'You had to do it, didn't you?' Bauer
responds with a simple 'yeah', but the audience is not relieved of its doubt
by this exchange.

When *24* takes us into the realm of revenge killing, it asks us to differentiate
Bauer's actions from those of his enemies. Bauer's acts are presented as
understandable, if not justifiable. The Drazens' actions, in contrast, are
treated as clearly wrong. Perhaps Victor Drazen's coldly calculated plot
makes the revenge too cold-blooded, whereas Bauer acts in the heat of the
moment. Or perhaps the Drazens' revenge is disproportionate because the
initial deaths were accidental, while the planned killings of Bauer's family
are intentional. Clearly none of these actions are morally justified: none are
protected by the criminal law. Nonetheless, *24* asks us to consider whether
there is a line between Bauer's actions and the Drazens'. The fact that Bauer
has so many fans, suggests that we do draw the line more or less where Bauer
does, and not necessarily in accordance with the criminal law.

CONCLUSION

In the intense, kill-or-be-killed world of *24*, Bauer and the other 'good
guys' are forced to make difficult decisions with enormous ramifications.
The choices and actions surrounding their killing of others range from
the obviously morally acceptable, like the self-defence killings involving
Teri, Kim, and Chloe, to Bauer's highly problematic acts of sacrificing
one person for the survival of many, and killing for revenge. In presenting
and exploring this range of homicides, *24* demands that we consider our
own sense of when killing becomes immoral. Sometimes mapping and
sometimes deviating from normal standards of criminal law, Bauer, the hero,
provides a particularly complex challenge to conventions of morality and

justifications. The effectiveness of his 'the ends justify the means' approach cannot be argued, yet the moral acceptability of many of his killings remains unresolved. As the hero, the audience will always applaud Bauer while, at the same time, we often question his methods. We perhaps regret the things he has to do to keep the world safe for another day yet, ultimately, we will always look forward to watching the next 24 hours.

'YOU'RE GOING TO TELL ME EVERYTHING YOU KNOW'

TORTURE AND MORALITY IN FOX'S 24

DOUGLAS L HOWARD

The following chapter takes place somewhere between moral justification and moral outrage. In a 2003 interview on *The Howard Stern Show*, Simon Cowell, the notoriously caustic judge and co-creator of *American Idol*, candidly admitted that the main reason why viewers tuned in to his show was not so much for the talent, but rather to watch the 'cruelty' that ensued as aspiring singers were coldly critiqued by the celebrity panel before America voted them off and sent them home ('Simon Cowell Comes In').[1] While it seems difficult to believe that the viewing public could, at heart, be so mean, *Idol*'s (and Cowell's) ratings success is hard to deny, and Fox seems to have picked up on this discovery with the other staple in its primetime schedule, the terrorist drama *24*. On a weekly basis, audiences are treated to a smorgasbord of violence, coercion, and torture, ranging from emotional blackmail and narcotic injections to graphic beatings, sensory disorientation, and electroshock treatments, all in the name of national security. Contestants can expect a brutal barb from Cowell if they hit a false note on *Idol*; on *24*, rarely do the terrorists and their supporters (or, for that matter, the agents themselves) ever get off so easily. Somewhere down the road, we may point to it as yet another milestone in the moral decline of our culture that we tuned in so faithfully to watch criminal masterminds and militant fanatics so viciously and mercilessly broken. Be that as it may, just try to turn away once the clock starts ticking.

If we take a look at how the writers and producers have incorporated torture into their plotlines over the years, before considering the moral implications of their use of it, we can see not only how it has evolved into one of the more central elements of the series, but also how the frequency and the nature of the tortures themselves have escalated in 24's constant attempt to raise the stakes and create realistic tension. The show's creators really do not begin to get a taste for it until Season Two, and, while Season One is high on drama, it is, in many ways, tame by comparison to the days that follow. In their attempt to break the conspirators who have kidnapped his family and are targeting presidential candidate David Palmer, Jack Bauer and his fellow agents largely use verbal threats and loud voices, and, though the threats themselves seem rather severe, the physical violence (and the visual horror for the audience) usually is not. When Jamey Farrell (Karina Arroyave) comes up with Nina Myers' name after analysing the encoded keycard (1.3), the worst that Bauer does is scowl and shout, and, from her wounded denial, he is willing to consider her story and investigate the possibilities. (Compare this response to a moment in Season Four, when CTU head Erin Driscoll (Alberta Watson) has agent Sarah Gavin (Lana Parrilla) 'tasered' by torture specialist Eric Richards (Butch Klein) because she appeared to be passing classified information, even after she, too, maintained her innocence and denied any wrongdoing (4.8).) After discovering Jamey's betrayal, Tony Almeida and Nina push her to breaking point by threatening to bring in her son, so that he can see 'his mother in restraints, arrested for being a traitor' (1.9). Along the same lines, Nina similarly advises Bauer, in his interrogation of the businessman Ted Cofell (Currie Graham), that, 'with people this tightly wound, the threat of pain can be more effective than pain itself' (1.11). Letting Cofell watch as he pours water out onto a bar towel, Bauer graphically describes a grisly Gulag torture that will pull out his stomach lining and make him die slowly and painfully.

Bauer similarly agrees to let Kevin Carroll (Richard Burgi), who earlier posed as Alan York, go in exchange for taking him to his wife and daughter, but warns that, if he does not cooperate, they will both find out how good Carroll really is 'at withstanding some pain' (1.11). As menacing as he may appear in these situations, though, Bauer never goes through with these threats (or is never put in a situation where he has to make good on them). Cofell, like Habib Marwan (Arnold Vosloo) in Season Four or, most recently, Walt Cummings (John Allen Nelson) in Season Five, essentially commits suicide, refusing medication in the midst of his heart attack, before Bauer can resort to more extreme measures, and Carroll wisely cooperates rather than testing the extent of his pain threshold by leading Bauer to Ira Gaines's (Michael Massee) North Valley compound. Even Alberta Green (Tamara Tunie), acting head of CTU in Bauer's absence, only threatens Nina and Almeida with being fired and prosecuted for withholding information about Bauer and for obstructing her investigation into the day's events (1.12). And when Bauer finally confronts Victor Drazen (Dennis Hopper) in his cell at the Saugus prison, he encourages a glaring Drazen, without violence, to make his sons call off their rescue attempt in order to save their lives, a request that Drazen immediately denies inasmuch as his sons are, in his mind, 'soldiers' (1.20).

By contrast, the terrorists themselves have no qualms about inflicting pain and no moral misgivings about torturing and killing the innocent in the service of their plot. Mandy (Mia Kirshner) sleeps with Martin Belkin (Rudolf Martin) in order to steal his press pass to Palmer's speech and then blows up their plane, killing everyone on board (1.1). An antsy Dan (Matthew Carey) callously breaks Janet's (Jacqui Maxwell) arm so that Kim will cooperate (1.2), and Gaines consistently threatens Bauer with the death of his family for the same reason (1.6; 1.7; 1.8). Kevin Carroll suffocates Janet in the hospital to keep her from talking (1.6). A host of CTU agents are murdered when the terrorists attack the safe house to get at Teri and Kim (1.16), and Nina lies to Bauer about the death of his daughter just so that the Drazens get one last shot at their revenge. And then, of course, Nina kills Teri because she knows too much about her escape plan (1.24). It is not so difficult to separate the heroes from the villains here; when it comes to harming others, the bad guys always cross the line.

With Season Two, however, the terms of 24 begin to change. The terrorists, of course, are as malicious and malevolent as ever. In two of the most brutal scenes in the series so far, the fanatical Syed Ali (Francesco Quinn) has his sadistic assistant Mohsen (Aki Avni) take a power tool to private investigator Paul Koplin (Al Sapienza) and rub lye on his wounds to make sure that he and Kate Warner (Sarah Wynter) are not on to his plans (2.9), and Ronnie Stark (Peter Outerbridge) literally tortures Bauer to death with a scalpel, a soldering iron, and a taser in an attempt to get the microchip that he recovered from Jonathan Wallace's (Gregg Henry) body (2.19).

However, as the terror threat escalates to a nuclear level, with Second Wave's plan to detonate a nuclear bomb in Los Angeles, the necessity of information becomes more urgent and, with more lives at stake, the agents have no choice but to respond in kind to get it. The season begins, in fact, with Korean agents desperately drugging and electrocuting a captured terrorist about the timing of the plot and Bauer killing cavalier government witness Marshall Goren (Carl Ciarfalio) during an interrogation, a dramatic sign of things to come (2.1). When Bauer now goes in to interrogate Nina, in one of the season's sure-fire highlights, he can no longer be so forgiving – Nina did, after all, kill his wife – and the tension in the room is palpable. Choking her up against the wall, he promises, 'You're going to tell me everything I want to know or, I swear to God, I will hurt you before I kill you' (2.6). Though Bauer is rationally using Nina's fear of him to gain a degree of control over her, even shrewd CTU head George Mason (Xander Berkeley) is convinced. When Bauer subsequently returns and fires his gun at the wall behind her, a shaken Nina provides him with more information about her contact in Visalia. From NSA Director Roger Stanton's (Harris Yulin) refusal to talk about his connection to the terror attack, Palmer instructs Secret Service Agent Ted Simmons (Steven Culp) to do 'whatever [he] need[s] to do' to get information from him. As Stanton sits with his feet in two buckets of water, Simmons methodically grills him with defibrillator paddles at the former director's temples. Meanwhile, Bauer, having captured Syed Ali, makes him reveal his plans by threatening the lives of his wife and children and effectively staging the execution of his son through a video feed (2.12). Later, Bauer refuses to treat the bullet wound in Marie Warner's (Laura Harris) arm until a crying, squealing Marie gives up the location of the bomb (2.14). Though the terrorists and their supporters are devoted to their cause, as Palmer soberly tells adviser Mike Novick (Jude Ciccollela), 'everyone breaks eventually' (2.12) and break they must for the greater good of the nation and its people. Ironically, President Logan's (Gregory Itzin) security aide Walt Cummings suggests that they kill Jack at the end of Season Four because he fears that the Chinese will break him, too (4.24).

With the risk of a deadly infectious virus in Season Three, the series follows a variation on the 'ticking bomb' scenario from Season Two, a variation that similarly justifies interrogation and torture to uncover the plot and prevent the outbreak. Wrapping his hand in a towel, CTU agent Chase Edmunds (James Badge Dale) tries to beat the whereabouts of Kyle Singer (Riley Smith), who may be a living host for the virus, out of drug lord Ramon Salazar (Joaquim de Almeida) in prison (3.3). When his information about terrorist contact Marcus Alvers' (Lothaire Bluteau) HIV treatment fails to make her cooperate, Almeida brings in the torture specialist Richards (a rather cold, quiet character whose introduction this season says a great deal about where the series is going)[2] to work on Nina and to inject chemicals into her neck (3.14). Since Michael Amador (Greg Ellis), who purchased the virus for Stephen Saunders (Paul Blackthorne), similarly refuses to tell Bauer where the virus is, Bauer holds him down while Edmunds cuts into his palm with a knife until he passes out (3.15). Once Amador regains consciousness, Bauer threatens to throw him into a room with an open incubator containing the virus (3.16). For the hundreds of thousands of lives on the line, Bauer frightens Stephen Saunders' daughter, Jane (Alexandra Lydon), with the thought that he will do whatever he has to do 'to acquire her cooperation' in his investigation (3.19), before horrifying her with the truth of her father's terrorist activities and a live feed from the infected Chandler Plaza Hotel (3.20). Though Saunders is willing to blackmail Almeida and kill millions to get his way and make his political statement, Bauer is just as willing to throw Jane into the hotel lobby (and force Saunders to 'watch her die' once she is infected) to get him to give up the remaining phials (3.23). Bauer even 'tortures himself' essentially in Season Three, by deliberately developing a heroin addiction to establish credibility with the Salazars, and he goes on to beat up (poor) Edmunds (3.4) and fire an unloaded gun at his head (3.8) for the same reason, before chopping his arm off to contain the virus in the final episode (3.24).

While Season Two is the most brutal in terms of the graphic nature of the tortures involved, Season Four is more violent in terms of the number of tortures that take place.[3] In more than half of the episodes, the plot revolves around some form of torture. The guilty certainly do get tortured. Ronnie Lobell (Shawn Doyle) has difficulty getting information from terrorist Thomas Sherek (Faran Tahir), even with the threat of thirty years in prison,

Bauer quickly learns about the attempt to kidnap Secretary Heller (William Devane) by shooting Sherek in the leg (4.1). Dismissing Richards and his more aggressive methods in this instance, Curtis Manning (Roger R Cross) tortures a distraught Richard Heller (Logan Marshall-Green) with sensory disorientation to find out if he had anything to do with the kidnapping (4.3), but he finally breaks after impassioned pleas from Audrey and his father (4.21). A desperate Agent Castle (Cameron Bancroft) presses on Dina Araz's (Shohreh Aghdashloo) bullet wound to get information about the Override device (4.9). Manning also gets the traitor Marianne Taylor (Aisha Tyler) to talk by wheeling in the dead body of her associate Henry Powell, a pointed commentary on the terrorists' intentions toward her (4.10). Almeida breaks Dina by promising to send her son Behrooz (Jonathan Ahdout) to prison for life, although he predicts that the teen will commit suicide from the horrific terms of his confinement (4.11), and Bauer later enlists her cooperation with the Marwan contact Joseph Fayed (Adam Alexi-Malle) by similarly warning that she will never see Behrooz again if she does not comply (4.14). In 4.18, an Amnesty Global lawyer prevents CTU from interrogating Joe Prado (John Thaddeus), who has ties to the terrorist leader, Marwan, so Bauer resigns, in the words of Division official Bill Buchanan (James Morrison), in order 'to take him on as a private citizen'. Breaking Prado's fingers one at a time and putting a knife to his throat, Bauer gives him 'something for the pain,' knocking him out after he reveals Marwan's next location. And after Bauer foils Mandy's attempt to kidnap Almeida and fake her own death, he offers her immunity in exchange for Marwan and spells out her options clearly with his gun at her head: 'You're either going to help me or I am going to kill you' (4.23).

But, while Marwan and his men do torture their fair share of people in Season Four – Forbes, for example, interrogates Manning when he brings Marianne to Powell's office (4.11),[4] and Marwan shoots Jason, who came across the Nuclear Football when President Keeler's plane crashed, in both his shoulder and his knee to get his wife Kelly to return the control board (4.17) – not all of the innocent or virtuous are tortured by terrorists. Bauer and his fellow agents torture the innocent and the guilty alike, in fact, in their attempt to thwart Marwan's plans. Sarah is brutally tortured by Richards after Marianne frames her (4.8), and, on Almeida's orders, Manning similarly has Richards work on the hapless Behrooz (who has already watched his girlfriend die and killed his father and who does not know that his mother is dead at Marwan's hands) in a failed attempt to find out more about Marwan's plans.

Frequently, the season plays off the dramatic tension that ensues, as Bauer must weigh the greater good against his own personal desires and his own personal happiness. As Kalil's (Anil Kumar) men beat Andrew Paige (Lukas Haas) senseless, Bauer (and, for that matter, the audience) can only sit by and watch because Kalil is his best lead to the kidnapped Heller (2.3). Since Paul Raines runs the company that owned the basement where Bauer found information about the power plant plot, Bauer electrocutes him with the cord from a lamp in his hotel room, even though Raines, as it turns out, is not working with the terrorists (4.11). Later, Bauer forces the CTU doctors to work on the Chinese scientist with information about Marwan, and abandon the wounded Paul Raines (4.20), who took a bullet for Bauer and dies as a result, a decision that ultimately costs Jack his relationship with Audrey.

At the time of writing, websites and message boards are abuzz with plot details and spoilers for Season Five; but, if the previous seasons and the first few episodes of this season are any indication, one thing is for sure: torture will, in one way or another, be a significant part of the day to come. In just the first eight hours of the new season, Bauer has threatened, tortured, and killed more than half a dozen people to get to the bottom of a nerve-gas plot that could kill hundreds of thousands of American citizens.

All of this, this four-year (and counting) catalogue of tortures, of course, ultimately raises the question of why the writers need to make torture such an integral part of their plots, year after year, and why we are eagerly tuning in to watch it. If Simon Cowell is right (and certainly this would be the greatest torture of all), then we are really watching because, on some level, we enjoy the cruelty, fictional though it may well be, and every cry and every scream scratches that secret sadistic itch that we consciously cannot dare to admit. The ratings for the series clearly support this awful idea. Where *Daily Variety*, after *24*'s first, more subdued season, called the show 'no breakthrough' and considered the ratings of the final episode that year 'underwhelming, given its strong lead-in [*That '70s Show*] and the serialized nature of the program' (Kissell: 2), it consistently made the Nielsen top twenty last year among the desirable demographic of 18 to 49-year-olds and 'ended its [2005] season a winner' (Kissell: 4). As the show has developed a following, fans have even set up websites and blogs, like the *Jack Bauer Torture Report* and the *Jack Bauer*

– *Kill Counter*, so that we can keep track of Jack's weekly abandonment of the 'Miranda rights' (to remain silent when being questioned or detained) and the US Constitution in the service of national security. The very fact that there would be a need to maintain these kinds of statistics admittedly speaks volumes about the series and its fan base. We probably would not be watching *in spite of* these elements, given their prevalence. Pretty much anyone who has seen a season knows what to expect when a witness refuses to cooperate with Bauer or when Richards is called into the interrogation room.

And, perhaps, this expectation is one of the more disturbing aspects of *24*, that it has, generally, desensitised us to these kinds of practices, however necessary they may be. Where Bauer's violent interrogation of a non-compliant witness or terrorist contact once seemed shocking and frightening, as we become used to the show, we now expect it as part of Bauer's and CTU's protocol in such situations. When Bauer warns the callous paedophile Jacob Rossler, 'You don't want to go down this road with me' (5.8), we know what is coming next. Some fans, moreover, are admittedly disappointed when these expectations are not realised and when the show does not follow 'protocol' under these circumstances. 'Melia', who provides running commentaries on the episodes on her *24Addict* website, for example, criticises Rossler for taking 'the wimpy way out [and asking] for a damn immunity deal', and 'Ted', who posts recaps of the episodes on the *Detroit Free Press 24* blog, similarly argues that 'most of us … are secretly glad when Rossler winces with pain' and that his call for immunity is a point of 'frustration and delay'.

Clearly, though, no one wants a Torture Channel added to their cable or satellite systems, just as no one wants to be complicit in their own homemade Abu Ghraib, and, in order to alleviate any guilt that we might openly feel in endorsing this behaviour, *24* cleverly couches its cruelty within the context of a timed crisis that makes it all morally acceptable. Since the terrorists typically will do almost anything to make sure that their plans succeed, Bauer and his fellow agents *must* do everything within their power to extract information from their prisoners. Although Frank Rich asserts that *24* 'shows but does not moralize about the use and abuse of torture by Americans interrogating terrorists' (Rich 2005), the character Mike Novick actually makes a case for it when he reassures a troubled Palmer about Bauer's torture of Syed Ali:

> Compare [the murder of Ali's family] to a weapons factory we
> discover is near a hospital – a situation we have faced. The bombing
> would still be ordered on the logic that many more people will be
> saved by the destruction of the factory. Now the numbers are even
> more compelling here [in the case of a nuclear disaster]. A few people
> may have to die to save millions. [2.12][5]

For Novick, this utilitarian 'greater good' determines and guides these more extreme measures, and 24 has continued to use this kind of reasoning to justify the hard decisions made by its protagonists.[6] To cite a recently broadcast example from the series, CTU head Lynn McGill (Sean Astin) convinces President Logan to allow terrorists to release nerve gas into a shopping mall, an act that would kill hundreds of men, women, and children in order to serve the 'greater good' and save hundreds of thousands by finding the remaining canisters. Bauer foils the attempt, but not before a small number of people are killed by the gas (5.8). The 'ticking bomb' argument may, as Richard Kim points out, be dangerous because 'it allows a plot dreamed up by Hollywood to determine the limits of moral authority' (2005); but, in escaping into the fictional reality of 24 and 'willingly suspending our disbelief' in its absurd plot possibilities, we accept the scenario that makes this utilitarian morality plausible and that frees us from any personal responsibility (or culpability) for what we are about to witness. Psychologically, we can rationalise the horror of what we are watching (and might, on some level, be enjoying) because the numbers mathematically make it okay and because the terrorists themselves have created the circumstances that demand this response. Although Bauer is the one who often conceives of and performs these tortures, he also places the blame for them onto his enemies, so why should we feel bad about it? As he tells Syed Ali before (mock) executing his son, 'I despise you for making me do this' (2.12). Since Ali is coordinating this attack, he, according to Bauer, is ultimately the one who is responsible for the consequences of his actions and for the torments that he faces, however perverse and horrific they might be. Not only does 24 give us our weekly dose of sadism, then, but it also painlessly reconciles it for us before our consciences ever kick in.

But is that all that the series, with all of its torture, is, just a thinly veiled attempt to gratify our voyeuristic desire for suffering, to watch villains bleed from the comfort of our living rooms content in the knowledge that they had it coming and that it is not real anyway? Does any of it serve a higher purpose? Before we begin running for the nearest confessional and doing penance for an unquenchable, vampiric bloodlust, we need to consider the socio-political context of 24 and its place within the public discourse, as some of the show's critics, in assessing its impact, have already started to do. Kevin Drum, commenting on the recurrence of torture in the middle of Season Four, believes that '[t]he real goal [of the show, in this regard] is to convince America that torture is (a) revolting and (b) doesn't work anyway' (2005). While many of the tortures do not work and while so many of the conspirators, like Ted Cofell or Nina or Marie Warner or Marwan, never talk and choose pain or death over confession, some of these threats and procedures actually do produce results and lead to positive ends.[7] Sherek, Dina Araz, Joe Prado, and Mandy all talk, just as Saunders and Syed Ali do in the previous seasons. Since their information does help Bauer and CTU to prevent these terrorist attacks from taking place, 24 could work as an endorsement of more extreme interrogation measures. Going back to Novick's justification, if just one of these tortures foiled a terrorist attack and saved lives, wouldn't that be worth the others that did not work? And if the writers and producers were trying to give us a negative example here, wouldn't we have got the message after a season or two?

Ultimately, 24's intentions, as far as torture goes, may be irrelevant. If the cultural critic Slavoj Žižek is right, just daring to consider the question (and, in this regard, this chapter is equally complicit) 'is even more dangerous than an explicit endorsement of torture' because it, like Bauer's rationalisation of torturing Syed Ali, 'allows us to entertain the idea while maintaining a pure conscience' (2002: 103–4). To this end, 24 fuels that debate by placing the topic within the public consciousness and, in what may well be Žižek's worst nightmare come true, making it fodder for dinner-table talk and water-cooler conversation. Whether we should be advocating torture in response to terrorism or not after seeing Bauer dispatch his nemesis of the day, we have incorporated these images and ideas into our psyches and, in doing so, could unknowingly be legitimising their use in the post-9/11 political landscape. Ironically, Žižek also sees the utilitarian point of torturing a prisoner 'whose words can save thousands' (2002: 103), provided, of course, that we do not talk about it and 'retain the sense of guilt' over what we have done.[8]

Inasmuch as it continues to respond to current events and international politics, 24 is still a fictional television show. In this case, though, the fiction becomes particularly relevant and personal because it directly refers to some very tangible, immediate fears and that parallel to the real makes the conversation about torture and terrorism (as opposed to the silence that Žižek would have us maintain) valuable because it forces us to face them. As the nations of the world continue to recuperate and recover from the horror of the 9/11 terrorist attacks, the suicide bombers in Israel, and the bombings in London in July 2005, 24 plays out nightmarish terror scenarios that dare us to imagine the very worst – that the terrorists are out there, in our cities and near our homes, armed and plotting and waiting to strike. (Shortly after 9/11, in fact, producers began the first season of 24 with an exploding plane, a chilling reminder of the attacks that took place several months earlier in Manhattan and Washington, DC.) But through its chaos and mayhem, through the tortures and violence that it demonstrates, and through the temporary suspension of standards of humanity, benevolence, and civility, the series ultimately works to reinforce the order that it threatens and calm the fears that it and our newspapers inspire.

After all, the government periodically raises our alert status without telling us what to look for or where we need to be on guard. We are under siege by enemies that we cannot see, and, if terrorist plots are being foiled and cells are being shut down, we may never hear the full story, as much for national and international security as to preserve our own piece of mind.[9] We stand on the sidelines, trying to watch a war that is being fought in the shadows. For all we know, our neighbourhoods, our businesses, and our highways have been or are being targeted even as we speak, but we are (and we must feel) powerless to protect ourselves from what we cannot see and what we do not know. While we might be feeding some sadistic appetite for destruction, 24, in all its violent glory, makes us believe that, if the terrorists are out there, something, everything, in fact, is being done to stop them and to keep us safe. Executive Producer Howard Gordon agrees that '24 taps into the public's 'fear-based wish fulfillment' of having protectors, such as Bauer, who will do whatever is necessary to save society from harm' (Keveney 2005). Audrey Raines essentially says as much when she tells Bauer, in ending their relationship, 'Thank God that there are people like you who can deal with [this] world' (4.24). Like Audrey, we may not be able to be party to all of it or to cope with the pain and suffering that Bauer must dish out, but we can take some comfort in knowing that he can and will on our behalf. So let the clock tick, and let the terrorists scream and break, and let their best laid plans collapse and fail in the course of a single day; regardless of how unrealistic and absurd it all may be, if *24* enables us to deal with that darker drama currently playing out in the streets and cities of the world, then, in the end, it is a guilty pleasure that is worth the time.

NOTES

1. Transcripts of the Stern show are not generally available, but Mark Mercer maintains a website (http://www.marksfriggin.com) that provides a daily recap of Stern's interviews and show events.

2. While Almeida introduces Richards to Nina as 'Darren' in this episode, he is called 'Eric' in Season Four and is still played by the same actor, Butch Klein.

3. Writing in *The Nation*, Richard Kim agrees that Season Four seems to outdo the previous three seasons as far as its use of torture goes, and that it occurs 'in so many episodes that it loses its shock value' (Kim, 'Pop Torture': http://www.thenation.com).

4. Although Forbes and his men clearly torture Manning, the producers never show it. They did film the torture scene, but, as producer Jon Cassar explains, with the pacing of the show, 'it felt a little slow,' so they decided not to use it ('Commentary on deleted scenes: 4:00–5:00 p.m.' Season Four DVD set).

5. The writers here are more than likely taking their inspiration for Bauer's use of Syed Ali's children (as well as Novick's justification of it) from the front pages and historical record, since governments have effectively used this kind of torture to get information from terrorists. As Jonathan Alter notes, 'Jordan broke the most notorious terrorist of the 1980s, Abu Nidal, by threatening his family' (2001: 45).

6. Jeremy Bentham himself allowed for torture in his philosophy and specifically conceived that it could be employed 'in cases which admit of no delay' (cited in Twining and Twining 1973: 313) and 'where the safety of the whole state may be endangered for want of the intelligence which it is the object of it to procure' (ibid: 315).

7. In their *Newsweek* article on 'The Debate Over Torture,' Evan Thomas and Michael Hirsh note that '[t]orture still works to extract the truth in the movies and on TV shows like the popular *24*, but [it is not as effective] in real life' and that prisoners 'will say (and make up) anything to make the pain stop' (2005: 26). US Senator John McCain, who is actually a fan of *24* and makes a cameo appearance this season in 5.7, has said that, while

he was being 'physically coerced to provide [his] enemies with the names of the members of [his] flight squadron, he '[i]nstead ... gave them the names of the Green Bay Packers' offensive line' (2005: 34).

8.   Sanford Levinson suggests that Žižek 'seems caught in a self-contradiction' here and that his position is analogous to the Clinton Administration's policy of 'don't ask, don't tell', 'with regard to gays and lesbians in the military' (2004: 31).

9.   Dodging questions about secret prisons in Europe for terrorist suspects (perhaps like the one that Bauer and Mason find at Saugus in Season One), US Secretary of State Condoleezza Rice recently talked about how the interrogation of terrorist suspects had 'stopped terrorist attacks and saved innocent lives – in Europe as well as in the United States and other countries,' but admitted that she could not 'discuss information that would compromise the success of intelligence, law enforcement, and military operations [and expected] that other nations [would] share this view' ('Rice defends US policy', 5 December 2005: http://www.bbcnews. co.uk).

PART 3
UNMASKING IDENTITIES
SEXUALITY, DIFFERENCE, CULTURE

00.12

DAMSELS
IN DISTRESS

FEMALE NARRATIVE
AUTHORITY AND KNOWLEDGE
IN 24

JANET McCABE

DIVIDE AND RULE: INTRODUCTION

No getting away from it: Kimberley Bauer infuriates me. Not since the hapless maidens of early film melodrama, wantonly throwing themselves into the evil grasp of dastardly villains, has a heroine got into so many scrapes. Near the end of Season Two, Kim returns to the house where, until twenty-hours before, she worked as a nanny, to pick up a few things (2.22). Once again, she falls into the clutches of violently psychotic, wife/child-beating and later spouse-murdering Gary Matheson (Billy Burke). Has she learnt nothing from past events? Her gallant escape with his daughter Megan (Skye McCole Bartusiak) was scuppered when she decided to take a short cut down an alley, straight into Gary's clutches for the first time (2.2); she ran off into the woods only to get into more trouble (2.10; 2.11; 2.12; 2.13; 2.14); and she managed to get taken hostage after brandishing a gun at someone clearly unstable and much stronger than herself (2.16; 2.17). To be fair to Kim not everything was entirely her fault. But really, these are textbook mistakes. Does the woman never read the patriarchal script? Has she not seen the movies? Did she not learn the lessons from old fairy tales like *Little Red Riding Hood?* Nothing good ever comes of a woman dashing into the entangled narrative forest without a sensible exit strategy.

24, superficially at least, seems to offer little of interest for the feminist television scholar. Populated with troublesome females – a delusional woman involved with political terrorists (Season Two), the naive girlfriend of a Central American drug baron losing her life trying to escape his clutches (Season Three), the senator's daughter unable to see the bigger picture (Season Four) – means Kim is not alone in exercising poor judgement and serving an oppressive narrative system. Working within a generic and narrative universe where male action is paramount – where heterosexual masculinity is a structuring norm in fact – the ladies seem little more than helpmates for the men. In truth, most of the women involved with Jack Bauer end up either dead or in captivity. 24 thus looks like a standard action thriller where characters and plots are sustained by suspense and convention dictates that women should await male assistance or face the consequences for defiantly going it alone. When terrorists conspire to threaten innocent American lives, the fate of the nation hangs in the balance and sleep is not an option, it appears only fitting to wait for Jack to make a decision. Doing the right thing for the country and those he loves, often at the expense of everything else, reveals the hero as a man above reproach, of unimpeachable integrity, impeccable (often physical) courage and strong moral fibre. Where power structures finding in favour of male authority and jurisdiction prevail, it does raise the question: how do women start carving out power and asserting narrative control *in* and *through* such a restrictive (male) generic and (patriarchal) narrative world that gives them little room to manoeuvre?

Struggle for female narrative authority (of any kind) is symptomatic of the broader post-feminist dilemma faced by women. Ambiguity and uncertainties continue to have an effect on and 'define' female identities at a time when women are told they have unlimited opportunities and no need for radical feminist politics. Contemporary femininity is a product of contradictory definitions of, and differences within, feminism, shaped by struggles between various strains of the discourse. This is to say nothing of the violent and sustained mainstream cultural backlash against feminism and activism, which has now gone on longer than the second-wave feminist movement. Coming to terms also with the continuously shifting base of power and oppression complicates our position even further. Strongly guided by the work of Michel Foucault on understanding how modern power relations work (1991; 2002), feminist scholarship (Bordo 2003) strives to understand discursive networks of power, conditioned by historical and political specificity, to consider how it produces and normalises female subjectivity to serve prevailing relations of dominance and subordination. Third-wave feminists in particular are keen to account for the paradox of our continued investment in power structures that are central to our survival but nonetheless offer us few favours, 'an often conscious knowledge of the ways in which we are compelled and constructed by the very things that undermine us' (Heywood and Drake 2003: 11).

The struggle faced by women in the 24 narrative, I suggest, is symptomatic of this uneasy post-feminist condition. Women may have attained influential authority – heading CTU (Counter Terrorist Unit), advising the President of the United States, coordinating information systems, protecting the nation – even as they paradoxically collude in sustaining sexism and sexist stereotypes. Rooted as they are in a tight-knit hierarchal (male) community, subject to the laws of alliance codified by government protocol, federal legislation and a (male) presidency, and locked into a generic world of the cause-and-effect suspense thriller where male problem-solving prevails, the women are further enclosed in a narrative territory where it is hard for them to think in terms of coalition, and where the 'f' word is never mentioned. At a time when mainstream hostility to feminism reaches a new peak, it is not too surprising that the women compete with each other rather than join forces. Competitiveness, backbiting, deep mistrust and guardedness define female relationships: Carrie Turner (Lourdes Benedicto) clashes with Michelle Dessler over remit and a man (2.14; 2.19); Carrie spies on Michelle and even betrays her to anyone willing to listen (2.16; 2.17; 2.18; 2.20; 2.22; 2.23); Chloe O'Brian has no time to sympathise with Kim (3.11); Kim, in turn, snitches on Chloe after finding out baby Angela is not hers (3.12); and Sherry Palmer works alone. Divided and contested, women may place their trust in a man, often at considerable personal risk, but not each other; and if they are not working under male supervision and/or with the men, then they are invariably up to no good.

However, on closer inspection, all is not as it seems in terms of gender politics and narrative authority in 24. Working within (rather than against) a compromised narrative and generic environment, firmly embedded and implicated in its power structures that they did not create and do not control, women are found to be engaged in an ambivalent and often paradoxical negotiation as they seek to access knowledge and assert power. We may be in a media territory where women traditionally do well – an open-ended, television serial narrative (Feuer 1984; Gledhill 1992) – but with a show obsessed with men working against the ticking clock, and a pervasive male policing of narrative knowledge, women find themselves in a precarious position. Inscribed into the very textual form of the female characters is a ceaseless dialogue between the different and sometimes apparently contradictory dimensions of women and their complex relationship to modern power relations and knowledge. So, for example, the female CTU analyst who rigorously follows protocol and unquestioningly does what the male hero asks, even to the point of putting her life and career at risk, discovers that doing so enables her to excel in what she does and assert herself more forcefully in the workplace.

PERILS OF KIM; OR, FOR THE LOVE OF MOTHER: NARRATIVE DISTRACTERS

But where was I? Oh yes, Kim. How many times in one day can a woman be abducted, rescued and seized again? Is she a victim of her own utter stupidity, or just craving male attention? She consistently chooses to ignore sensible counsel – about sneaking out after midnight (Season One), about leaving LA when a nuclear bomb is just about to detonate (Season Two), about choosing to tell her dad of a clandestine office romance despite being warned that it might not be a good day for such news (Season Three). She has a terrible habit of ringing her father for help at the most inopportune moments, such as when she calls to say she is trapped with Gary just as Jack is trying to preserve his last link with those trying to trigger a full-scale war in the Middle East (2.22). If that was not bad enough, she switches her mobile phone onto voicemail when someone, normally her dad, urgently needs to contact her. Has she no sense of timing?

She stretches my patience. She really does.

Maybe, but her actions also stretch the plot. Getting into trouble with those time-consuming antics, distracting CTU and her father at a time when they are striving to thwart assassins and terrorist action, diverting resources away from time-sensitive undercover operations, initiates an unforeseen chain of events and postpones narrative closure (Stanley 2003). Her mother was the same. Believing her daughter to have perished after their car toppled over an embankment and burst into flames, Teri fell into a dead faint (1.16). Good grief. Coming-to, she remembered nothing – neither her name nor what had happened to her (1.17). Teri's convenient bout of amnesia prevented her from sharing crucial narrative details with others, inadvertently putting the lives of innocent men at risk in the process. To this extent, women like Kim and Teri act as narrative distracters, as saving someone takes time, sidetracking the plot and delaying resolution, leading to further complications and narrative hitches invariably requiring male action.

Delaying tactics allow the damsel in distress to assert control over initiating narrative events. Season One, for example, finds Kim kidnapped, taken hostage, threatened with rape (1.10), liberated by her father (1.12) and air-lifted to safety after a dramatic shoot-out involving CTU operatives (1.13); only to go missing again and find herself on the run from assassins (1.16), held captive by small-time drug dealers (1.18; 1.19), mistakenly arrested on drug charges and incarcerated (1.20; 1.21), pulled from the van taking her to CTU (1.21) and finally falling into the clutches of Victor Drazen (Dennis Hopper) (1.22). Phew! Exhausting. Persistently requiring help means Kim (as well as her mother) retells the same predictable story over and over again within the twenty-four-hour time span. This repeatedly re-enacts a standard patriarchal plot about fantasies of (male) power and (female) powerlessness, in which narrative hurdles are surmounted and terrible ordeals test the hero. It is a familiar Oedipal tale where the Law of the Father quite literally prevails and the female cedes her (narrative) authority to the male – but at what cost? It is apparent that female agency may be achieved at the level of facilitating an alternative problem-solving narrative, prolonging the drama for as long as possible, but it is predicated on having little or no authority over the events she initiates. Her voice is without legitimacy, easily discredited; and her presence to a certain extent simply acts as a way of giving the hero his appeal and strengthening appropriate masculinities. Teri's amnesia, which finds her wandering aimlessly through the narrative until her memory returns, becomes a broader metaphor for how such heroines 'relinquish their own plots so that others may have theirs' (Modleski 1999: 10).

Tales of dashing heroes and naive heroines, and the damsel-in-distress type in particular, offer us a perspective on the discord separating the 24 women. Women's squabbling, over men and male approval, is carried out in a context in which the supremacy and importance of the male – as object of desire, as embodying omnipotent power – go unquestioned. Bauer may have cheated on Teri, and she may have forgiven him, but it is she and not her husband who Kim blames for the temporary expulsion of her father

from the family home (1.1). It is the familiar Freudian story in which the
girl must turn away from her mother on discovering lack, her own and her
mother's, and side with the father instead. Aligning with powerful men
bestows privilege even as it shores up patriarchy and discredits other women
in the process; and it is interesting to note how the two most vulnerable yet
privileged (both textually and in the credits) women – the fragile wife and
the self-centred daughter – belong to Bauer, the heterosexual über-male and
narrative power-centre. Little wonder these women can marshal substantial
(narrative) resources when it comes to facilitating their rescue.

Women have long persisted in delighting at, and participating in, these
masochistic narratives that find one woman pitted against another over the
erotic charge of being owned: the vain and green-eyed older stepmother doing
away with her much younger rival with a dodgy apple, or the crone putting
a sleeping curse on a fair maiden to eliminate her from the dating game.
It is no small coincidence that it is Bauer's ex-lover, Nina Myers, who ends
Teri's narrative meanderings by killing her (1.24). But taking revenge on the
privileged patriarchal woman is no easy matter. Precisely because the damsel-
in-distress type exerts such a culturally sentimental and strong psychic hold
over most of us, and because she is so integral to dominant heterosexual-
based fantasies of dominance and submission, and crucial to legitimising
patriarchal power to which she is aligned, the woman neutralising her does
so at considerable personal peril. The crime of matricide – the woman was
with Bauer's child for goodness' sake – cannot go unpunished; and textual
retribution will be exacted at some point.

Another perspective on how the naive heroine divides women is how other
female types in the series call Teri into question. They expose her inability to
acquire knowledge beyond her role as self-sacrificing mother and wife (asking
about Kim is one thing but enquiring into the investigation is quite another),
and make known what an anachronistic and truly destabilising force she
really is. Existing beyond political machination means neither Teri nor Kim
are subject to the same rules as those women working inside CTU or close
to the presidency. Ignorance of protocol allows them to break narrative rules
(do not bother Bauer at work, for example), but also makes them vulnerable
without a male guide for protection. So, for instance, at the moment when
Nina is attempting to cover her traitorous tracks, Bauer's hapless wife
stumbles in wanting information on her husband (1.24). Overhearing Nina
speaking Serbian, Teri puts aside her surprise to ask instead about what has

happened to her husband. Fatal mistake. Positioned as she now is in Nina's sights, a powerful gaze able to determine action precisely because it is privy to knowledge which the virtuous wife has no access, Teri's downfall stems from her inability to understand protocol, acquire relevant information, read the narrative clues, impose meaning without male assistance – and wandering into a narrative terrain unaided by Bauer.

FOR YOUR GENTLE EYES ONLY: WORKING GIRLS AND NARRATIVE ENABLERS

Not that being near the epicentre of narrative knowledge is any less precarious for women working at CTU or for the President. Insofar as each woman is highly skilled and self-disciplined (although Kim's CV might require closer scrutiny), and must pledge allegiance to serving the interests of an organisation that enables while restricting her, female access to knowledge and the power she can claim is highly circumscribed and heavily policed. How each handles information and makes use of it ultimately determines her fate. But such a process for women is at the same time a struggle involving values 'defining' what constitutes appropriate feminine identities and behaviours in relation to the politics of the modern workplace. So, when Erin Driscoll (Alberta Watson) is summarily removed as CTU Director, it is in part as cultural retribution for failing to take proper care of her schizophrenic daughter, Maya (Angela Goethals), but also in part – and possibly more importantly – as textual reckoning for dismissing Bauer over that small matter concerning his heroin addiction.

Women tend to do well when adopting a fairly traditional role, as helpers to the male hero. Female information gathering and dissemination serving the interests of the male investigation – helping it proceed briskly, anticipating potential trouble-spots, negotiating blockages, providing crucial evidence, giving essential directions – navigates the male hero through hazardous and uncharted narrative territory as he races against time to stop political assassins and assorted terrorists threatening to detonate nuclear bombs or release deadly viruses. Without Nina Myers in Season One, Bauer could not have multi-tasked so well, pursuing the kidnappers of his wife and daughter while thwarting the attempt on Senator David Palmer's life; in Season Two, Michelle Dessler takes on the role as she passes on crucial messages, alerts the hero – Bauer and/or Tony Almeida – when something important is about to happen, and briefs Bauer on the whereabouts of the various game-players as he hunts down those willing to risk lives and compromise American interests in the Middle East. Chloe proves her worth in Seasons Three, Four and Five with her finely honed computer skills able to decrypt the most impenetrable of information systems. Unquestioned loyalty and unwavering obedience to the male hero (rather than the organisation) are essential qualities for survival. These women know when to keep their counsel, and are prepared to be led away in handcuffs for insubordination as long as it protects the integrity of Bauer's mission. Benched maybe, but these women are rarely out of the game for long.

Most troubling, however, are the ways in which these women never quite belong. In the case of some, the more competence they possess the more excluded they eventually become. Being at the top wins few friends. Paula Schaeffer (Sara Gilbert) is a new CTU recruit in the second season, hired to fill the position previously held by the deceased Jamey Farrell (Karina Arroyave). Highly competent at her job and having waited two years for the CTU assignment, she desperately wants to prove her worth. Not long after her arrival, Michelle has to tell her to stop trying so hard (2.1). Given an opportunity at last, and charged with the task of transferring the CTU data on the impending crisis to the NSA server, Paula insists on staying at her workstation despite evacuation warnings (2.3). Her dedication to duty means she is still there when the bomb goes off, and she is eventually pulled from the wreckage with internal haemorrhaging. Kept alive long enough to reveal the decryption key reveals the textual sacrifices made for crucial information. But her death is also the price she must pay for being so annoyingly obsessive and good at her job (2.4). Season Three sees the introduction of über-techno-geek Chloe. She may constantly worry that she is in trouble for the slightest infringement of protocol but she remains the best at what she does. No one else can set up audio filters (3.11; 3.12), encrypt files or navigate the network like Chloe. But her drive, her obsession with rules and protocol, and her over-analytical mind means she is only ever tolerated in the workplace. Having to be better than her male colleagues, and often involved in petty squabbles with female ones over the opportunity to work more important assignments, positions her as forever on the margins, socially awkward and dysfunctional. Easily discredited and often removed from her workstation for the least violation in procedure, despite the important information gathering role she performs in the 24 text, Chloe is constantly *contained* and *represented* by dominant institutional frameworks that define her as a problem. Viewed as deviating from social 'norms', and thus accorded an inferior status, Chloe, as Paula before her, is perceived as having a 'compulsive' personality, which neutralises her and keeps her in a non-threatening place endlessly requiring male validation. No wonder both are obsessed with the rules, as they more than anyone know how their voices carry little veracity without male authority backing them up.

Problems of legitimacy are not only suffered by the likes of Chloe and Paula. Key political female players, such as Michelle or Lynne Kresge (Michelle Forbes), consistently find themselves struggling for creditability. On the surface at least, each woman is a skilled negotiator, able to mediate delicate office politics and diplomatically convey information without causing discord. But stepping out of the mediating role and questioning the reliability of intelligence and/or the integrity of a political strategy is risky business. Michelle is, for example, the first inside CTU to question the veracity of the Cyprus tapes (2.16). Believing Syed Ali (Francesco Quinn) is telling the truth, she goes against the official assessment that the tapes are genuine. Almeida may doubt her judgement based on considered opinions from the technical team, but Carrie Turner (Lourdes Benedicto) goes even further to dispute her right to draw such a conclusion in the first place. Carrie immediately discredits Michelle's voice, casting doubt on her interrogation skills and highlighting her general lack of experience. Difference, friction and disagreement based on nothing more than personal animosity and professional jealousy prompts Carrie to question Michelle's reliability and motives. Similar issues over trustworthiness and who has the right to speak resurface between Lynne and Sherry Palmer as the two women clash over who is best able to advise the President (Season Two). It cannot be stressed enough that these verbal brawls are nothing compared to the retribution women face when challenging male claims to 'defining' truth. Fallen women – their broken bodies (Lynne, Marianne Taylor [Aisha Tyler]), their expulsion from the building (Carrie, Chloe), their exclusion from knowledge (Michelle, Chloe) – quite literally litter the narrative as a consequence of defiantly disputing powerful men.

LADY MACBETH RIDES IN A GOLF CART: COVERT OPERATIONS AND TEXTUAL RETRIBUTION

A moment of confession: my world was rocked when I learnt stalwart counter-terrorist agent, and trustworthy companion to Bauer, Nina Myers was the mole. Who would have guessed? No clue was given that she was a Serbian-speaking, rogue double agent named Yelena, part of a dastardly plot to assassinate presidential candidate Senator Palmer, or her role in the apparent suicide of Jamey Farrell (1.24). A traitor to her country; a murderer of women getting in her way; a betrayer of the 24 narrative. It is enough to make you lose faith completely. But is this not the point? In a narrative and generic format that seemingly gives women little to do – either susceptible damsels needing rescue or helpmates facilitating male action – some are often driven to extreme measures to assert narrative control and locate power for themselves, to the point of undermining the ability of the patriarchal narrative to tell its story. If 'trust no one' is the central premise, then these women are responsible for shaking our confidence. Never again will I trust the 24 narrative.

Time and again, women are to blame for those astonishing, 180-degree plot twists, those jaw-dropping moments. Who can forget when blonde, seemingly sweet-natured, WASP-ish bride-to-be Marie Warner (Laura Harris) arrives just as fiancé Reza Naiyeer (Phillip Rhys) figures out her involvement in processing the incriminating shipping order – and shoots him dead (2.10)? Or when assassin Mandy (Mia Kirshner) makes another surprise return only to deliver a deadly handshake to President Palmer (2.24)? But these acts pale in significance compared to the shenanigans of Nina, and Lady Macbeth herself, Sherry Palmer. TV critic Wendy Lesser predicted that before the first season ended Sherry, because her deceit can no longer be tolerated, and Nina, because with Jack and Teri back together her status as ex-girlfriend troubles the marital reconciliation plot, might die. 'Such are the rules of conventional television morality, and mortality' (2002: 27, 37). How wrong can you be? Sidelined maybe, but both remain in the game for a little longer.

Any struggle for power, Michel Foucault contends, is both systematic and hidden; and certainly, in the beginning, Sherry and Nina diligently work undetected at the margins while biding their time. Secrecy and silence are indispensable for success. Attention to small detail, hinting that neither can see the broader picture nor the dangers ahead, preoccupies them: Sherry focuses on the wellbeing of her husband and protecting her children, and Nina concentrates on decrypting data to guide Bauer through his most gruelling day. Both appear content to follow generic protocol and tow the patriarchal line. But, before the first 24 hours have drawn to a close Sherry is unmasked as capable of doing just about anything to get her husband elected, and Nina is exposed as willing to sacrifice anyone and everything for substantial financial gain. The damage that their will to narrative power inflicts upon the socio-cultural and textual world of 24 is the chaos that ensues as a consequence of their involvement. Uttering the truth behind their treachery, making known what they had done even before the clock started ticking, immediately ascribes them with the desire for power and knowledge; their intentions are known and both become subject to various contesting laws that will seek to *contain* and *represent* these women forever more as trouble *in* the text and troubling *to* the generic and narrative rules of 24. Over the next two seasons their struggle to survive – to acquire political/personal leverage, to work while under surveillance, to bargain with information and to rewrite the script – reveals how women's will to power remains heavily compromised in and through the way 'power acts by laying down' rules neither sex can escape (Foucault 1998: 83).

Seasons Two and Three find Sherry back in the political fold after her expulsion from politics and from her marriage to Palmer. She returns under the pretext of warning Palmer that someone in his Defense Department is working against him and could jeopardise his presidency (2.6). Only needing five minutes of his time, she convinces him that he *needs* her; she knows *exactly* what is happening and, more than anyone else, can help. Palmer may be suspicious but he knows she has access to information that others (including himself) do not. Never letting him forget that he has enemies within his own government allows Sherry to generate, manipulate and sustain an uneasy climate of political deception, internal intrigue and personal treachery. She cuts a deal with detained journalist Ron Wieland (Michael Holden) behind closed doors (2.8); she manages to get back into the inner circle with provisional security clearance (2.10); she skilfully handles the information flow, releasing details of back-channel communications implicating cabinet minister Roger Stanton (Harris Yulin), thus trading Stanton with whom she is in league to gain Palmer's trust (2.10; 2.11); and she deftly distances herself from Stanton's subsequent allegations incriminating her, saying that his team tried to recruit her four months earlier to work against Palmer (2.14). What slowly unfolds is how Sherry is constructing and orchestrating the conspiracy. She is adept at passing on reliable information and correctly identifying conspirators precisely because she is implicated in engineering the crisis in the first place. Revenge may be her motive, and events may spiral beyond her control, but creating an atmosphere of paranoia, confusion and uncertainty is the reason for her existence in the narrative.

Mike Novick (Jude Ciccolella) may say she has her own agenda, and Palmer may claim to have her on a tight leash (2.7), but Sherry can only shape narrative events in the first place because she is speaking through her exalted role as mother and former consort to the President. But playing power politics is a dangerous game for any woman identified first and foremost as a loyal wife and loving mother. Look at the fate of Hillary Rodham Clinton, where her role as First Lady, involved in policy decision-making and the law, provoked nothing but suspicion, hostility and vitriolic media backlash. On the one hand Sherry functions as the gendered inverse of Bauer, working hard to protect the integrity of male power – how many times have we heard Sherry or Bauer tell Palmer that they kept knowledge from him in order to safeguard his political virtue and the sanctity of his office? On the other hand, whereas Bauer can get away with outrageous violations in protocol because generic rules grant him immunity, Sherry is not so lucky because convention dictates that loving wives and self-sacrificing mothers are not supposed to do what she does. The implication here is that Sherry emerges as 'calculating' and 'manipulative' precisely because the power structures in which she functions cannot tolerate any transgression against conventional codes of feminine behaviour.

24's deep textual investment in familial obligation enables Sherry to remain in its narrative world. When she claims her right to speak to Palmer because she is his wife (2.7), she establishes the terms on which she is allowed to remain. He may correct her, calling her his 'ex-wife', but no matter: she loves him and always will; and he needs to give her a second chance, as everything she has ever done has been for him. Endlessly evoking marital faithfulness and sexual fidelity invokes her privileged agency as stalwart guardian of patriarchal law: a law informed by the male roles of husband, father and by extension, the President. It is a shrewd tactical move that gives her political (and even personal) leverage while enabling her to avoid prosecution at the end of Season Two and to be back working her angles in Season Three. Lady Macbeth is not easy to depose. But she overplays her hand when she causes the literal collapse of another powerful patriarch, Alan Milliken (Albert Hall). Sent to neutralise Milliken, who is threatening to spoil Palmer's re-election campaign, she precipitates his death after a heated argument ensues where she taunts his masculinity (never wise for any woman), exacerbates an existing medical condition (as he struggles to breathe), and prevents his wife (Gina Torres) from dispensing lifesaving medicine (3.13). Ironically, her death is not at the hands of a man – for who could eliminate a woman with the knowledge and ability to topple presidencies and discredit influential men – but another woman with a powerful husband and nothing to lose. Sherry initially persuades Julia to withhold Alan's medication, saying that his death will free her from an intolerable marriage. But unable to live with the guilt of her own complicity, Julia exacts textual retribution by shooting Sherry before turning the gun on herself (3.23). No feminine loyalty here – only patriarchal recrimination and revenge for removing one woman's power base, however compromised it may be.

Attempts to carve out power and narrative agency (however limited) emerge as indicative of the dense and deeply entangled gendered politics at work in the 24 text. These reproduce modern gendered power relations in which female agency involves a continual but ambivalent struggle in resisting *and* reproducing entrenched patriarchal culture that, while oppressive, is necessary for personal success – and narrative survival. Different feminine subject perspectives, split loyalties, and little if no solidarity reveal the multiple feminine subjectivities negotiating the constraints in generic and narrative form – some experience it as liberating, others as a tactical alliance and a few resist. Diverse archetypes emerge, in which various models of femininity and female subjectivity operating in the text contribute to a particular ideological construction of what constitutes and 'defines' women and their conflicting relationship to power and knowledge at this historical moment.

In Season Five, Michelle is dead: if only she'd listened to Almeida about not returning to CTU. Chloe is out in the field helping Bauer: smart girl. Audrey Heller Raines (Kim Raver) is back at CTU co-ordinating security systems for an important presidential summit. The new First Lady acts more like a hysterical heroine from Victorian sentimental melodrama than the despotic power-crazed mistress of Glamis Castle. Derek Huxley (Brady Corbet) looks set to irritate me no end with his annoying habit of being in the wrong place at the wrong time; although I suspect Kim will return this season to show him how it is done properly – and to grate further on my nerves. And the clock is ticking. But as the women teach us, nothing is ever as it seems; and I wait for them to defy my expectations yet again.

Except, let's face it, we are all damsels in distress.

FATHER KNOWS BEST?

THE POST-FEMINIST MALE AND PARENTING IN 24

JOKE HERMES

The Fox real-time action drama *24* is easily read as celebrating traditional and conservative notions of masculinity. The central male characters display ruthlessness and rationality in equal measure, in a series filled with violence and machismo. At face value, there is little to suggest that *24* could be considered as a 'usable fiction' from a feminist perspective (Mepham 1990). Yet, there is more to be said and seen, especially if one reads *24* as playing with traditional televisual and cinematic conceptions of masculinity. That is to say, *24* invests itself in *performances* of masculinity, roles formed from an adherence to established generic conventions and attributes of 'the male', and from traditional principles of parenting and fatherhood.

In the case of the analysis presented here, the character of Jack Bauer in the first four seasons of *24* constitutes the primary subject of scrutiny. The analysis is, in turn, informed by a critical understanding of how popular culture both produces and reflects social constructions of masculinity. In particular, to explore these codes and conventions of masculinity in a work of popular television, it appears both appropriate and fruitful to consider corresponding codes and conventions of genre. Genre dictates how a series may tell a story as well as what is to be expected of characters and the relationships they enter into. Analysing the genres that shape *24* will help give due weight to how gendered qualities in Jack's character can be understood. As an exemplary version of many contemporary successful television series, 24 references more than one genre, and mixes codes in unexpected ways (Feuer 1998). 24's unusual combination of genres, such as the Western and the soap opera, more than warrant a closer look from a feminist perspective, and particularly in terms of how masculinity is performed. Through its hybrid mix of genres and associated generic principles of masculinity and femininity, 24 invites us to reconsider the meanings of gender in relation to professionalism, and of masculinity to parenting. It thus helps us 'work through' (Ellis 1999) a central, post-feminist anxiety of our time by fictionally rehearsing possible solutions to how men might be turned into good 'mothers' while women go about making careers.

In its narrative arcs, 24 poses an unexpected question: whilst many of its female characters climb the professional hierarchies of CTU and the US government (to name two organisations under constant survey in the series), who is taking care of the children? And how? The answer to this question is partly to be found in the conveyed masculinity of 24's central protagonist, Jack Bauer. As becomes a series comprising a generic hybrid, Bauer's masculinity is forged from past conventions. As an amalgam of conventions, his masculinity can be seen as a *bricolage* of these forms. Whilst acknowledging that the generic forms and codes of maleness bleed together in the series, it is useful to isolate qualities derived from particular, distinct genres: the action series (made manifest in facets of Bauer's cold-blooded professionalism), the Western (conveyed in his sense of individualism) and the soap opera (Bauer as family man). Each in turn helps to make sense of 24's post-feminist involvement with masculinity. Together, they also show what 24 suggests 'male parenting' might look like.

THE PATRIOTIC PROFESSIONAL

First, 24 can be classified as a television action-adventure series. As an overarching 'trend' incorporating generic forms such as the crime series, the detective or spy series, and the TV thriller, the action-adventure pinpoints a set of characteristics common to all, including 'a propensity for spectacular physical action, [and] a narrative structure involving fights, chases and explosions' (Neale 2000: 52). However, according to Toby Miller, action series are 'largely over as far as broadcast television is concerned' (2001: 17). 24 proves him, at least partly, wrong. The type of crime fought, the evil conglomerates threatening North America, the link to political shenanigans and especially Bauer's cool professionalism and ability to remain level-headed and focused on the job 'no matter what' are easily reminiscent of espionage series such as *The Man from UNCLE* and other 1960s fare. Napoleon Solo (Robert Vaughn) and Illya Kuryakin (David McCallum) were more suave and had an easier time of it, cast as they were in a less realist (and realistic) world. Bauer does, however, share particular aspects of the former spies' male-ness: as predominantly well-mannered yet bordering on anarchistic (or at least unconventional) practice; always acknowledging the presence of a hierarchical structure of action and command, but believing that to 'bow' to it is a personal choice. Further, all these 'action heroes' share a governing view that the downfall of western democracy and welfare must be avoided at all cost, particularly from the attacks of jealous outsiders.

Like his predecessors Solo and Kuryakin, Bauer never doubts his own world-view. He always knows right from wrong. Correspondingly, *24* paints a landscape of terror and terrorism in 'prime colours' to parallel and justify Bauer's stark distinctions. In the world of *24*, the United States of America still has unquestioned moral authority and must be defended at all cost against amoral others, whether of East European or Arab descent. In the 1960s TV spy-world, this required unflappable and dedicatedly patriotic officers working closely together, using the most advanced technology on offer. In this world, the male action heroes reigned supreme, at the helm of a techno-state, guarded by the bureaucratic networks of power (Miller 2001: 18). In *24* the same mould holds true. Jack is forged a patriot and, initially, an employee in a vast bureaucracy. Mobile phones, faxes, GPS tracking systems and other spy toys are always at hand.

Further connections can be made between the historical context of previous male-dominated spy series such as *The Man from UNCLE*, and our man at CTU. The 1960s were also the era of sexual liberation (Osgerby 2001) and second-wave feminism, which together provided male professionals with another set of challenges while saving the country. Initially, traditional masculine disdain cloaked as chivalry continued to 'do the job' for such action figures as *The Persuaders!* Bauer, however, is a post-feminist professional, yet problems remain. Although respectful of his female bosses, the overall narrative arc sides with Bauer. Those women questioning his actions soon find Bauer proved right and their authority undermined. In short, Bauer still commands the field of action.

While Bauer knows absolutely what it takes to get the job done, affairs of the heart elude him. That is to say, he lacks the ability to commit to relationships with women because of the relentless demands of his job. He loses his wife twice – first to the job, and then because of his inability to save her – and is reluctant to commit, knowing that as long as he works for CTU the job precludes relationships. This is evidenced in the travails of Kim and Edmunds in Season Four, and Bauer's own short-lived connections with Kate Warner (Sarah Wynter, in Season Two); Audrey Raines (Kim Raver, in Season Four); and Diane (Connie Britton, in Season Five). It appears that sentimentality and emotions are anathema to the true 'cold-blooded' professional.

To continue to trace the historical formation of the 'action hero', Bauer does, however, appear to have advanced beyond the figures of the 1990s. Initially, the action heroes of Bauer and, for example, John McClane (Bruce Willis) in the *Die Hard* trilogy appear bound by type, actions and reactions to corresponding circumstances. For example, Yvonne Tasker suggests that 'a lack of control, accompanied by a sense of placelessness, is a defining feature of the action hero in films such as *Die Hard*, in which John McClane (Bruce Willis) finds himself in an impossible situation controlled by an incompetent bureaucracy' (1993: 114). Equally, Bauer is confronted by myriad 'impossible situations', day after day, constantly held back from action by the bureaucratic networks surrounding each nightmarish scenario. Yet, at the same time, there are marked differences. Unlike McClane or Danny Riggs (Mel Gibson) in the *Lethal Weapon* cycle, Bauer refuses to become a cynic. He continues to believe passionately in his work and in being needed by his country. That is to say, the distinction lies in McClane and Riggs' cynicism for humanity and the social order extending to dispirited thoughts about work and country, whereas Bauer continues to believe in the merits of both, rather than in their essential futility and rottenness.

Further, unlike his witty antecedents, Bauer does not joke about life or the vicissitudes of his job. There is no humour in 24 to undercut the dramatic effects of the plots and of the fighting. In this sense, masculinity is not reduced to masquerade. With its sense of seriousness, and the personal investment of Bauer in gravely making his professional patriotism into a personal quest, 24 reaches towards another generic format and figure, that of the cowboy. Not the cheerful gunslingers of 1950s television, but the desperate male figures made mythic by Clint Eastwood on the big screen, in works such as *High Plains Drifter* and *Pale Rider*. Drawing on characteristics of Eastwood's lone gunman, Bauer can be seen as a true, urban cowboy.

THE URBAN COWBOY

The abduction of his daughter and wife in Season One is staged to force Bauer, as head of CTU, into cooperation with the criminals. Rather than seeking assistance and surrounding himself with the powers of bureaucracy (of governmental and military networks), Bauer decides to confront the situation by 'going it alone'. In that moment 24 recasts its central protagonist in the generic format of the Western (see Cawelti 1976; Matheson 2005). Later seasons have seen Bauer adopt the trappings, increasingly, of the 'urban cowboy': a lonely male riding out to do justice, to revenge the attack on his (otherwise absent) family (Neale 2000: 223). The fact that Bauer's wife dies at the end of the first season provides more grounding for this particular genre-led reading. In the 'pure' Western, the hero's wife and children are not permitted to survive. The tragedy of a family's massacre informs a strong sense of male heroism, which befits the 'intensely male orientation of many post-war Westerns' (Neale 2000: 141–2).

24 adopts further characteristics of the 'pure' Western, informing, in turn, Bauer's masculinity. Just as the cowboy mediates between civilisation and wilderness, Bauer crosses similar borders and boundaries, both geographical and attitudinal. Through each season, Bauer crosses and recrosses the topographical terrain of Los Angeles (and further afield), from the seats of power of civilised society and of the western world (governmental headquarters; the White House), to the 'heart of darkness' (for example, the Drazens' desert lair in Season One). Equally, instances abound of Bauer transgressing the *behavioural* boundaries of civilisation and 'the wild'. In Season Two, Bauer brutally murders a group of malcontent criminals-for-hire. More broadly, across the seasons, Bauer does not hesitate to kill when necessary, or torture those he thinks are withholding information vital to his investigation. Although, at the beginning of Season Four, Bauer is working security detail for a top government minister and displays the outward signs of professional corporate masculinity, it does not take long before he has gone rogue, working in 'the wilderness' with corresponding signs of wildness: roughly seizing, amongst other instances, a witness from the Chinese Embassy. In moving between civilisation and the wilderness, in location and action, Bauer epitomises the 'frontier myth' of the pure

Western: living to protect the community, yet existing outside of the group, constantly alone.

While the spy series produces an outwardly polished form of masculinity, the Western takes its examination of maleness further. Many Westerns revel in violence and glorify it; but those films that underscore how tragedy and triumph are one and the same in their conceptions of manhood make a more lasting impression. To take a relatively recent example: Clint Eastwood as William Munny is a sorry figure in *Unforgiven* (1992). The film initially sets him up as a loser, only to show him prevailing once he kills his arch enemy. Hurdles, as the genre dictates, must be taken in order for the protagonist to become a 'real man': 'for manhood in Westerns to be achieved, the male body must be challenged, beaten, convalesce and recuperate to ultimately earn the mantle of manhood' (Motley 2004: 4). It is in this mould that one can understand Bauer's many physical trials and tribulations. He is tortured and hunted, goes 'cold turkey' to conquer his heroin addiction, and bears the personal *and* physical responsibility for finding and disarming nuclear and biological weapons that could harm the nation.

Crucially, Bauer does *not* succeed in his mission from a position of unquestioned strength. At the end of Season One and into Season Two he is emotionally broken. In Season Three, he is battling drug dependence and is later tortured to the point that his heart stops beating. It appears that, in what he must endure in terms of physical ordeals and emotional torments, Bauer-as-cowboy is moving towards earning the 'mantle of manhood'. Yet, at the same time, this collation of physical endurance and the trials of the 'loner' are troubled by a further twist to Bauer's professional patriotism and maverick character: he is a father. Whilst suffering the crucial western trial with the death of his wife, Bauer problematises the generic connection by working, ceaselessly, to protect his daughter, Kim.

THE CARING FATHER

While a tale of violence, in which authority and social order are upheld by means of rough justice, and a celebration of embedded aspects of masculinity, 24 is more than this. Although the violence in 24 suggests that the ideological work performed by the show is to strengthen traditional and conservative notions of masculinity, there are other ways to understand the series. Beneath the surface, 24 experiments with the gender inscriptions of its characters. If gender is not understood as describing individuals but social subjects, that is to say that if we understand identities to be shaped via social relations and not as the result of bodily attributes or one-dimensional social roles, a different story emerges. A series of questions can thus be posed: why is Jack Bauer (as well as other characters like President David Palmer) portrayed as a family man? Why do storylines interweave the male figures' private and public lives rather than erect a wall between them? Why do these 'cold-blooded professional men' yield to explicit and outward displays of emotion when their families are placed in jeopardy? To ask these questions is to ask another: why, in short, does 24 follow the generic codes of the soap opera?

To conceive of 24's relationship with the soap opera genre one need only note the series' preoccupation with (and prominent placement of) families: the Bauers, the Drazens, the Palmers, the Warners, the Araz family – the list goes on. By holding its attention on the multiple members and intricate interrelations of these families, 24 adds another layer to its male characters. The result is a new mix of generic characteristics and, in turn, markers of masculinity. What happens when a spy or 'lone rider' has parental responsibilities? The act of adding unexpected genre ingredients to the mix changes characters. It extends the range of their responsibilities, and invites them into new experiential realms; equally, they may be faced with new choices. Above all, in its soap mode, 24 uses children to complicate a character's position.

To have children, 24 suggests, is something of a burden. Bauer has the never-ending responsibility of rearing, chasing and protecting his ill-fated (and profoundly irritating) daughter, Kim. In Season One, the machinations and misadventures of Palmer's daughter and son almost lose him his candidacy and his bid to become the President of the United States. Although their children may be a little older, the Drazens, Warners and Arazs also experience parental grief. Outside of these extended families, further examples of child-as-burden abound in the series. Kim's boyfriend Chase Edmunds (James Badge Dale) turns out to have a baby in Season Three, brought to CTU headquarters, drawing people away from their professional duties to act as ad hoc babysitters. In Season Four, 24 introduces the mentally unstable daughter of CTU boss Erin Driscoll, in which Maya's psychotic episode and later suicide make it impossible for Driscoll to continue in her job. Children, by their actions or simply by their very existence, have a way of complicating storylines.

Children redefine professionals as parents, whether crime fighters or terrorists. This does more than rebuild characters, it opens up interesting ideological possibilities. 24 makes use of these possibilities in a rather audacious fashion, daring to portray cold-blooded killer-for-the-right-cause Jack Bauer as a 'new father'. 24 no less than suggests that we might broaden our notion of what parenting could look like if we were to give up on the preconceived notions that revolve around mothers and mothering, regardless of whether it is women or men taking care of children (Woodward 1997). Bauer's qualities as a father are quite remarkable but perhaps not clearly visible behind his hyper-masculine behaviour and the smoke screen of irritation caused by Kim in the first two seasons. However, Bauer's continuing loyalty to his daughter, and Kim's impressive survival skills (in the face of kidnapping, murderous employers and wild animals) suggest that she is a positive example of the effects of fatherly care. This, then, might be 24's usable fiction. As soap, 24 suggests that Jack Bauer be understood in terms of male mothering. In turn, the series can help us rethink parenting away from conservative gendered notions by showing us that dedicated professionals can also be parents, and that parenting need not necessarily be conceived (and performed) in markers of femininity and masculinity, as distinct forms.

As a father, Bauer is not always available but he does stay in touch, mainly by the ubiquitous mobile phone. He loves his daughter regardless of her ill-advised behaviour. He seems to expect Kim to learn by experience rather than by formal schooling, offering 'shop floor socialisation' for her as a young professional. Most of all, he does not 'treat her as a girl' when she is in danger. In the second season there is a strong example of Bauer's lack of sexism regarding his daughter. In 2.13, Kim faces the murderous father of a little girl she has been babysitting. The man is a psychopath: he abused and killed his wife, and was stopped by Kim from doing the same to his daughter. Instructed by Bauer over the phone (of course), she manages to shoot him and kill him. In this moment, 24 brings together father and daughter in an explosive manner. It shows Kim following in her father's footsteps, doing what a man (and at times a girl) needs to do.

It should not have come as a surprise to the viewer that Kim returns in the third season as a CTU agent, working on the computer mainframe. Here too is an important moment that rewrites prescribed notions of fatherhood. Bauer does not forbid Kim to see her boyfriend, Edmunds. But Bauer does shield him from danger (against the young man's wishes) while warning Kim that as a father he is in a 'tough position'. This is not symptomatic behaviour of an emotionally distanced 'cold professional' or a hardened cowboy for whom fatherhood is an impossible mission. This is a new father who, against 'hands-on' care, suggests that the parenting of teenagers can be a mixture of close ties and mutual freedom.

If Bauer is presented as a 'new' father, then the question is raised of how 'being a child' can also be (re)defined. In the first season, children are mostly and explicitly presented as vulnerable beings, requiring constant care and control, regardless of the fact that they are well past the age of fifteen. Kim gets abducted; Palmer's daughter raped; and Palmer's son is implicated in the death of the rapist. But from Season Two onwards children are defined differently. They are presented as adults who have not yet acquired the markers or behavioural and social encoding of professionalism. Through their entangled position within deadly scenarios, these mini-adults come to adulthood through their individually determined actions. A good example is offered in Season Four, when teenager Behrooz Araz (Jonathan Ahdout) literally shoots his way out of childhood in his Oedipal rebellion against his parents and their terrorist mission.

Returning to Kim, Bauer-as-father can be judged as having created a diligent and discerning 'mini-adult'. After landing in situations that suggest a fair degree of stupidity, Kim passes several tests that result in her becoming a CTU agent. An independent, thinking professional, much like her father, she dares to challenge him and others when she thinks they are not doing the right thing. By the fourth season she temporarily disappears after serving the unlikely purpose of making us think about how the type of masculinity men like Jack Bauer represent might be richer and more complex than suggested by the second-wave feminist denunciation of machismo and male conceit (my own included).

To conclude: all of the afore-mentioned generic markers and models of responsibility inform our understanding of masculinity as presented in 24, as forms of 'being Bauer'. At first sight, Jack Bauer is presented as a dedicated law-enforcement professional who happens to have a family. Attention to the series' careful balancing and mixing of generic traits leads to a reversal of this perception, allowing us to understand Bauer as a 'new father'. To get us there, 24 draws on key characteristics of the action-adventure series (incorporating elements of the spy thriller), and of the Western. Bauer's character performs and references codes of masculinity associated with these generic forms: as the hardened, streetwise, serious spy; as the lone rider mediating between civilisation and the wilderness, in location and action. Drawing on traits of his generic predecessors, Bauer appears exemplary in his ability to shield emotion and cultivate ruthlessness rather than empathy, beholden to no one but the 'greater cause'. His masculinity is bound with tragedy and physical endurance, as a means to access the 'mantle of manhood'.

With many thanks to Steven Peacock.

00.14

TECHNO-SOAP

24, MASCULINITY AND HYBRID FORM[1]

TARA McPHERSON

When *24* burst onto the US broadcast landscape in November 2001, it was quickly hailed as something radically new for television. Writing for *The Boston Globe*, critic Matthew Gilbert proclaimed, 'Strong adjectives such as 'riveting' and 'gripping' and 'compelling' are shamelessly overused in the critical vernacular ... But it's time to reinvest in their stock when it comes to *24*, a riveting, gripping, and altogether compelling new suspense drama ... An innovative and expertly executed hour of suspense, *24* is without question the best premiere of the fall season' (2001). Such praise was typical, and the series went on to accrue great critical acclaim, an eventually solid viewership, and no small amount of scholarly attention (as evidenced, of course, by collections like this one.)[2] *24* was thus one of several recent series framed via a rhetoric of newly emergent televisual quality, as a kind of benchmark of 'good TV' that might be distinguished from the ever-growing tendency toward reality programming. As a feminist who has watched the show with great ambivalence, often recoiling from its flat characterisations of women and its troubling nationalism, I am particularly interested in the way frequently voiced perceptions of the show's innovation and quality may serve to mask its deployment of what has long been seen as a particularly feminised form, the soap opera. Further, I query what role this new inflection of male melodrama might play in at once fixing and troubling masculinity in the era of global capitalism and national insecurity.

This chapter then considers 24 as a hybrid form, a kind of convergence parable that brings together elements of the soap opera, reality television, and 'quality' drama within a formal structure that emphasises technological innovation and change. In particular, I am interested in the ways in which the series undertakes a re-masculinisation of serialised melodrama via a very particular deployment of both narrative and style. In the drama's narrative structure, a relentless focus on certain tropes of masculinity and nation works to distance criticisms that might be aimed at the programme's use of a serial form that shares much with both daytime and primetime soap operas, even as the soapy content helps secure the series' most reactionary moments. At the level of stylistic or aesthetic innovation, the series deploys technology (from the trope of liveness activated by its real-time countdown to the featured use of split-screen videography) to distance further the 'feminine' form of the serial, reinstalling a very particular vision of the white, male post-9/11 hero. This dual strategy also serves to protect television itself (often theorised as feminine) from the perceived threats posed, first, to the industry by new media technologies like the Internet and, second, to the 'serious' or 'quality' drama by reality TV, (itself a televisual response to the threat of digital media). I will return to the question of 'quality' television as this chapter draws to a close, querying the work such a concept does for both broadcast television and for television studies.

'24 IS ITS OWN RNIMAL': LIVENESS, TECHNOLOGY, AND SERIAL FORM

If critic Matthew Gilbert initially praised 24 as it premiered for being the best that television could be, by Season Two he was gently mocking the narrative for having 'its share of Aaron Spelling moments' even as he continued to laud the show as 'ambitious' (2002). Gilbert seemed willing to call a soap a soap, a tendency many of his fellow journalists avoided. For instance, writing in *The Atlanta Journal-Constitution*, Phil Kloer describes 'the series' multiple plot lines' and 'the sadistic way the writers keep piling stress on their beleaguered characters' while also portraying the 24 viewer as a 'junkie craving a fix' (2002b). Even as he ponders whether or not 'there has ever been a series that had more viewers shouting advice to the characters,' he refrains from commenting on the soap-like features of the drama or from drawing references to soap operas. Still, from Teri's amnesia and hidden pregnancy in Season One to the obligatory wedding scenarios of Season Two, 24 draws much of its narrative force and story content from terrain familiar from soap operas, even while it also draws from cop dramas and action films to prop up its investigations of masculinity.

Given its elaborate and often ridiculous plot twists and in its interlocking, ongoing narratives, 24 clearly depends on the serial form of the soap and on the conceptual terrain of melodrama, extending the ongoing serialisation of primetime US television that Jane Feuer, Lynne Joyrich and others have noted is constitutive of television since the Reagan era. As Joyrich notes, melodrama is 'the preferred form for television' (1996: 46), spreading across the televisual landscape in a diverse array of forms and genres. Yet, even with this generalised diffusion of melodrama throughout television's many formats, 24 is more than simply melodramatic. Its narrative structure conforms closely to the serialised form of soap operas. If many of today's television shows attempt a series/serial hybrid, allowing closure week to week while also continuing key storylines, this Fox drama deploys pure serial structure. This structure was duly noted by network executives who, hoping to allow casual viewers to drop in on the series, pressured the show's creators to move toward a more episodic structure after Season Two, a move the creative team resisted.

This is not to say that 24's producers were eager to have the show labelled a soap. Creator and executive producer Bob Cochran acknowledges in an interview that, while 'just about every show on TV ... has some degree of serialization, ... serialization [on 24] is obviously much more prominent.' But, even as he goes on to note that his first staff job as a writer was on the night-time soap, Falcon Crest, he maintains that the connection between his show and soaps 'can be overstated. What soaps don't have that we do is time continuity ... in that sense, 24 is its own animal.'[3] In fact, we might read the series' aggressive production techniques – including its split-screen showiness and its conceit of running in real-time – as attempts to distance the show from its debased and feminised narrative form. Thus, its trope of liveness and its technological fetishism come together to function as a prophylaxis against the debased form of the soap while also shoring television up against the incursions of new digital forms like the Internet into domestic spaces that were once the near-exclusive domain of television. The show is defended as 'quality' (by its creators and most critics) precisely because it is figured as different from soap operas, and its 'quality' status is established in the ways that it is not like debased melodramatic forms (be they soap operas or that other form of television that now also trades in simulated liveness, the reality TV show).

In her examinations of melodrama and postmodern television, Joyrich consistently reminds us that 'sexual difference(s) in the TV melodrama ... invite further investigation' (1996: 46), and this is certainly true of 24's remaking of the soap opera. There is a re-masculinisation of TV at work here, both in the near-obsessive explorations of the twenty-first century contours of maleness that the show undertakes and in its hyper-technologised formal strategies, both of which suggest an overcompensation for the series' abduction of what has long been seen as a highly feminised form. Initially, I had (and sometimes still have) a hard time watching the series because of its figuration of the women characters, particularly the blondest, dumbest ones, but I have slowly come to think this is not an especially telling aspect of the drama. In fact, the serial form of 24 seems to demand a certain deployment of fairly predictable representations, as form and representation reinforce one another. Its stock female characters are not that surprising given the show's reworking of the soap opera (hence its use of delicious villainesses and sacrificing mothers) and its deep investment in investigating masculinity (particularly via its blend of action and melodrama).[4] Put differently, I'm not sure the old feminist critique – 'These are degraded images of women' – really tells us anything very useful or interesting about 24. A different (and, I would say, more useful) critical project might be to explore the series' relationships to both masculinity and technology, particularly as they interconnect via new generic hybrids and as they speak to the shifting conditions of daily life at a particular moment in late capitalism.

These relationships are quite complex. Many of the series' formal strategies and production techniques pay homage to new digital forms, displaying a certain high-tech aesthetic, from the 'countdown' clock to the split-screen videography techniques. Screens multiply across the *mise-en-scène*, with mobile phones, computer monitors, and surveillance devices figuring prominently in the visual field. Despite this recurring techno-fetishism, the storylines often enact a subtle critique of technology, ranging from faulty phone systems to frozen computer networks. In crucial moments, high technology breaks down; for instance, in Season Two, Nina's spy-toy surveillance necklace gives out at just the wrong moment, leaving the agents in the lurch (2.7). Mobile phones lose reception or are left at home;

networks are busy and can't receive calls. At the level of narrative, Bauer's successes often derive not from a deployment of high-tech gadgetry à la James Bond or McGyver, but from individual ingenuity and courage, guts and guns. In one of the series' more gruesome moments, Bauer defeats new technology with a knife, carving an embedded microchip from an enemy's flesh (3.13).[5] As likely as not, high-tech equipment fails him when he needs it most. This troubling of the status of technology recurs and intensifies across the series' development; while technology often worked on the side of 'good' in Season One, by Season Two, technology seems to be the province of the villains or proves to be highly unreliable. Even the vast computational powers of networked systems that might save the world remain idle without the password sequence retained in the frail, embodied human memory of girl computer geek Paula Schaeffer (Sara Gilbert).

Further, the series often returns to a fairly 'old' technology as our most cutting-edge resource in times of trouble. The opening episode of Season Two features several minutes of high-tech imaging technology that allows the President and his advisers to zoom in on images of Second Wave terrorist camps in an unidentified Middle Eastern country. The CTU offices are resplendent with computer monitors (2.1). But, despite this immersion in high-tech networks, in moments of real crisis, characters repeatedly learn about breaking news from the familiar space of television. Even at the glitzy, screen-saturated NSA, the President and his team get their news from Fox TV. Perhaps not surprisingly, television here offers itself up as the most relevant and timely source of information, framing network news as the 'killer app' that occupies all those big screens at mission control.[6] Thus, there is a disjuncture in the show between its formal strategies (that largely celebrate the digital and the language of screens) and a recurring narrative troubling of the value of new technologies, technologies that are as likely to advance the goals of the villains as those of Bauer and the good guys. Technology is treated with a high degree of uncertainty and ambivalence in the many plot strands.

Theories of melodrama offer one way to think about this seemingly schizophrenic figuring of technology. In theorising melodrama, critics have repeatedly noted that, in films like those of Douglas Sirk, a certain ideological leakage is made manifest in a hyperbolic *mise-en-scène*, structuring a visual excess that might call into question the films' neat and tidy endings. Affect and emotion are mapped over objects and settings, transferring or displacing an exploration of social relations onto material objects or visual settings that are excessively rendered. In 24, that excess might be read as an excess of technologically slick style: the multiple-window display technique that does very little by way of servicing the story (and is typically not scripted in advance but added in post-production, like a special effect) signals that something is going on beyond the confines of the narrative. What are we to make of such excess? By reading this excess and its complicated relationship to narrative, we might begin to move beyond my first reaction to the show – a rather obvious critique of its images of women or its representations of a certain hyper-masculinity – to think about what larger cultural anxieties are writ large across these figurations as well as across the frenetic spaces, style and pace of 24.

While the series narratively celebrates old-fashioned technologies like 'hero television' and intrepid, lone-wolf masculinity, stylistically and formally it sculpts a loving look at the dispersion of screen languages into everyday life: as noted above, windows and screens proliferate in 24, both in the mise-en-scène and in its formal structures.[7] Additionally, the official website and DVDs all capitalise on the digital technology and gadgetry, illustrating once again TV's well-recognised capacity to spin meaning in many directions at once and to multiply contradiction. What are we to make of this doubled, seemingly contradictory, strategy of technological embrace and containment? At one level, television's primacy – as a source of cutting-edge information that even the President turns to – is assured: TV trumps new technology as the place we all go for real-time information in times of trouble. (Of course, in an era when the US government's agenda is piped directly to Fox News, imagining that information sometimes flows the other way might also speak to our desires to have 'independent' journalism once again.) On another level, by situating this narrative critique of new technology within a formal and stylistic embrace of digital media, the series also naturalises a particular version of convergence, one in which TV and new technologies seamlessly blend in order to offer up a particular version of the future: unidirectional broadcast and linear narrative all dressed up in an illusion of choice, multiplicity, and liveness.

Elsewhere, I've theorised several key modalities promised by new information technologies. Briefly put, one of these central modalities is a repackaging of the lure of liveness. Liveness has been central to theorisations of TV's specificity, and liveness remains a key dimension of our experiences of the Internet, a medium that also promotes itself as essentially up-to-the-minute ideology once again masquerading as ontology, to borrow from Jane Feuer's trenchant analysis of television. But, if TV traded in tropes of liveness, the forms of the Internet couple this feeling of presence to a sense of choice and possibility. As such, the web's liveness feels both mobile and driven by our own desires, structuring a mobilised liveness that we imagine we can invoke, and impact, with a simple, tactile mouse click. This sensation is a kind of *volitional mobility*, foregrounding choice and mobile presence, creating a sensation of liveness on demand. Thus, while television insisted that it brought the world live to us, the web weds causality and liveness to mobility, often structuring a feeling that our own desire drives the movement. The web is in process, in motion, and under our control. In its frenetic split-screen technology, 24 hails this new form of mediated, mobile liveness. If the web seeks to appropriate TV's long-standing relationship with liveness by offering up a volitional mobility, 24 fights back from the space of the television screen, claiming this enhanced and mobile liveness for itself.

Volitional mobility is a property specific to new technologies themselves, derived from their very forms and materiality and, in some ways, independent of content. But it is also an ideological force, packaged and promoted within certain digital media as a corporate strategy and mode of address. In a sense, it is always an illusion even if also an ontological property. But this sense of volitional mobility is perhaps even more illusory in the space of network television than on the web, for here it morphs into pure visual effect, an effect that works to hide a championing of a unidirectional broadcast model. While the series uses split-screen to suggest multiple storylines and the kind of always-emergent potential promised by the interactive narratives of gaming or the Internet, the plot is, of course, tightly controlled.[8] When offered up a screen of four simultaneous storylines, we can hardly choose which story we would like to follow or pursue the story at our own pace, at least at the moment of broadcast. (That said, I did often deploy my Tivo to fast forward through all scenes featuring Kim, particularly if they also involved mountain lions.) Even the official series website offers up minimal interactivity in most of its features (like Kim's cell phone or Jack's desk). In fact, the real-time conceit of the series serves to heighten its tight linearity, despite its split-screen window dressing, reinstalling a strict temporal progress as the 24 hours rapidly tick by. This clock only moves in one direction, taking us along as it goes, reducing interactivity to the viewers' previously mentioned desire to shout at the screen as the characters endlessly get embroiled in soap-like plotlines, tragedies, and crises.

Thus, while the critique of new technologies deployed at the narrative level in 24 does make manifest some cultural anxieties about life in the digital age, the series is not defined by or contained within this critique. In some ways this critique simply acts as a cover story for corporate strategies of media convergence and monopoly, moving us toward a digital future that promises minimal interactivity beyond the options offered up by the DVD box sets viewers of the show eagerly purchase. Of course, three decades of cultural studies scholarship reminds us that this containment is never total: for instance, 'unofficial' websites foster vibrant fan communities that are highly 'interactive,' and my own DVR-fuelled viewing strategies suggest my developing desire to watch television only on my own terms. Still, all the fast-forwarding and blogging in the world won't turn Kim into a character I would enjoy or re-jig the right-wing bias of Fox News. My ability to control my TV is clearly limited. Here, the stylistic and visual excesses of melodramatic narrative seem to stitch us back into capitalism's illusions even while feeling riveting and new.

'A MAN WHO KNOWS NO LIMITS': MASCULINITY IN THE ERA OF GLOBAL CAPITAL.[9]

Even while 24 at one level might be read as a celebratory tale of convergent media, the series' reworking of gender via a technologised soap opera form also indicates a certain troubling of the contours of masculinity. If the soap opera has been theorised as particularly feminine in its lack of closure and resolution, what might we make of the masculinist project of 24, a project that is deeply invested in exploring shifting patterns of maleness and manhood? I first read the series as a kind of cultural return to the hard-bodied, hyper-masculinity that so characterised the first Bush (and Reagan) era. Clearly Bauer's lone-wolf figuration does aim at a certain tough-guy status, but this status is never secured in the series. The drama certainly displays moments of longing for an inviolate, quick-witted, gun-toting male, but this is not the hyper-masculinity of *Rambo* or of *Die Hard*. There are both continuities and differences between Bauer's tortured masculinity and the masculine projects of the first Bush regime.

Unlike the heroes of the 1980s private investigator (PI) dramas from which 24 partially draws, Bauer is less caught up in navigating the homosocial bonds of (often interracial) masculinity than in parsing the kind of familial tangles long familiar from daytime soap operas. In tracking the figuration of masculinity during the first Gulf War, Robyn Wiegman reflects upon the interpenetration of masculinity and melodrama across the media landscape, arguing that the maleness this first Middle East conflict constructed was all about dissolving the 'often accepted ... [binaries] of masculine/public and feminine/private' (1994: 178). In such modes, there is a 'narration of geopolitical crisis as private and domestic', as melodrama moves from its traditional concern with the feminine and the household to a pointed exploration of masculinity in both private *and public* realms. In many ways, the character of Bauer perfectly illustrates this bleed. His workplace and familial lives consistently blur together in endless feedback loops. Other characters, like George Mason (Xander Berkeley) or President Palmer, also attempt familial reconciliation and model different modes of husbandly or paternal behaviour, although I would argue that the series frames geopolitical crises as at once public and private occupations, as various nations and ethnicities are investigated for potential enemy status.

We might push Wiegman's analysis further, thinking through why such a dissolution of binaries has a particular purchase in the 1990s and beyond, particularly in a post-9/11 USA; I would argue that the series very much represents and responds to life in a post-Fordist economy. In their insightful article, 'The Luster of Capital', Eric Alliez and Michel Feher describe the neo-Fordist economy as a shift away from the massive scale of factory production in the Fordist era toward a regime marked by a more supple capitalism. This includes a turn to flexible specialisation, niche marketing, service industries, and an increasing valorisation of information as the product 'par excellence' of capitalism. The separation of the spaces and times of production from those of reproduction (or leisure) that was central to an earlier mode of capitalism is replaced by a new spatio-temporal configuration in which the differences between work and leisure blur. 'Capital claims to be a provider of time' (1987: 316), and a 'vast network' emerges 'for the productive circulation of information,' structuring people and machines as interchangeable, equivalent 'relays in the capitalist social machine' (ibid). Rather than being *subjected* to capitalism, privileged workers are now *incorporated* into capitalism, made to feel responsible for the corporation's success. Put differently they are at the beck and call of capitalism 24/7, round the clock and counting down the hours.

Bauer and the denizens of 24 seem to have emerged from the pages of Alliez and Feher's astute analysis. Not only do the worlds of work and home constantly intertwine and overlap in 24 (and to a degree much greater than in earlier cop or PI shows like *McGyver* or *Miami Vice*); the series as a whole also displays an extraordinary obsession with time. From the drama's pretense of real-time structure to the frenetic pace of the plot, managing time becomes a clear goal of both the characters and the show itself. This endless focus on time hints at the heightened temporal stakes of US life in the era of late capitalism when those lucky enough to be employed are tethered to the workplace by laptop computers, networked mobile phones, and increasingly ubiquitous wi-fi. Critics reviewing the series endlessly commented on the ways in which the characters, especially Bauer, seemed to be sleep deprived and 'cranking on No-Doz' (Collins 2001: 39), with Wendy Lesser observing that 'time is the dominant character' in the series (2002: 27). While our fearless hero manages to beat the clock at the end of every season, we do witness the emotional toll that working 24/7 takes on the hero's psyche. Many of the series' most sympathetic characters often seem just moments from coming undone, barely able to keep up with the pace (and anxieties) of daily life in the twenty-first century.

Melodrama seems to have its greatest purchase at moments of disruption in the social order. In Peter Brooks' terms, melodrama seeks 'to demonstrate, to "prove" the existence of a moral universe' (1976: 20). In his analysis of *Miami Vice*, Scott Benjamin King highlights our current moment of disruption as 'a crisis of shifting definitions of masculinity' in postmodern times, a crisis that 'is also a crisis in the concept of work' (1990: 286). Alliez and Feher signal a crisis in labour as a hallmark of our post-Fordist times, a crisis heightened by the pressures of the globalisation of capitalism and the diffusion of information across networked economies. Although Alliez and Feher wrote their analysis well before 9/11, the anxieties they analyse have only accelerated since the Twin Towers fell. By calling endless attention to the stresses produced for Bauer by living in our moment of convergence, particularly on the home front, 24 seems to be pushing back against Bauer's total incorporation into capitalism, trying to carve out a space to live differently.

Bauer can be seen as a liminal figure of masculinity, at once inside and outside of the law and social conformity, leaving and rejoining CTU, working as both a team leader and as a renegade loner. Indeed, this inside/

outside status exists in interesting feedback loops with the series' blurring of private and public realms and of national and domestic contexts. Bauer has a privileged position as a bridging agent between various domains: legality/ illegality; hero/torturer; authority/individuality; public/private; national/ domestic. Several models of masculinity are presented by the show across its multiple seasons, but Bauer's position is a privileged and highly mobile one, transiting across various circuits of exchange and meaning. Other male and female characters remain more fixed, casting Bauer's mobility into greater relief while also highlighting the emotional costs of such movement.

In his investigation of 1950s representations of masculinity, Steven Cohan productively examines the ways in which filmic representations of the period both reveal and manage a larger cultural crisis in masculinity, at least partially brought on by new conditions of labour in the emergent cold war economy. He writes 'the discourse of masculinity crisis registered as a problem of gender what were, more subtly, social contradictions pressuring the ideological function of 'the new American domesticated male,' as *Life* named the middle-class breadwinner in confirmation of his typicality' (1997: xix). Masculinity was perceived to be in crisis precisely because men were moving to positions of consumption from earlier labour as producers. Cohan devotes considerable space to an analysis of Cary Grant's Roger Thornhill in *North by Northwest* (Alfred Hitchcock, 1959). Thornhill is the prototypical 'man in the gray flannel suit' of the period, working in advertising, and Cohan suggests that the 'film's depiction [of Thornhill] ... locate[s] masculinity in representation while revealing its place there to be highly problematic.' Of course, the ad man was a perfect symbol for these shifting conditions of labour, working as he did in images at what was the very beginning of the emergent service economies of post-Fordism. *24* unfolds at the other end of this era, when the image rules fully supreme and the information economy is in complete (if unevenly distributed) ascendancy. Bauer's workplace at CTU trades largely in information, data displayed across the multiple screens that comprise the office setting, coursing through networks that join the global economy, but both Bauer and the series at large are as ambivalent about these forces as Hitchcock's hero, Roger Thornhill, was about his own time. In moving from the 1950s to a new millennium, we transit from cold war global politics to a new American isolationism wrought by the Bush years, once again tracking the close intertwining of masculinity and geopolitics.

If Roger Thornhill spoke to and tried to contain society's worries over man's place in a world moving toward an ascendant middle class, i.e., over his transformation into a consuming subject, 24 might be read as taking up this question for a new era in a nation strongly polarised over questions of gay marriage and urban masculinity. Social anxieties over hetero-normative masculinity are reflected in public conversations and confusion over the meaning of the metrosexual, particularly as reflected in reality television series like *Queer Eye for the Straight Guy*. Part of the lure of the volitional mobility that so characterises our current moment is an increasing belief in the mutability of the self. The 'transformations' featured on shows ranging from *Extreme Makeover* to *Plastic Surgery Beverly Hills* (shows which also makeover men) highlight the malleability of the self. Bodies become one with the bitstream, as easily morphed as a Photoshop file. The very forms of electronic culture (and, especially, of digital culture) help naturalise this process, shifting our understandings of what constitutes the self and working in tight feedback loops with shifting modes of economic production and emergent media ecologies. The bleed between work and leisure and between old and new bodies can be seen as equipping us for the new modes of living demanded by post-Fordist economies, modes that require a new relationship to our corporeal selves.[10]

But, if Bauer is caught up in these blurred modes, his relationship to them is neither easy nor seamless. By Season Two, Bauer emerges as a rugged alternative to the metrosexual, a decidedly unmade self whose body is constantly battered, embattled, and in need of a shave. While occasionally stylish, his frequent fights and physicality seem to relocate him as embodied, sexed, and gendered. Bauer is not exactly hyper-masculine, but neither is he easily read as an urban metrosexual. He is also more rugged and casual (and less suited) than many of his CIA counterparts and was described in several reviews of the show both as 'puffy' and as an unexpected choice for a male lead, particularly because he was not conventionally handsome. One review in *The New York Times* remarked that Sutherland played the role with 'a notable lack of vanity' (James 2002b), while another mentions his 'red-gold beard' and 'plaid work jacket' (Ruch 2002: 33). Bauer is never fully converted in the course of the series, staging a form of masculinity that resists the beck and call of easy transformation proffered by digital technologies and reality television. Bauer may consume technology and information, but the series seems to suggest that he is less susceptible to consumption than those more feminine fellows populating reality television.

The series plays with and pushes against the temporalities and mutable selves of neo-capitalism even while its formal structures, production techniques, and *mise-en-scène* embrace the very technologies that underwrite this post-Fordist turn. In its obsessive tracking of various modes of masculinity, *24* seems to be working through and modelling different possibilities for networked subjectivity, a condition of contemporary life for the privileged mobile subject which means that closure and neat separations between work and leisure or public and private are no longer real possibilities. In an era of convergence, media monopolies, and diffuse networks of power, stand-alone masculinity really won't take you very far, but the series can't quite imagine and sustain a new mode of masculinity either (even as it attempts to image more 'integrated' landscapes). While America has entered a phase of retrenched isolationism, the ascendancy of globalised capitalism always threatens to unravel the borders of the nation-state, a reality brought home when George W Bush defended the outsourcing of US port operations to Arab nations in March 2005.[11]

The status of masculinity in the twenty-first century USA is particularly complicated by the national anxieties spawned by 9/11 and its aftermath. The series attempts to work through these anxieties in a variety of ways, mapping its more reactionary moments alongside Bauer's most sustained performances of tough-guy status. Throughout its many seasons, *24* consistently offers up rationales for torture and for operating outside the law, even as this torture is often revealed to be unnecessary, echoing our own government's game-playing with the very definitions and morality of torture. Even CTU agents and their relatives are fair targets for brutality if they are thought to *know things*, adding a new level of horrifying nuance to what it means to trade in information in our post-Fordist era. If power and capital are diffuse in such an economy, so is the enemy; they must be pursued by any means necessary. Slavoj Žižek has recently written that the 'depraved heroes of *24* are the Himmlers of Hollywood,' commenting that their ability to perform heinous acts 'while being loving husbands, good parents and close friends ... is the ultimate confirmation of moral depravity' (2006).

In many ways, the unstable figure of masculinity that the series deploys allows Bauer's relative morality to be mapped across different narrative structures and domains. His supposed humanity is confirmed by his anxiety and his familial bonds, narrative aspects most clearly tied to the serialised, soap opera format of the show. The series' action narratives figure Bauer differently, as a man perfectly capable of 'doing what has to be done.' When newspaper critics and fans reflect at all on the series' soapiest moments, they often bemoan that such plotlines even exist, but, in the logic of the series, these moments are a necessary flipside of its lone-wolf, renegade masculinity. The two narratives threads depend upon one another, intertwining home and homeland security. Put differently, Bauer's familial status authorises his ability to operate outside the law (yet in its service), granting him a kind of moral authority within the series' bizarre (if hauntingly familiar) ethical universe. Still, I don't think 24 offers us a fixed ideological position on these post-Fordist, post-9/11 developments in form and meaning or gender and genre, even as its plotlines are often skewed in reactionary ideological directions, advocating an 'anything-goes-in-defence-of-the-nation' mentality. Rather, its masculine melodramas might be read as symptomatic of the unstable contours of masculinity in the twenty-first century and of our national anxieties over labour, security, and morality. Below Bauer's scruffy exterior, one might even sense a latent longing for different possibilities, for new ways of being a man.

Finally, we can read this multifaceted ambivalence as a manifestation of (and perhaps a latent critique of) a broad cultural and individual sense of having lost control: of information, of time, of technology, of gender boundaries, of the comforts of genre, of our work lives, of our government. While the series does not articulate a progressive agenda, we might see beneath its high-tech surfaces and multiplying screens, the contours of a desire to challenge the relentless pace of life and create new circuits of meaning for masculinity that can navigate the demands of both home and family. One hopes that such a desire might be mobilised differently.

SOME CLOSING THOUGHTS ON THE WORK OF QUALITY IN THE ERA OF ELECTRONIC CULTURE

The origin of this chapter was a talk for a 2004 conference on American quality television held in Dublin, Ireland. The possibility of this volume was first broached there, and several of the chapters included here were presented in earlier versions at that time. While concerns about quality may seem only tangentially related to this chapter's current form, I would argue that the designation 'quality' helps function to secure 24's masculinised ethos. The series is at least partially framed as 'quality' because of its formal and aesthetic innovations, technological interventions that help stave off the association with soap opera that might overtly highlight the series' embrace of serial form. But, rather than simply arguing that the series is a testosterone-driven revamp of a soap opera and, thus, *not* quality television, might we instead query what work the category 'quality' actually performs within the series, within the TV industry, and within our scholarly industries themselves?

We need to examine the work that the designation 'quality' performs, both within the mainstream reception of television programmes and within academic publishing. Why are television executives (and media scholars) particularly interested in 'quality' at this moment in time – as television (and TV studies) increasingly feel at threat from new media studies? A sustained examination of a series like 24 can help us to understand how such a term conceals as much as it reveals about contemporary issues of globalisation and digital convergence, as well as about the shifting relations of gender, genre, and nation. One prominent theme of the Dublin conference was a sustained denigration of reality television, an argument that largely worked to binarise the two forms of television. To defend quality TV as diametrically opposed to other forms of television like reality television is to miss a central point about the diffusion of both digital forms and melodramatic structures across culture in the present moment. In fact, in their highly serialised, melodramatic nature, reality shows like *Survivor* or *American Idol* share a great deal with the serialised storylines of 24 and other examples of quality television like *The Sopranos*. Further, the 'beat-the-clock' feel of 24 and its technological glitziness share formal strategies with the revitalisation of the game show in the past several years, particularly in a series like *Who Wants to Be a Millionaire*. A singular focus on (and privileging of) quality television might even serve to lead us astray, allowing us to overlook the degree to which 'high' and 'low' genres actually share key traits and serve to support one another, particularly in relation to cultural anxieties about new technological forms, missing the larger issues at hand in an industrial drive toward convergence.

Seeing Bauer as a kindred spirit to all those guys the *Queer Eye* fellows are intent on making over, as someone equally struggling with what it means to be a man while racing against the clock, might also help to illuminate the stakes of masculinity for our era. In many ways the reality show is a bit more straightforward in its representations of masculinity in crisis than is

24, although each series is invested in versions of heterosexual masculinity, if differently so. As Steve Cohan observes, 'a culture's hegemonic masculinity has to appear to accommodate competing masculinities' even as it attempts to secure dominants modes of maleness (1997: 35). Thus, we can more clearly understand the role of Bauer's grim and gritty masculinity when we examine it in relation to other prominent representations of contemporary men. In staging a rugged maleness for Bauer, 24 seems to be insulating its protagonist from certain crises of male labour (or male fashion) that destabilise masculinity while also protecting 'serious' television from the incursions and popularity of reality TV.

In a prescient essay on the relationship of television scholarship to broad market forces, Amelie Hastie maintains that some scholarly volumes focused on particular cult or quality TV shows might be read as 'fairly transparent examples of an attempt to capitalize on a show's popularity', as scholarly productions that thus participate in the very consumerist nature of television at large, functioning as a kind of 'tie-in.' Further, the focus on 'quality' series in these volumes can reinforce 'a hierarchical understanding of television' (Hastie 2006). I think such series-based volumes and a focus on quality TV also serve to insulate television studies, itself a field long struggling to prove its worth, from the ascendancy of new media studies as a field of academic enquiry. These volumes reflect a desire to conserve TV as innovative (and 'gripping' and 'compelling') at the moment when the boundaries of television blur amid other popular elements of digital culture. The lustre of writing about quality television may be the very way in which it allows us to sidestep our own incorporation into ascendant forms of capitalism, forms that depend upon knowledge production as a key form of exchange. Perhaps we find Bauer such a 'compelling' figure precisely because his 24/7 work habits so parallel our own working conditions, where even the leisure time of television viewing exists in tight circuits of exchange with our own scholarly labour. Bauer may not be the only networked subject in town.

NOTES

1. This chapter emerged from ongoing conversations with various friends about the series 24. I especially thank Rob Knaack for watching 24 with me, Daniel Chamberlain and Scott Ruston for urging me to attend the Dublin conference, and Amelie Hastie for her suggestions on an earlier draft of this essay.

2.   The series faced cancellation after its first season as it averaged a relatively small US viewing audience of about 8.6 million viewers per week. Despite garnering critical raves and Emmy awards, it had the smallest audience of any drama picked up for renewal after the 2001–2002 series.

3.   This interview with Cochran was conducted via email by USC graduate student Christopher Cooling on 4 June 2003. I thank Chris for so graciously sharing the transcript with me.

4.   For a now-classic investigation of the pleasures of the villainess in soap operas, see Tania Modleski's *Loving with a Vengeance*. Creator Bob Cochran defends the show against accusations of misogyny by arguing that 'Everybody on our show is duplicitous, not just the female characters ... They are not helpless victims or impossibly noble, any more than the men are.' One wonders if Cochran actually watched the scenes of Kim and Teri in Season One or read reviews like the one by Matthew Gilbert which summarised the Kim plotlines thusly: 'See Kim. See Kim run. See the Bad Man chase Kim down the alley' (2002). (Perhaps he did, as Kim morphed into an unlikely CTU computer expert by Season Three.) Viewers posting to the popular *Television Without Pity* site took to referring to Kim as 'Spawn', while another critic referred to her as 'MacIdiot' (Stanley).

5.   In 3.14, Bauer outsmarts a tracking device embedded in the chip via old-fashioned, low-tech ingenuity and intelligence.

6.   The phrase 'killer app' derives from the era of the Silicon Valley dot.com boom. A 'killer app' was a phrase used to describe that holy grail of the moment, the software application that would fully capitalise (in all senses) on the techno-lust and rampant greed of the period.

7.   'Hero television' here refers to a long history of 'action' TV involving detectives, government agents, and cops, a genre that often privileges tough guys who act both within and outside of the law.

8.   This is not to say that websites or interactive games are not themselves highly scripted; they are. But, typically, they allow a greater degree of perceived choice in terms of narrative flow than your typical television show.

9.   This phrase comes from the promotional material for the third season of *24*. Several national magazines in the USA included a DVD of 'exclusive' previews for that season, a DVD sponsored by Ford that hyped the new F-150 truck. (Ford also sponsored the first episode of that season, an episode that was presented 'without commercial interruption,' further cementing the series' real-time feel.) The DVD packaging included the tagline: 'To

stop a weapon that has no cure ... you need a man who knows no limits.'

10. I explore these ideas further in a piece in the online journal, *Flow*.

11. A controversy erupted in the US in March 2006 when it was widely reported that the Bush administration had permitted Dubai Ports World, controlled by one of the United Arab Emirates' seven city-states, to purchase a company that manages the terminals at many US ports. The Congress immediately crafted a bi-partisan plan to block the transfer, and the struggle was widely reported in the press. While it may seem that Bush's support of the Dubai company ran afoul of his often-isolationist rhetoric, it makes perfect sense given the global flow of oil and capital. For one take on the controversy, see White, 2006.

00.15
'SHE MAY BE A LITTLE WEIRD'
CHLOE O'BRIAN

PAUL DELANY

When someone tells us we should watch a new television show, our first question will probably be: 'What's it about?' For *24*, some answers might be that it's about office politics, mobile phones, gun control, time, dangerous and helpful foreigners, parents and children ... one could go on. But a successful US primetime series is likely to be about, in the first instance, America and Americanism.[1] Within this requirement of national and cultural self-definition, *24* belongs to the tradition of the Western, as described by Robert Warshow. We recognise in Jack Bauer a contemporary exemplar of 'a single man who wears a gun on his thigh. The gun tells us that he lives in a world of violence' (Warshow 1964: 105).

Singleness is the key: the Western hero answers only to his personal code of honour, not to the laws of settled society. His acts often appear to be those of an outlaw, yet these transgressions are the means of purging an evil that conventional laws are powerless to defeat. In a phrase that often recurs in *24*, the Western hero is one who says 'you do what you have to do.' He embodies the violence and spontaneity of nature and is opposed by 'the schoolmarm,' who stands for the restraint and order of culture. In *24*, the schoolmarm is no longer a single, censorious female; she has been generalised into the multitude who try to control Bauer – his superiors first of all, then bureaucrats, lawyers and craven politicians. This is no longer a gendered conflict because the women of 24 are on both sides. Some fight side by side with Bauer, others fight him with equal ruthlessness.[2]

Within the scheme of 24 as Western, Chloe O'Brian (Mary Lynn Rajskub) descends from another stock figure of the genre: the telegraph operator. In the first scene of the first Western – *The Great Train Robbery* – a telegraph operator is held at gunpoint and forced to send a false message. Even in the black-and-white society of the Old West, heroes face such problems as locating evildoers, finding out when a bank will be robbed, or tracking those who have been kidnapped. The cowboy hero needs actionable information, and it is the telegraph operator who controls the flow of knowledge in and out of the town. He is traditionally an eccentric, cowardly and physically weak figure (qualities taken to extremes in Sergio Leone's Spaghetti Westerns). The stigmatising of the telegraph operator reflects the anti-intellectualism of frontier society, where only warrior virtues are held in esteem, and anyone sedentary is despised.

From the beginning, 24 has been a thriller in which communication systems have played a central role in counter-terrorist operations. All the main characters have had technical skills, to supplement their prowess with guns. A key scriptwriter for 24 has been Michael Loceff, who teaches computer science at Foothills College in Silicon Valley. We can assume that he has been responsible for making computers, networks, satellites and mobile phones an integral part of 24's hectic plots. The inner workings of these devices are presented with a wealth of detail, creating a milieu that is fascinating in its own right. However, 24 is rigorously contemporary in its technologies: the show stays away from science fiction speculations about things not yet invented.

For the first two seasons of 24, computer skills were mainly just another attribute of the man or woman of action. But in Season Three a computer geek, Chloe O'Brian, appears as a major character.[3] Her personality is inseparable from the technology she deploys, and we are led to believe that skill with computers comes at the expense of full social involvement in the human realm. Chloe understands everything about machines, but very little about the emotional concerns of other people. In Season Four, Edgar Stiles (Louis Lombardi) is introduced as Chloe's partner, an anxious and obese individual who is clearly unfit for action. He suffers from his own set of postmodern ailments: weak nerves, low blood sugar, panic attacks. From

Season Four onwards, Chloe and Stiles form a distinct geek subculture within CTU.

If one sees *24* as simply a drama of redemptive violence – what DH Lawrence called 'the fatal glamour of militarism' – then Chloe and Stiles remain marginal figures who provide a touch of humour and eccentricity, like Shakespearean clowns. Yet, *24* is also about the nagging limitations on American power in the new century. The global 'war on terror' is also a war of intelligence, and even its most avid supporters would have to admit that things on the latter front have not been going well. *24* might be characterised as a Western whose action plays out in the 'information society'. Before CTU agents can torture a terrorist, or retaliate against an attack, they have to address such questions as: 'which side is this person on?'; 'what is their real name?'; 'what is their history?'; 'what enemy agents may have infiltrated CTU?'

CTU's geeks are there to provide answers to these questions, and it is the discovery of new information that provides the stream of reversals and surprises that sustain the action of *24*. Television viewers now know that evildoers are not caught by the cop on the beat, but by databases, phone records, and surveillance cameras. Many of the attacks on CTU are accordingly directed against their information resources. In parallel with the war of field agents against terrorists, there is a war between each side's geeks. At CTU, Chloe and Stiles are often the first to identify a threat and initiate counter-measures. They also have the Orwellian task of reconstructing the records when something has to be covered up. The computer keyboard becomes a weapon of both offence and defence, and is handled under conditions similar to those prevailing for actual weapons, under extreme pressures of time, and with suspense over the outcome. When Chloe picks up an automatic rifle in 4.19 and uses it to deadly effect, this may be seen as 'out of character.' But the qualities she displays – manual dexterity, coolness under pressure, the ability to quickly enter the code for the rifle's safety lock – are not that different from her skills when sitting in front of her terminal. Although geeks are supposed to be in a different class from field agents, we never see them being relaxed or merely thoughtful; their life may be safer than those who go out into the field, but it is no less frantic.

Soon after Chloe's arrival at CTU, Tony Almeida remarks that she 'may be a little weird, but she knows her stuff' (3.1). Chloe's weirdness takes a specific form, which I would trace back to an article in *Wired* on 'The Geek Syndrome' (Silberman 2001). This article reported that a spectre was haunting Silicon Valley: more and more children were being diagnosed with 'autistic spectrum disorders.' Psychiatrists suggested that these disorders lay on a continuum, extending from uncommunicative and unreachable children to those who were just socially awkward and had obsessive interests in technology, role-playing games, or fantasy. These milder conditions were first defined as 'Asperger's Syndrome' in 1944.[4]

The rise in diagnoses of autism and Asperger's has created panic in many Silicon Valley parents, especially since no definite cause has been found. People have blamed side effects from immunisation, pollutants emitted from chip foundries, or 'assortative mating' (geeks marrying geeks). Whatever the cause, there is fear that the world capital of technology is an abnormal environment, especially threatening to children. In reaction against the Asperger's panic, some have tried to redefine disability as simply difference. They emphasise the special talents associated with Asperger's, and suggest that these children may be the creative vanguard of technological civilisation. Figures like Newton, Mozart and Einstein have been posthumously diagnosed as having Asperger's, which becomes a 'disease of genius.' The debate over Asperger's reflects the rise of a distinct 'geek culture,' and the enormous success of geekish entrepreneurs like Bill Gates, or Larry Page and Sergey Brin of Google. Rather than being scorned as social misfits, geeks may be envied for their wealth and power.

One reading of Chloe's 'weirdness' might be through Hollywood's positive narratives of disability or discrimination. Such characters are at first marginalised by their failure to measure up to conventional norms. As the plot develops, their special talents become manifest; by the end, the disabled person is celebrated and welcomed into the dominant group. When it is a case of mental disability, there is often a compensating emphasis on idiot savantism (the possession of extraordinary abilities in memory or calculation). As Stuart Murray observes, 'Hollywood narratives indulge in a clear fascination with the supposedly exceptional skills of the autist' (2005). The audience for a film like *Rain Man* (Barry Levinson, 1988) moves from feeling superior to the mentally impaired person, to appreciation of their surprising talents.

Yet, *24* consistently rejects that kind of mainstream sentimentality. It is set in a ruthless world where the weak do not survive. People with emotional problems are repeatedly shown as making trouble for those who care about them. Secretary Heller's troubled son gets his father and sister kidnapped in

Season Four. Maya (Angela Goethals), the schizophrenic daughter of Erin Driscoll (Alberta Watson), is brought into CTU; she creates chaos in CTU's work and finally kills herself (4.5–4.11). In Season Five, Martha Logan (Jean Smart) is an apparently bi-polar presidential consort who may have to be sectioned to keep her under control (5.1–5.7). All these episodes confirm prejudices about mental illness rather than challenging them; they seem to propose a Nietzschean ethic, that the weak are the greatest danger to the strong. We notice also that 24's villains are never given troubled childhoods or other psychological excuses; they are inhumanly effective psychopaths who would be impervious to therapy. In a choice between kill and cure, they can only be killed.

With Chloe, though, the story is not so simple. Her disability is neither obvious nor pitiable; rather, it is one of the vague and contested contemporary pathologies. If we identify her problem as Asperger's Syndrome, she may be the victim of some genetic flaw or environmental toxin. Alternative diagnoses, if we consulted the *DSM* (*Diagnostic and Statistical Manual of Mental Disorders*) – *IV*, might be 'Avoidant Personality Disorder' or 'Oppositional Defiant Disorder': as Bill Buchanan (James Morrison) snaps at her, 'We don't have time for your personality disorder' (4.21). Symptoms of these disorders include fear of social interaction, clinging to rules and routine, and reflexive unwillingness to do what one is asked. Or perhaps Chloe is just what Ryan Chappelle (Paul Schulze) calls her, a 'pain in the ass' (3.7). If so, her role is to support 24's 'office-from-hell' theme, where at any time people may be denounced, tortured, betrayed or shot by their fellow workers.

It is unusual for network television that 24 should have a central character who is as awkward and uncooperative as Chloe. Some shows pay tribute to disability through occasional appearances by actors like Marlee Matlin (in *The West Wing* as Joey Lucas), who is hearing-impaired in real life. Such casting cannot easily escape the charge of mass-media tokenism: physical flawlessness is the rule, which the exception only confirms. Chloe's unkempt appearance and strange personality signal her possession of extraordinary mental powers, for which she gains respect, though not love or acceptance. 24 also draws on the tradition, in American action movies, of glorifying a crew of scruffy and rebellious outsiders who are more effective than conventional combat units (*The Devil's Brigade*, *The Dirty Dozen*, etc).

When Chloe first appeared on 24, we were given no clear indication of her moral standing. Her trademark facial expression might convey sadness, hostility, or puzzlement at the antics of those around her. Most of 24's characters carry a fixed look that either suppresses emotion, or is a mask of deception (Sherry Palmer, for example, looks sweet but really is sour). Unlike her somewhat wooden colleagues, Chloe provides the viewer with comic relief. She is the only childish character in the series, with her look of smug triumph when she defeats her rival geek, Stiles.

Chloe's eccentricity is both generic, and a way of playing with generic expectations. Our uncertainty about whether Chloe is nasty or nice contributes to the general edginess of the CTU culture. Chloe's supposed personality disorder is hardly shocking when she belongs to such a collectively dysfunctional organisation. As a group, the agents are wildly unstable and unpredictable – perhaps because they never eat or sleep, unless they have been suspended and have to stay at home. Not that home is any more normal. In Season Four, Almeida appears in a domestic setting of alcoholic disorder, with a stripper girlfriend (4.8). Chloe is a bizarre contrast, seen in a romantic boudoir with her hair down and wearing a 'Sweet Mermaid' T-shirt (4.14).

If the geeks are so crucial to the action of 24, why are they the exception to the rule that everyone on television has to be 'hot'? A character in Douglas Coupland's Microserfs observes that 'Many geeks don't really have a sexuality – they just have work' (1995: 227). The nubile Kim Bauer was reincarnated as a geek in Season Three, but she never carried much conviction in the role. Sexuality in 24 can only be aroused by situations of violence, and only the violent have the right to be sexual; you have to be blooded before you can go to bed. Chloe's pulling the trigger in 4.19 leads to her sexual flowering in Season Five. Meanwhile, her unravelling bun, or Stiles' trousers pulled above the navel, give us what we expect and want to see in geek self-presentation. On-screen, intelligence is often signified by bad grooming. The only woman Stiles loves (and who loves him) is his mother; Chloe's sexual interests seem restricted to a secretive fantasy-life. She has to confess that she doesn't have a boyfriend in Season Three's 'mystery baby' episodes. CTU bears out the truism that everything in American life is a continuation of high school, with its division between jocks, prom queens, and asexual nerds.

Bureaucracy and rule-bound behaviour are opposed, in 24, to the imperative of 'doing what you have to do' (which Bauer takes as his rule at all times). Within this foundational conflict of the series – 'the rules' versus virtuous action – Chloe begins by occupying a distinctive niche. Most of the time she is on the side of the rules, but not because of any truly bureaucratic disposition. Rather, she invokes the rules in order to satisfy her instinct for denying any request that is made of her. She is a descendant of Melville's Bartleby the Scrivener, whose response to all demands is that he 'prefers not to.' Yet Chloe's fractiousness is redeemed by the fact that she does eventually do what is needed, once she has indulged her compulsion to resist orders. Her resistance and her competence are not in conflict.

Thematically, Chloe's dislike of authority aligns her with similar, more extreme traits in Bauer. Paul Raines (James Frain) sees Bauer as no more than 'a thug with a badge' (4.11). Yet, his sociopathic tendencies are always vindicated by events. Secretary of Defence Heller (William Devane) says of him, 'we need people like that' (4.13): under present circumstances, America must become a sociopathic nation if it is to survive. Even beyond the context of the 'war on terror', Bauer seems to represent a new type of male hero in American mass culture, one with 'strikingly anti-social tendencies' (St John 2005). The viewer – especially the young male demographic – can identify with the outlaw, but also with the state power that finds a use for him.

In Season Four, and continuing to develop in Season Five, Chloe is being normalised: she becomes steadily less eccentric and moves towards participation in sexuality and violence. She expresses her anti-social tendencies by forming a close alliance with Bauer. In the early episodes of Season Four, she regularly disobeys instructions from her superior, Erin Driscoll, in order to support Bauer's improvisations in the field. As usual in 24, though, her motives are unclear. When she is helping Bauer to track a terrorist suspect, Stiles remarks that 'Chloe's acting kind of strange,' to which the reply is: 'That's nothing new' (4.3). She is acting strangely in order to cover up a rational decision – that Bauer has a better chance of rescuing Heller than Erin Driscoll believes. But there is also the possibility that Chloe is backing Bauer for a purely personal reason – because she is in love with him. In 4.21, she makes something close to a declaration of love: 'Jack, if you ever need anyone to talk to, as a friend, I'm here for you.' This may be a revelation that, beneath her geekish exterior, there beats the heart of a true woman. Or perhaps Chloe is just making one of her robot-like attempts at behaving like a normal, sympathetic person.

Chloe moves onto a higher plane altogether in 4.19, when she wipes out two of Marwan's (Arnold Vosloo) hired assassins. As usual she whines about accepting the assignment to look at a suspect laptop, insisting that she is 'not a field agent.' But when she is ambushed her killer instinct emerges, and she proves to be as adept with an automatic rifle as with a keyboard. Once back at CTU, her Asperger's symptoms recur, as she tries to find the appropriate emotional response to her experience: 'I'm not used to the idea I just killed somebody ... I'm trying not to think about what just happened ... I'll process it later ... I didn't feel anything at all ... I hope I'm not some kind of psychopath' (4.20). Yet, Chloe's difficulties with affect are endearing rather than sinister. She is like a child who still needs to be instructed in how to behave, but who is eager to learn.

Season Five confirms the convergence of Chloe and Bauer. When they first met, there was a complete opposition between the neurotic geek and the man of action (3.1). Bauer had no patience with Chloe; he cut off her delaying tactics with the command 'just do it now.' By 4.3, when he is breaking the rules to save Heller, he says to Chloe: 'I can't do this without you.' In 4.24, when Bauer stages his own death to avoid being assassinated by the Secret Service, Chloe is one of his three confidants, along with Almeida and Michelle Dessler. Once she has been 'blooded' by killing Marwan's men in 4.19, Chloe can follow up by putting a bullet into the assassin of President Palmer (5.1). We have come to realise that Chloe occupies a similar position among CTU's analysts that Bauer occupies among its field agents. Both are temperamentally insubordinate, supremely confident in their abilities, and scornful of conventional wisdom. There is a family resemblance between their trademark expressions of sulky defiance: each has the charisma of the adult in whom the child is still present.[5]

In Season Five, there is also a shift from the disability model of geek culture to something more typical of everyday office life: the geek as an overworked and irritable figure, resentful of those who make demands on his or her services. These traits bring about Stiles' death in 5.11. The new geek, Carrie (Danielle Burgio), warns him that someone may have infiltrated CTU. Stiles brushes her off, and realises too late that she is in danger. He then dies heroically, trying to atone for his mistake. Chloe also becomes less of a geek and more of a field agent. She goes into shock over Stiles' death, but resists the efforts of the psychologist, Barry (C. Thomas Howell), to medicalise her condition. 'Shrinks are always giving advice that they probably don't follow themselves,' she retorts, and goes back to work.

Chloe's sexual dimension becomes prominent from the beginning of Season Five. She first appears in bed with her good-looking subordinate,

Spenser Wolff (Jonah Lotan), though we discover that he only slept with her as part of a plot to infiltrate CTU. She brings him back from custody when she needs his help to penetrate a terrorist firewall; once he has done the job she discards him, much to Stiles' satisfaction. Sexually, she has assumed the 'male' role by first using Wolff and then rejecting him. Stiles gazes longingly at Chloe; her appearance becomes more conventionally female and her behaviour assertive rather than sulky or disagreeable. The stereotype of the geek is being replaced by something less interesting: the stereotype of the hero's loyal sidekick. *24*'s scriptwriters seem to be following the usual imperative: when a character becomes popular with viewers, she is given more to do and is shown in a more positive light. The trouble with this evolution is that if Chloe is no longer weird and no longer contrary, she is no longer the true geek with whom we first bonded in Season Three.

NOTES

1. This need not be literally true, as we see from the prominence in *24* of what my colleague Susan Brook calls 'stealth Canadians'. In addition to Kiefer Sutherland there are Leslie Hope (Teri Bauer); Elisha Cuthbert (Kim Bauer); Mia Kirshner (Mandy); Wendy Crewson (Dr Anne Packard); Alberta Watson (Erin Driscoll); and Roger Cross (Curtis Manning). But there are no identifiably Canadian characters in the show, in contrast to various snooty or villainous Brits.

2. Female allies include Chloe O'Brian, Michelle Dessler and Audrey Raines; notable adversaries are Nina Myers and Sherry Palmer.

3. In the computer world, 'geek' is more acceptable as a self-identifier than 'nerd', so that is the term I use in this chapter. The origins of both words remain obscure.

4. The Cambridge Lifespan Asperger Syndrome Service (CLASS) offers a checklist to help identify those individuals who fit the common characteristics of Asperger's patients. Statements that seem to fit Chloe include:
    *I am good at picking up details and facts.
    *I find it hard to work out what other people are thinking and feeling.
    *I can focus on certain things for very long periods.
    *People often say I was rude even when this was not intended.
    *I have unusually strong, narrow interests.
    *I do certain things in an inflexible, repetitive way.

5.   When Chloe is reprimanded by Erin Driscoll in 4.2, she says that she shouldn't be treated like a student called in to the Principal's office. But this only makes us wonder if Chloe still feels herself to be a disobedient child.

00.16
24 AND POST-NATIONAL AMERICAN IDENTITIES

CHRISTOPHER GAIR

It is probably self-evident that American popular culture has always responded to (and helped to shape) shifting economic and ideological relations. For example, in the new millennium, globalisation and the erasure of regionalism within the United States have had an impact on American 'quality' television in a variety of ways. Factors beyond 'entertainment' have brought about change: as has been the case with the George W Bush presidency, American television's traditional desire for isolation – or else, simplistic narratives of American supremacy – has been overwhelmed by the post-9/11 realisation of the impossibility of avoiding the negative as well as the positive (in hegemonic US terms) ramifications of the post-cold war world order. As such, there has been a move from 'personal' narratives representing uniquely 'American' experiences – such as most of the Westerns and detective series of the 1960s to 1980s – to movies and series that deploy these tropes in attempts to interrogate other spatial and cultural boundaries.

As so often, however, there is a cultural lag between shifts in international and transnational relations, and popular cultural understanding of these shifts: old master narratives continue to be mapped on to new realities by both politicians and the creators of popular entertainment in ways that (often unintentionally) subvert original structures. Thus, although the second (post-9/11) series of *24* represents moments of inter-ethnic and international cooperation in response to the threats of a nuclear attack on Los Angeles and military reprisals by America against three Middle Eastern countries, it privileges Jack Bauer's feelings of individual grief, isolation, and partial redemption within allegories of a nation ultimately celebrated despite its contradictions and weaknesses.

This chapter will argue that the perspective adopted by *24* depends upon a nostalgic understanding of US history that revisits the dominant ideologies of the nineteenth and twentieth centuries and accommodates freethinking and independent individualists alongside career politicians as 'patriots'. Thus, the intertextual references associated with Bauer and Senator/President David Palmer in *24* project a vision of an 'innocent' United States, and suggest that this innocence can be regained – problematically, even through the use of multiple murder and torture – by re-enacting key gestures from earlier American culture. Like so many of its ideological predecessors, *24* proposes that Bauer's position is the truly patriotic one, and that it is the government and military (with the exception of a President who is at one point summarily removed from office) that has strayed from the ideals of American nationhood in ways that include corruption, indolence and misunderstanding of 'American' values.

In many ways, *24* draws upon the generic staples of earlier popular culture from the dime novel and the Western, to the hard-boiled detective novel and the buddy movie. At the most elementary level, it adopts the mythemes (unchanging elements in the study of mythology) summed up by John Carlos Rowe as 'self-reliant individualism, masculine potency, technical ingenuity, and perseverance' (Rowe 2002: xi) to construct in Bauer a *near*-archetypal American hero. In order to illustrate the point, but also to demonstrate just how important that '*near*' is, and to show why the series rewrites these conventions, I will offer an assessment of its intertextual allusions to canonical examples of the Western and (more briefly) to the hard-boiled novel (and film), and of the generic discontinuities that emerge in its efforts to map popular master narratives on to the contemporary American scene.

I would like to suggest that the Western to which *24* bears greatest similarity both ideologically and structurally is Fred Zinnemann's *High Noon* (1952). In part, of course, the similarity is a result of both taking place in (or very close to) real-time, with the camera's repeated return to the clock reminding the viewer of the increasingly urgent need for the hero to act.

In addition, both function as what Richard Slotkin calls 'town-tamer' narratives, although both also complicate the notion that one man can clean up communal disorder through strength of character alone.

There are also more specific links: in Season One of *24*, the impetus for the plot to kill Bauer and Palmer stems from Victor Drazen's (Dennis Hopper) desire for revenge against them, just as, in *High Noon*, Frank Miller (Ian MacDonald) returns to Hadleyville to kill those who overthrew him and put *him* in jail. Although Bauer is rather keener than Will Kane (the hero of *High Noon*, played by Gary Cooper) to confront Drazen, he, too, is distracted by a wife who counsels against such intervention and desires that he retire into the secure comfort of the domestic space. Furthermore, like Kane, Bauer is alienated from the community by the very qualities that make him appear 'heroic' to the viewer and, again like Kane, he does not discover the extent of this isolation until moments of crisis, when he is unable to rely upon social solidarity to support his actions. Again, both plots stage a series of meetings in which a range of potential allies refuse to assist in confronting the enemy. Both Kane and Bauer have to go it alone – the latter repeatedly – since they are stripped of their official positions and serve, effectively, as vigilantes, acting on the principle that in moments of crisis, as Slotkin puts it in his reading of *High Noon*, 'the defence of "civilization" is more important than the procedures of "democracy"' (Slotkin 1992: 393).

Finally, there is a sense that Kane and Bauer overcome Miller and Drazen because they share a particular brand of 'masculine' virtue – a combination of 'knowledge, skill, and power' coupled with a conscience that, to cite Slotkin, means (in cases like this) 'possession of the power to act entails an absolute responsibility to act, whether or not the action is legal or acceptable to the public' (1992: 393). In both cases, the triumph is represented through a form of doubling between 'hero' and 'villain' – there are many clues that suggest Kane has his own dark side; and, like Drazen, Bauer is frequently driven by the revenge motive, in the belief (real or mistaken) that he is avenging the death of a family member. But both Kane and Bauer are redeemed by their '"essential' goodness and manliness' of character, which provide an authority to which they can appeal 'in justification of [their] actions' (Slotkin 1992: 394).

As such, both *High Noon* and *24* unravel the central values of American democracy, exposing the tension between, on the one hand, faith in the will of the people, and, on the other, the notion that the democratic process must be defended by individual or group actions that fall outside or beyond that will. Thus, both suggest that at moments of supreme crisis, only 'a gun in the hands of the right man' (Slotkin 1992: 396) is effective in protecting a community confronted by evil. Nevertheless, there are also significant differences between the two texts, largely as a result of the extremely dissimilar historical conditions of their production. *High Noon* is generally read as a leftist allegory of Hollywood's capitulation to McCarthyism, in which the very people who had once overcome fascism have become too complacent to confront the new threat in their midst. *24* uses the same idea, stripped of its leftist subtext, but suggests that the world has become more complex than that of the cold war past – instead of being too old, frightened, or jealous to act, the community is fragmented and has a plethora of reasons for leaving Bauer to his fate. These range from the ruthless political ambition of Sherry Palmer, to the treachery of Nina Myers, and to the over-dependency on the rule book demonstrated by several senior figures at CTU, all staged within a narrative where it is never entirely clear whether these characters are acting alone or with others; for shady government organisations or for economic or politically motivated terrorists; for or against the ultimate good of the equally fragmented nation.

There are also clear differences between the small community of Hadleyville and Bauer's LA. The former represents an almost all-white society, engaging in a narrative of nation-building only interrupted by the presence of Helen Ramirez (Katy Jurado), who is rejected by Kane in favour of his Quaker wife (played by Grace Kelly). Kane's choice is relatively simple – he must choose between the 'dark' outsider and the 'white' woman, although it is, of course, noteworthy that Mrs Kane is converted to her husband's ways at the end of the film when she shoots one of Miller's men in the back.

Although frontier mythologies have been transplanted into threatening urban environments since at least the 1890s, they assume new significance in *24* and other similar movies and series. Instead of a straightforward national narrative, the LA of *24* represents a fragmented, multi-lingual, multi-ethnic space of social and cognitive conflict where class, political, national and transnational boundaries are constantly destabilised. Although Bauer also has to choose between two women, their symbolic differences only emerge late in Season One, since Nina's 'darkness' is masked by an apparently 'white' devotion to duty and by her willingness to support the man she has surrendered back to his wife. In a twist on the traditional closure in which, after a captivity/rescue scene (as where Miller uses Mrs Kane as a shield, before he is killed by Kane), the gunfighter is reunited with his wife or family in a domestic environment now made secure from the fragmented space of the streets, Teri is murdered by Nina, whose own ruthless transformation into cold-blooded killer is given none of the moral validation used to support Jack's earlier actions (1: 24). Ideologically, however, the closure is the same – both Kane and Bauer (if we leap ahead to the start of Season Two) reject the people that they have saved, with Kane dropping his badge in the dirt and Bauer appearing to want no more to do with CTU and other government organisations (2: 1). In each case, the message appears to be that the rescued community is of less value than the man who saved it, and does not deserve him.

The more complex manner in which the female characters are constructed in *24* points toward the series' other obvious generic prototype; that is, the hard-boiled detective story. Although there is not space here for a detailed look at how *24* appropriates and updates all the requisites of the genre, I would like (very briefly) to examine three aspects of this process as a way to lead into my conclusions about the programme's conflicting messages. First, as my comparison of Hadleyville and LA has already suggested, urban space in *24* bears close resemblance to the world of Raymond Chandler's Philip Marlowe and Dashiell Hammett's Sam Spade, in that it is suffused with a pervasive air of corruption and criminality. Like Marlowe's earlier LA, it is an environment marked by violence, cynicism and multiple murders, where the line between respectability and crime is frequently breeched by a mixture of Americans and foreigners. As such, it is hardly surprising that what Northrop Frye identifies as the 'wavering finger of suspicion' hovering over a series of suspects is as evident in *24* as in hard-boiled narratives (Cawelti 1976: 142).

Like Marlowe, Bauer also unearths an apparently never-ending sequence of plots and crimes beyond his original investigation and, like him, Bauer must make personal choices that necessitate tackling assault, capture, and attempted assassination. It is unsurprising, therefore, that Bauer manifests the same series of antithetical traits – identified by John Cawelti as 'cynicism and honor', 'brutality and sentimentality', 'failure and success' – as those found in Noir detectives. Indeed, in an obvious nod to Chandler, George Mason tells Nina that, 'Jack's not the knight in shining armour you think he is.' Of course, these features are also staples of the Western hero who, as we have seen, also tends to be a 'man of virtue in an amoral and corrupt world' (Cawelti 1976: 149; 152). And, although Bauer works for a government unit rather than as a Private Investigator, 24 adopts the same stance towards institutional authority – as inefficient, decadent and corrupt – as that imagined by Chandler and Hammett.

But what marks the urban crime text as a particularly significant precursor of 24 in a way that does differ from High Noon is its representation of women. Despite what I have already acknowledged as a resemblance between female roles in High Noon and 24, the latter's depiction of women – especially the pivotal roles of the duplicitous betrayers, Nina Myers and Sherry Palmer – closely mirrors hard-boiled misogyny. In 24, women are either needy and incapable of self-preservation, as with Bauer's daughter, Kim, whose one mission in life seems to be to break the record for being kidnapped most often in a single day, or attractive and dangerous, as with Nina and Sherry. As with the majority of Noir detective narratives, there are no representatives of 'ideal' American womanhood, able to provide firm moral guidance but always ultimately submissive to incorruptible male authority. Nina, of course, embodies the femme fatale in that she has already seduced the hero away from respectable family life, and uses the memory of this relationship to deflect any suspicion that she is the traitor. Nina resembles The Maltese Falcon's Brigid O'Shaughnessy (Mary Astor) in her ability to conceal her 'true' self – the nature of which we are never entirely certain, even at the end of Season One – beneath a veneer of loyalty, repeatedly thwarting his quest for justice by distracting his attention or providing false information.

Sherry Palmer is potentially even more subversive than Nina, not only because she appears for most of Season One to be on the brink of becoming the First Lady – a position whose name implies its highly charged if imprecisely defined responsibilities – but also because she conceals her own 'evil' intentions behind the supremely respectable role of wife, mother, and domestic support for her husband's presidential campaign. As such, her role combines the most 'serious' crimes imaginable for a wife – within the conservative narrative of 'ideal' womanhood – in putting her own ambitions above those of her husband and placing personal success above the best interests of her family. The fact that she is willing to sacrifice Kim is only confirmation of what we already know – that, in a narrative structured around long-standing 'American' cultural conventions, Sherry has no right to be associated with her husband and his idealistic ambitions.

But if we have established the links between earlier formula fictions and *24*, there is also a need to examine how generic staples have been updated to take account of changed national and global relations. Most obviously, the relationship between Bauer and Palmer rejects both the lone individualist narrative of the Western and hard-boiled format and the 'buddy' movies that have appeared since the 1960s. Although, as George Mason (Xander Berkeley) suggests, Bauer is a 'loose cannon' that 'does what he wants when he wants,' he does remain loyal to Palmer, who also retains his respect for Bauer's judgements and actions. Given the unequal nature of their relationship – and the fact that they are very rarely on screen at the same time – it seems mistaken to place them alongside, say, Butch and Sundance, but their mutual dependency does indicate that this is no longer a world where one man can work entirely alone.

The relationship between the two men also points to the fundamental instability at the heart of the show since Bauer and Palmer's own acts allegorise recent US foreign and domestic policies, although in Season Two Palmer is temporarily removed from office (through use of state powers that are uncomfortably reminiscent of the nineteenth-century internment of 'uppity' fugitive slaves), and subsequently condemns the overly hawkish behaviour of his Cabinet. Furthermore, it is clear that Season Two (scripted and shot post-9/11) encourages us to endorse – or, at the very least, to contemplate the acceptability of – much higher levels of 'permissible' violence in pursuit of 'justice' on the part of Bauer and on the orders of Palmer than were witnessed in Season One. Although there are clear signposts directing the audience to be appalled by the Cabinet's hasty and ill-conceived detention of the President and deployment of force to the Middle East, the attention paid to Palmer's essential moral decency encourages us to accept his 'reluctant' decision to use torture to extract information from a political colleague. Likewise, Bauer's brutal execution and decapitation of a prisoner is represented as an unfortunate but necessary consequence of the need to deal with ruthless enemies (2.1). In consequence, *24*'s other message is that there is no point in negotiating with either 'terrorists' or 'hostile' foreign powers, since greater and greater exhibitions of force bring the only hope of success. Even where these exhibitions later prove to be deceptive – as with the faked threat to kill an Arab's family in Season Two – they depend upon the belief held by others that the US *would* act in such a ruthless manner. At heart, *24* seems uncomfortably close to official state policy and rhetoric, and it is no coincidence that it frames atrocities carried out in the name of the 'state' – even by a 'loose cannon' like Bauer – as patriotic duty, while similar behaviour by anyone else is an 'act of terrorism.' And, although it does its best to keep them separate, it is plain that the consequences of US imperialism abroad are, as Amy Kaplan has suggested in a discussion of nineteenth-century American imperialism, 'inseparable from the social relations and cultural discourses of race, gender, ethnicity, and class at home' (Kaplan 1993: 15, 16). If it were not for the sheer complexity of these relations, it would not be possible to imagine so many potential enemies of 'the state'. In addition, in order to pursue the American and 'foreign' suspects, Bauer must travel through the very urban spaces that reveal the failures of US domestic policy – a narrative that makes 24's premise of an African-American President almost risible. In short, the conflicts and tensions within this space illustrate the impossibility of ever separating the 'domestic' and the 'foreign'.

To conclude, for Bauer to triumph, the counter to patriotic tub-thumping comes from a (characteristically, yet paradoxically, 'American') rejection of democratic principles and the turn to individual conscience to dictate action. On the one hand, 24 – which, as we have seen, reiterates many of the central generic features of the classic Western – indicates that such a turn will result in a revisionist American history (and a new sense of 'nationhood') that pays lip service to inter-ethnic and international cooperation, but ultimately imagines an America re-invented and redeemed from within, through the deployment of 'traditional' values. But in so doing, it also reaffirms precisely those values and acts – macho conduct over diplomacy; ever-increasing use of force as the only way to solve regional and (implicitly) global conflicts – that President Palmer appears to condemn.

00.17
AFTERWORD

DAVID LAVERY

> When all the archetypes burst out shamelessly, we
> plumb Homeric profundity. Two clichés make us
> laugh but a hundred clichés move us because we sense
> dimly that the clichés are talking among themselves,
> celebrating a reunion.
> Umberto Eco, 'Casablanca: Cult Movies and
> Intertextual Collage'

I have watched every hour of 24, heard every nervous tick, from the beginning, and almost from the outset I have told anyone who cared to listen that I would probably never write about the series. A scholar-fan of such television programmes as Buffy the Vampire Slayer, The Sopranos, Deadwood, Twin Peaks, The X-Files, and Lost, my strong preference has been for quality television offering richly imaginative, genre-bending, abundantly intertextual teleuniverses with fascinating, inimitable characters and inspired writing. It's not that I didn't like 24 – indeed I loved it and still do, a third of the way through Day Five as I write.

Day Five (Season Five) of 24 indeed seems better than ever. Beginning, in January 2006, much later than the competition,[1] the new season commences fourteen months after Day Four (Season Four). Someone is killing off those who know Jack Bauer is still alive, and before the first hour has run its course three major 24 regulars are dead (whether for diegetic or non-diegetic reasons is subject to question). Audrey Heller Raines (Kim Raver) learns that Bauer is still alive, but his heart may belong to another – Diane Huxley (Connie

Britton), his landlady during his fugitive period. Chloe has a boyfriend (not
named Edgar), who of course proves to be untrustworthy. President Logan
shows himself to be even more of a detestable wuss than on Day Four, and
now has a possibly unhinged first lady (Martha) to test his spineless mettle.
His chief of staff, Walt Cummings (John Allen Nelson), who had ordered
Bauer terminated on Day Four, is clearly a traitor, and a new man from
District (played by *Lord of the Rings*' Sean Astin) may or may not be cut from
the same cloth as all his boss-from-hell predecessors. Oh, and canisters of
nerve gas are on the loose – in the possession of Russian separatists. Eight
episodes in, however, the true enemy has yet to reveal itself.

In basic agreement with Chamberlain and Ruston's discerning
conclusions in these pages – that *24* 'both seems like quality television
and the farthest thing from it', that it 'represents a break from traditional
academic discussions of quality television', 'does not share many of the
generic traits which often serve as markers for quality television, and ... is
often fantastic and excessive in spite of its appeals to realism' – I felt no
need to engage the series in any other way than as a fan. As a lapsed English
professor now immersed in television studies, I was especially enthralled
by the capable-of-any-savagery (decapitation, torture, eyeball removal) Bauer,
who, I was shocked to learn in the Season One tie-in book *24: The House
Special Subcommittee's Findings at CTU*, earned a BA in English at UCLA
(Cerasini 2003). But *24* itself, despite its English major hero, didn't seem to
call for a close reading.

And yet here I am, contrite, having the last word in a book of insightful
and eye-opening (not just about the programme but about television)
studies of *24*. Who knew that examining *24*'s innovative use of split-screen
in the context of the history of western painting, cinema, and cartooning,
contemplating its political themes in light of its sponsors and the popularity
of the SUV, considering women's narrative authority in a very male story,
debating the post-Abu Ghraib ethics of its use of torture, diagnosing Chloe
(Asperger's Syndrome?), or interrogating its surprising genre affiliations
would yield such remarkable, ingenious results? Why hadn't I thought of
all this smart TV crit?

Though I have watched *24* ardently, my suspension of disbelief has not
always been willing. My attachment to the series has not prevented me from
(like most viewers) staring in disbelief at the off-the-scale implausible perils
of Kim, incredulously questioning the time it takes in the *24*verse to cross

Los Angeles by car or return to the city from the Mojave, wondering how CTU could be so ludicrously incompetent, puzzling how Mike Novick could serve so many roles in so many administrations, wincing at Teri's soap-opera-esque amnesia (*and* pregnancy), Chase Edmunds' secret love child, or Jack's miraculous return from the dead and astonishing on-the-run recovery from an addiction to smack, mystified at the tendency of each day's breakneck events to peak, like clockwork, at the top of the hour, and achieve climax at the end of 24.[2]

In a famous passage in *The Poetics* Aristotle had observed (with Greek tragedy and not television narrative in mind) that 'With respect to the requirements of art, a probable impossibility is to be preferred to a thing improbable and yet possible.' '[P]lot,' the Greek philosopher was convinced, 'must not be composed of irrational parts. Everything irrational should, if possible, be excluded; or, at all events, it should lie outside the action of the play ... But once the irrational has been introduced and an air of likelihood imparted to it, we must accept it in spite of the absurdity' (Trans. Butcher 1971: 47). Does 24 pass Aristotle's test?

In the age of the Internet we have a new name for the failure to do so. Thanks to Jon Hein's popular website (and later book) jumptheshark.com, it has now become common, after a telling moment on *Happy Days* when Fonzie actually did leap over said marine predator, to speak of the moment when a good television show goes bad – when we realise our 'favorite show has lost its magic, has begun the long, painful slide to the TV graveyard' (Hein 2002). 24 has, of course, inspired its own entries on the website, but revealingly the majority of visitors have insisted the series has yet to take the leap.

It is hard to believe that those who find 24 still shark-free are watching the same series I am. 24, a show that, as numerous chapters in this book demonstrate, experiments radically with the nature and form of televisuality, has likewise taken shark-jumping to a new level. By jumping the shark incessantly, like clockwork, 24 has transformed the vault into a leap of narrative faith in which the viewer, as breathless and unremitting as the story itself, plunges on, untroubled by doubt or disbelief, misgivings or qualms. Umberto Eco was thinking of one of the great, transcendent films when he observed that '[t]wo clichés make us laugh but a hundred clichés move us because we sense dimly that the clichés are talking among themselves, celebrating a reunion' (1971: 197). The equally transcendent 24 is such a reunion.

NOTES

1. In an experimental, ratings-successful innovation, Fox decided to delay airing Seasons Four and Five in the US until January, giving *24*'s creative team enough time to have enough episodes in the can to air, after an initial screening of four episodes on consecutive nights, an entire season without interruption over 21 consecutive weeks.

2. For an especially perceptive reading of each and every episode of *24*, taking special note of improbabilities and inconsistencies, see M Giant's always snarky *Television Without Pity* recaps: http://www.televisionwithoutpity. com/show.cgi?show=73.

00.18
SEASON
GUIDE

24 (FOX Entertainment Group)

Creators: Joel Surnow, Robert Cochran

Writers: Joel Surnow, Robert Cochran, Remi Aubuchon, Manny Coto, Duppy Demetrius, Matt Michnovetz, Andrea Newman

Producers: Remi Aubuchon, Chris Cheramie, Robert Cochran, Brian Grazer, Ron Howard, Stephen Kronish, Norman S Powell, Joel Surnow, Danielle Weistsch

SEASON ONE

Original air-date (1.1): 6 November 2001

Season summary: events start at 12 a.m. Jack Bauer leads the Los Angeles branch of the US Counter-Terrorist Agency. Information is received from 'their man in Kuala Lumpur' confirming an attempt is to be made on the life of presidential nominee David Palmer. Bauer helms the response, working to stop a criminal group run by the Drazen family. Meanwhile, his strained marriage to his wife, Teri, is taken to breaking point by the sudden disappearance of their troubled teenage daughter, Kim. The Bauer family becomes separated, and Kim and Teri are kidnapped. As events ensue, rogue agents or 'moles' are uncovered at work within CTU headquarters: first Jamey Farrell, then Nina Myers, Bauer's (ex-)lover. Averting the assassination attempt and connected threats to national security, Bauer must endure the death of his wife, at the hands of the treacherous Myers.

SEASON TWO

Original air-date (2.1): 29 October 2002

Season summary: events start at 8 a.m. and take place a year after those of Season One. A nuclear bomb is planted in Los Angeles, forcing new head of CTU George Mason into action, drawing again on the field skills of Jack Bauer. Meanwhile, Kim is on the run from her psychopathic employer, who has threatened to kill her. Bauer must protect his daughter, and the state of the nation, by relying on information from the woman who murdered his wife: Nina Myers. As the nuclear bomb is detonated over the Mojave desert in a life-giving act of bravery by Mason, a greater plot reveals itself: the manipulation of the US government by a criminal corporate syndicate to enter into an international war. The fate of civilisation rests in the hands of Bauer, and the duplicitous (ex-)wife of the President, Sherry Palmer, in a final race against time. Temporarily relieved of his duties by Vice-President Jim Prescott, David Palmer finally and jubilantly regains control of the country, only to be struck down in the dying seconds of the season by a poisoned handshake.

SEASON THREE

Original air-date (3.1): 28 October 2003

Season summary: events start at 1 p.m. and take place three years after those of Season Two. Jack Bauer returns to work in CTU following a prolonged period 'undercover' at the heart of a South American drugs cartel, run by the Salazar family. Bauer, suffering from heroin withdrawal (a habit picked up whilst with the Salazar clan to strengthen his cover story) is now joined at the helm by his daughter, Kim, as a CTU analyst, and her boyfriend (and field agent) Chase Edmunds. The day turns on Bauer's attempts (together with CTU regulars Tony Almeida and Michelle Dessler) to counter the cartel's threats to release a deadly virus. In the year of re-election, matters are made worse for President Palmer, through a vicious and potentially deadly smear campaign organised by his political rivals.

SEASON FOUR

Original air-date (4.1): 9 January 2005

Season summary: events start at 7 a.m., and take place 18 months after those of Season Three. Bauer has been fired by new CTU head Erin Driscoll, and works as a private bodyguard for Secretary of Defense James Heller.

He is also conducting a secret affair with Heller's daughter, Audrey Raines. However, the kidnapping of Heller and Raines by a group of fundamentalist terrorists suddenly places Bauer back in the centre of the action, at CTU. Rescuing the Secretary and his daughter brings Bauer, and CTU, closer to the greater threat: the proposed meltdown of nuclear reactors across the United States of America. The Araz family is at the heart of the proposed terrorist activity, and as Bauer works to gain information from them, it is revealed that Audrey's ex-husband, Paul Raines, is also implicated. Bauer seeks help from retired CTU agent Tony Almeida, whilst the suddenly instated President Logan calls on the support of ex-President David Palmer. Averting the disaster of the reactors, Bauer lays himself open to arrest and imprisonment by the Chinese government. To escape, his loyal colleagues help him to fake his own death, and Bauer disappears, as a 'dead man'.

SEASON FIVE

Original air-date (5.1): 15 January 2006

Season summary: events start at 7 a.m. and take place 18 months after those of Season Four. Bauer, having faked his own death, lives in refuge in California with his lover and her son. Yet, he is brought back to the centre of downtown LA following the assassination of President Palmer, and the car-bombing of his colleagues, Tony Almeida and Michelle Dessler. Framed for the assassination of Palmer, Bauer works to clear his name, whilst protecting his assumed identity. The murders connect rogue agents within the US government, led by CIA agent Walt Cummings, and members of a radical, Soviet separatist group. The group gains control of a consignment of nerve gas, threatening to release it across the States if the Russian President is not given up for assassination. As CTU headquarters is made the target of the gas, Bauer must confront those closest to him, including Kim and Audrey. As events unfold, President Logan's involvement becomes ever more questionable. The supply of nerve gas to terrorists is part of a much larger political plan, which rapidly deteriorates with disastrous consequences for all involved. Factions threaten permanent divisions: between CTU and Homeland Security, the President and his wife, of Bauer and his dedicated allies. Bauer must work under the radar to bring down the corrupt Logan and stop the terrorists. A final twist marks the return of some old enemies, and the disappearance of Jack Bauer, beaten and alone.

00.19
FILM AND TV INDEX

Fatal Hour, The (DW Griffith, 1908)

FOX News (FOX Entertainment Group, 1996–)

Gilmore Girls (CBS/Warner Bros. Television, 2000–)

Great Train Robbery, The (Edwin Porter, 1903)

Happy Days (ABC, 1974–1984)

High Noon (Fred Zinnemann, 1952)

High Plains Drifter (Clint Eastwood, 1973)

Hill Street Blues (MTM Enterprises/NBC, 1981–1987)

Law and Order (Dick Wolf, 1990–)

Lethal Weapon (1–4) (Richard Donner, 1987, 1989, 1992, 1998)

Life of an American Fireman (George S Fleming, 1903)

Lord of the Rings Trilogy, The (Peter Jackson, 2001, 2002, 2003)

Lost (Bad Robot Productions/Touchstone Television, 2004–)

Maltese Falcon, The (John Huston, 1941)

Man from UNCLE, The (NBC, 1964–1968)

Matrix, The (Andy and Larry Wachowski, 1999)

MacGyver (Vin di Bona, 1985)

Miami Vice (Michael Mann Productions, 1984–1990)

Napoleon (Abel Gance, 1927)

Nick of Time (John Badham, 1995)

North by Northwest (Alfred Hitchcock, 1959)

Northern Exposure (Brand/CBS, 1990–1995)

O. C., The (FOX Entertainment Group, 2003–)

Pale Rider (Clint Eastwood, 1985)

Persuaders!, The (ITC Entertainment, 1971–1972)

Psycho (Alfred Hitchcock, 1960)

Pulp Fiction (Quentin Tarantino, 1994)

Pure 24 (BBC, 2003)

Queer Eye for the Straight Guy (Scout Productions, 2003–)

Rain Man (Barry Levinson, 1988)

Rambo: First Blood Part II (George P Cosmatos, 1985)

Rope (Alfred Hitchcock, 1948)

Salon, The (Endemol, 2003–2004)

Simpsons, The (Gracie Films, 1989–)

Six Feet Under (HBO, 2001–2005)

Sopranos, The (HBO, 1999–)

Special Bulletin (National Broadcast Company, 1983)

Anon. 'A Strong Start for "24" on Fox'. *New York Times*. 31 October 2002.

Anon. *Diagnostic and Statistical Manual of Mental Disorders – Fourth Edition* (DSM-IV). American Psychiatric Association, Washington DC, 1994.

Anon. 'Fox Series *24* a Timely Reflection of our Fears'. *The Vancouver Province* . 4 April 2003.

Anon. 'Gas Taxes: Lesser Evil, Greater Good'. *New York Times*. 24 October 2005.

Anon. 'Green Light for Guzzlers'. *The Washington Post*. 29 August 2005.

Anon. 'Multiple-Image Technique for *The Boston Strangler*'. *American Cinematographer*. February, 1969: 202–5, 228, 238–41, 245.

Anon. 'Not Everything's A Terrorism Issue'. *Dayton Daily News*. 11 January 2003.

Adam, Barbara. *Time and Social Theory*. Cambridge: Polity Press, 1990.

Adam, Barbara. *Timewatch: The Social Analysis of Time*. Cambridge: Polity Press, 1995.

Agamben, Giorgio. *Homo Sacer: Sovereign Power and Bare Life*. Stanford, CA: Stanford University Press, 1998.

Agamben, Giorgio. *The State of Exception*. Trans. Kevin Attell. Chicago: University of Chicago Press, 2005.

Allen, Michael. *Family Secrets: The Feature Films of D. W. Griffith*. London: BFI Publishing, 1999.

Alliez, Eric and Michel Feher. 'The Luster of Capital'. Trans. Alyson Waters. *Zone* 1 and 2 (1987): 315–59.

Alter, Jonathan. 'Time to Think About Torture'. *Newsweek*. 5 November 2001.

Altheide, David L. *Terrorism and the Politics of Fear*. Lanham, MD: AltaMira Press, 2006.

Altman, Rick. 'A Semantic/Syntactic Approach to Film Genre'. In *Film/Genre*. London: BFI Publishing, 1999. 216-26.

Amatangelo, Amy. 'Duct and Coverage: Fiction, Reality Blurred Further as More Dramas Weave Current Events into Plot Lines'. *The Boston Herald*. 18 February 2003.

Aristotle. 'Poetics'. Trans. SH Butcher. *Critical Theory Since Plato.*, ed. Hazard Adams. New York, HBJ, 1971. 47-66.

Baer, Robert. *Sleeping With the Devil: How Washington Sold Our Soul for Saudi Crude*. New York: Three Rivers Press, 2003.

Baker, Peter. 'President Acknowledges Approving Secretive Eavesdropping'. *Washington Post*. 18 December 2005.

Bankston, Douglas. 'On the Clock'. *American Cinematographer*. February 2004.

Barnett, Erica C. 'Axles of You-Know-What'. *Seattle Weekly*. 5 March 2003.

Bazin, Andre. 'The Evolution of the Language of Cinema', in *What is Cinema Vol. 1*. Berkeley: University of California Press, 1967. 23-40.

Bianculli, David. *N.Y. Daily News*, 5 November 2001.

Billen, Andrew. 'Twenty-four Hours To Go; Television – Arab Government Backs Band of Terrorists. Relax, it's Just Drama'. *The New Statesman*. 24 February 2003.

Bordo, Susan. *Unbearable Weight: Feminism, Western Culture, and The Body*. Berkeley: University of California Press, 2003.

Bordwell, David. *Narration in the Fiction Film*. London: Routledge, 1985.

Boyd-Bowman, Susan. "The Day After': Representations of Nuclear Holocaust'. *Screen*. 25: 4-5. July–October 1984.

Bradsher, Keith. 'Ford Said to Plan Improved Mileage in Sport Utilities'. *New York Times*. 27 July 2000.

Brooks, Peter. *The Melodramatic Imagination: Balzac, Henry James, Melodrama and the Mode of Excess*. New Haven: Yale University Press, 1976.

Brownlow, Kevin. *Napoleon*. London: Jonathan Cape, 1983.

Caldwell, John Thornton. *Televisuality: Style Crisis and Authority in American Television*. New Brunswick, NJ: Rutgers University Press, 1995.

Caldwell, John. 'Prime-Time Television Theorizes the Docu-Real'. In James Friedman, ed. *Reality Squared: Televisual Discourse on the Real*. New Brunswick: Rutgers University Press, 2002. 259-92.

Campbell, Duncan. 'The Truth is Out There'. *The Observer*. 16 February 2003.

Campbell, Jan. *Film and Cinema Spectatorship*. Cambridge: Polity Press, 2005.

Caughie, John. *Television Drama*. Oxford: Oxford University Press, 2000: 122.

Cawelti, John G. *Adventure, Mystery and Romance: Formula Stories as Art and Popular Culture*. Chicago: University of Chicago Press, 1976.

Cerasini, Marc. 24: The House Special Subcommittee's Findings at CTU. New York: HarperEntertainment, 2003.

Chambers, Samuel and Daniel Williford. 'Anti-Imperialism in the Buffyverse: A Challenge to the Mythos of Bush as Vampire-Slayer'. Poroi. 3.2. 2004.

Chatman, Seymour. Story and Discourse: Narrative Structure in Fiction and Film. Ithaca and London: Cornell University Press, 1978.

Chemerinsky, Edwin et al. 'Symposium: The Second Amendment and the Future of Gun Regulation: Historical, Legal, Policy, and Cultural Perspectives'. Fordham Law Review. 73:2 (November 2004): 475-730.

Cherpack, Clifton. The Call of Blood in French Classical Tragedy. Baltimore: John Hopkins Press, 1958.

Christie, George C. 'The Defence of Necessity Considered from the Legal and Moral Points of View'. Duke Law Journal, 48: 2000. 975-1072.

Cohan, Steven. Masked Men: Masculinity and the Movies in the Fifties. Bloomington, IN: Indiana University Press, 1997.

Collins, Monica. 'Grim themes of 24 and NYPD Blue premieres are painfully familiar'. The Boston Herald. 6 November 2001.

Corsi, Jeremy R and Craig R Smith. Black Gold Stranglehold: The Myth of Scarcity and the Politics of Oil. Nashville: WND Books, 2005.

Coupland, Douglas. Microserfs. Toronto: HarperCollins, 1995.

Davis, Walter E. 'September 11 and the Bush Administration: Compelling Evidence for Complicity?' In Bernd Hamm, ed. Devastating Society: the Neoconservative Assault on Democracy and Justice. London: Pluto Press, 2005: 67-87.

Derrida, Jacques. 'Force of Law: The "Mystical Foundation of Authority"'. In Deconstruction and the Possibility of Justice, eds. Drucilla Cornell, Michael Rosenfeld, and David Gray Carlson. London: Routledge, 1992.

Dickens, Charles. Bleak House. Harmondsworth: Penguin Books, 1971.

Doane, Mary Ann. 'Information, Crisis, Catastrophe'. In Patricia Mellencamp, ed. Logics of Television. Bloomington: Indiana University Press, 1990. 222-39.

Doane, Mary Ann. The Emergence of Cinematic Time: Modernity, Contingency, the Archive. Cambridge, MA and London, 2002.

Eco, Umberto. 'Casablanca: Cult Movies and Intertextual Collage'. Travels in Hyper Reality. Trans. William Weaver. New York: Harcourt, Brace Jovanovich, 1986: 197-211.

Eliot, TS. 'The Love Song of J. Alfred Prufrock'. Prufrock and Other Observations. London: The Egoist, 1919; New York: Bartleby, 2000.

Ellis, John. *Visible Fictions: Cinema, Television, Video*. London: Routledge, 1982, 1984. 128–37.

Ellis, John. *Seeing Things: Television in the Age of Uncertainty*. London: I.B.Tauris, 1999.

English, Bella. 'A Groundswell Against SUVs: King-Size Vehicles Stir Some Large Resentment'. *The Boston Globe*. 10 February 2003.

Evans, Joyce A. *Celluloid Mushroom Clouds: Hollywood and the Atomic Bomb*. Boulder, CO: Westview Press, 1998.

Feuer, Jane. 'The Concept of Live Television: Ontology as Ideology'. In E Ann Kaplan, ed. *Regarding Television Critical Approaches: An Anthology*. Frederick, MD: University Publications of America, 1983. 12–22.

Feuer, Jane. 'Melodrama, Serial Form and Television Today'. *Screen*. 25. 1984.

Feuer, Jane. 'The MTM Style'. In Jane Feuer, Paul Kerr and Tise Vahimagi, eds. *MTM: Quality Television*. London: BFI, 1984. 32–60.

Feuer, Jane. 'Genre'. In Richard Allen, ed. *Channels of Discourse, Reassembled: Television and Contemporary Criticism*. London: Routledge, 1992 (second edition).

Fisher, Eric. 'Ford's New Mega-SUV Irks Safety Green Groups'. *The Washington Times*. 26 February 1999.

Fisher, Louis. *Presidential War Power: 2nd Edition*. Lawrence, KS: University Press of Kansas, 2004.

Ford, Royal. 'Ford's Risky Redesign of F-150 Pays Off Beautifully'. *The Boston Globe*. 19 October 2003.

Foucault, Michel. *Discipline and Punish: The Birth of the Prison*. Trans. Alan Sheridan. London: Penguin, 1991.

Foucault, Michel. *The Will to Knowledge. History of Sexuality. vol. 1*. Trans. Robert Hurley. London: Penguin Books, 1998.

Foucault, Michel. *Power: The Essential Works of Michel Foucault: 1954–1984, vol. 3.*, ed. James D Faubion. London: Penguin, 2002.

Frank, John N. 'SUVs – Automakers Need to Drive Home Message on SUVs'. *PR Week*. 3 March 2003.

Gallo, Phil. Review of *24*. *Daily Variety*. 2 November 2001.

Genette, Gérard. *Narrative Discourse: An Essay in Method*. Trans. Jane E Lewin. Ithica, NY: Cornell University Press, 1983.

Gilbert, Matthew. 'Tight *24* Makes Every Second Count'. *The Boston Globe*. 6 November 2001, 3rd Edition.

Gilbert, Matthew. '*24* Continues To Be Time Well Spent'. *The Boston Globe*. October 29, 2002, 3rd Edition.

Gledhill, Christine. 'Speculations on the Relationship Between Soap Opera and Melodrama'. *Quarterly Review of Film and Video*. 14. 1–2. July 1992.

Gleick, James. *Faster: The Acceleration of Just About Everything*. London: Abacus, 2000.

Gordon, Dillian. *Making and Meaning: The Wilton Diptych*. London: National Gallery Publications, 1993.

Graser, Marc. 'Driven Heroes'. *Variety*. 4–10 November 2002: 7.

Grossberg, Larry. *We Gotta Get Out of this Place*. New York: Routledge, 1992.

Hark, Ina Rae. "Today is the Longest Day of My Life': 24 as Mirror Narrative of 9/11'. In Wheeler Winston Dixon, ed. *Film and Television After 9/11*. Carbondale, IL: Southern Illinois University Press, 2004: 121–41.

Hastie, Amelie. 'The Epistemological Stakes of *Buffy the Vampire Slayer*: Television Criticism and Marketing Demands'. In Elana Levine and Lisa Parks, eds. *Undead TV: Critical Writings on Buffy the Vampire Slayer*. Durham, NC: Duke University Press, 2006.

Healey, James R. 'Ford CEO Pushes Government to Put on an Energy Summit'. *USA Today*. 23 November 2005.

Hedges, Chris. *War is A Force That Gives Us Meaning*. New York: Anchor Press, 2003.

Hein, Jon. *Jump the Shark*. New York: Plume Books, 2002.

Hermes, Joke. *Rereading Popular Culture*. Cambridge: Blackwell, 2005.

Heywood, Leslie and Jennifer Drake. 'Introduction'. In Heywood and Drake, eds. *Third Wave Agenda: Being Feminist, Doing Feminism*. Minneapolis: University of Minnesota, 2003: 1–24.

Holmes, Su. '"But this time you choose!" Approaching the "interactive" audience in reality TV'. *International Journal of Cultural Studies*, 7: 2 (2004).

Hurley, Michelle. 'A Short History of Brevity'. *The Times Magazine*. 23 June 2001.

James, Caryn. 'Television, Like the Country, Loses Its Footing'. *New York Times*. 4 November 2001.

James, Caryn. 'Television Review; Clock Reset, Agent Bauer Returns to Work'. *New York Times*. 29 October 2002.

Jancovich, Mark and James Lyons, eds. *Quality Popular Television: Cult TV, the Industry and Fans*. London: BFI, 2003.

Jensen, Jens F. 'The Concept of Interactivity in "Interactive Television" and "Interactive Media"'. In Jensen, Jens F and Cathy Toscan, eds. *Interactive Television: TV of the Future or the Future of TV?* Aalborg: Aalborg University Press, 1999. 25–66.

Jermyn, Deborah and Su Holmes. 'The audience is dead: Long live the audience! – Interactivity, "telephilia" and the contemporary television audience'. *Critical Studies in Television*, 1:1 (2006).

Johnson, Steven. *Everything Bad is Good for You*. London: Allen Lane/Penguin, 2005.

Joyrich, Lynne. *Reviewing Reception: Television, Gender, and Postmodern Culture*. Bloomington, IN: Indiana University Press, 1996.

Kennedy Jr., Robert F. 'Crimes Against Nature'. *Rolling Stone*. 11 December 2003.

King, Scott Benjamin. 'Sonny's Virtues: the Gender Negotiations of Miami Vice'. *Screen* 31, 3. 1990.

Kiousis, Spiro. 'Interactivity: A Concept Explication'. *New Media and Society*. 4:3 (2002): 355–83.

Kissel, Rick. 'No breakthrough, but *24* beats drama rivals'. *Daily Variety*. 23 May 2002.

Kissel, Rick. 'Eye 'Loves' Finales'. *Daily Variety*. 25 May 2005.

Klare, Michael T. *Blood and Oil: The Dangers and Consequences of America's Growing Dependency on Foreign Petroleum*. New York: Henry Holt, 2004.

Kloer, Phil. '*24* Fans Anticipate Payback in Finale'. *The Atlanta Journal-Constitution*. 21 May 2002.

Kloer, Phil. 'Terrorists move in for next *24* hours'. *The Atlanta Journal-Constitution*. 29 October 2002. Home Edition.

Kundera, Milan. *Slowness*. New York: HarperCollins, 1996.

Lesser, Wendy. 'The Thrills and the Chill of *24*'. *New York Times*. 31 March 2002.

Levinson, Sanford. 'Contemplating Torture: An Introduction'. In Sanford Levinson, ed., *Torture: A Collection*. New York and Oxford: Oxford University Press, 2004: 23–43.

Lothe, Jakob. *Narrative in Fiction and Film: An Introduction*. Oxford: Oxford University Press, 2000.

Lury, Karen. *Interpreting Television*. London: Hodder Education, 2005.

Marshall, P David. *New Media Cultures*. London: Arnold, 2004.

Matheson, Richard. 'The West Hard-boiled: Adaptations of Film Noir elements, existentialism and ethics in John Wayne's Westerns'. In *Journal of Popular Culture* 38 (5).

McCain, John. 'Torture's Terrible Toll'. *Newsweek*. 21 November 2005: 34.

McCarthy, Michael. 'Turn on *24* and You'll Also Catch a 6-min. Film-ercial'. *USA Today*. 27 October 2003.

McCloud, Scott. *Understanding Comics*. New York: Harper Perennial, 1994.

McKinnon, John D and Yochi Dreazen. 'Bush Concedes Intelligence Flaws Played Part
in War'. *The Wall Street Journal*. 15 December 2005.

McPherson, Tara. 'Reload: Liveness, Mobility, and the Web'. In Wendy Hui Kyong Chun and Thomas Keenan, eds. *New Media, Old Media: A History and Theory Reader*. New York, NY: Routledge University Press, 2005.

Meacher, Michael. 'This War on Terrorism is Bogus'. *The Guardian*. 6 September 2003.

Mellencamp, Patricia. 'TV Time and Catastrophe'. In Patricia Mellencamp, ed. *Logics of Television*. Bloomington, IN: Indiana University Press, 1990. 240-66.

Mellinkoff, Ruth. *The Devil at Isenheim: Reflections of Popular Belief in Grunewald's Altarpiece*. Berkeley, LA and London: University of California Press, 1988.

Mepham, J. 'The ethics of quality'. In Geoff Mulgan, ed. *The Question of Quality*, London: BFI, 1990. 56-72.

Miller, Toby. 'The action season'. In Glen Creeber, ed. *The Television Genre Book*. London: BFI, 2001. 16-18.

Modleski, Tania. *Old Wives Tales: Feminist Re-Visions of Film and Other Fictions*. London: I.B.Tauris, 1999.

Monahan, Torin, ed. *Surveillance and Security: Technological Politics and Power in Everyday Life*. New York: Routledge, 2006.

Mulgan, Geoff. 'Television's Holy Grail: Seven Types of Quality'. In Geoff Mulgan, ed. *The Question of Quality*. London: BFI, 1990. 4-32.

Musser, Charles. *Before the Nickelodeon: Edwin S. Porter and the Edison Manufacturing Company*. Berkeley, CA: University of California Press, 1991.

Neale, Steve. *Genre and Hollywood*. London: Routledge, 2000.

Norris, Andrew. 'Giorgio Agamben and the Politics of the Living Dead'. *Diacritics* 30 (2000): 38-58.

Osgerby, Bill. *Playboys in Paradise*. London: Berg, 2001.

Page, Jeffrey. 'SUV Drivers, Their Critics Need Attitude Adjustment'. *The Record* Bergen County, NJ. 12 January 2003.

Parry, Vivienne. *The Times*. 4 February 2006.

Patocka, Jan. 'Wars of the 20th Century and the 20th Century as War'. In *Heretical Essays in the Philosophy of History*. Trans. Erazim Kohak. Chicago: Open Court, 1996.

Perkins, VF. 'Rope'. In Ian Cameron, ed. *Movie Reader*. London: November Books, 1972.

Perrine, Toni A. *Film and the Nuclear Age: Representing Cultural Anxiety*. New York: Garland Publishing, 1998.

Phoenix, Laurel. 'Dissenting Groups and Movements'. In Bernd Hamm, ed. *Devastating Society: the Neoconservative Assault on Democracy and Justice*. London: Pluto Press, 2005: 267–89.

Poniewozik, James. 'The Time of Their Lives'. *Time Magazine*. 12 November 2001.

Rice, Lynnette. 'Sensitive Material: The New Spy Shows'. *Entertainment Weekly*. 28 September 2001.

Rimmon-Kenan, Shlomith. *Narrative Fiction: Contemporary Poetics*. London and New York: Routledge, 1983.

Roberts, Paul. *The End of Oil: On the Edge of a Perilous New World*. New York: Houghton Mifflin, 2004, 2005.

Ronell, Avital. *The Telephone Book: Technology – Schizophrenia – Electric Speech*. Lincoln: University of Nebraska Press, 1989.

Ruch, John. 'Thrills Work Overtime in *24*'. *The Boston Herald*. 28 October 2002.

Ruth, Daniel. 'Jack-Booted Goons Of Political Correctness Strike Again'. *Tampa Tribune*. 12 January 2003.

Shapiro, Jerome F. *Atomic Bomb Cinema: The Apocalyptic Imagination on Film*. London: Routledge, 2002.

Sheridan, Mary Beth. '15 Hijackers Obtained Visas in Saudi Arabia; Most Citizens of That Country Seeking to Visit US Are Approved Without Interviews'. *The Washington Post*. 31 October 2001.

Shulze, Laurie. 'The Made-for-TV Movie: Industrial Practice, Cultural Form, Popular Reception'. In Horace Newcomb, ed. *Television: The Critical View*. Fifth, ed. New York: Oxford University Press, 1994: 155–75.

Silberman, Steve. 'The Geek Syndrome'. *Wired* 9: 12. 2001.

Simon, William H. 'Moral Pluck: Legal Ethics in Popular Culture'. *Columbia Law Review*. 101: 2001.

St John, Warren. 'What Men Want: Neanderthal TV'. *New York Times*, 11 December 2005.

Stanley, Alessandra. 'Countering Terrorists, and a Dense Daughter'. *New York Times*. 28 October 2003.

Strachan, Alex. 'Ad Sales Out Of This World for *24*'s Next Season'. *The Vancouver Sun*. 25 May 2002.

Talen, Julie. 'Video Visions: Beyond Monovision'. *Village Voice*. 29 March 1984.

Tasker, Yvonne. *Spectacular Bodies*. London: Routledge, 1993.

Teather, David. 'Republicans Turn on the Oil Industry as Petrol Prices Soar'. *The Guardian*. 10 November 2005.

Thomas, Evan, and Michael Hirsh. 'The Debate Over Torture'. *Newsweek*. 21 November 2005.

Thompson, Robert J. 'Television's Second Golden Age: The Quality Shows'. *Television Quarterly*. 28:3. 1996.

Thomson, David. 'At the end of the day'. *The Independent Review*. 16 August 2002.

Thomson, David. 'Shock around the clock'. *Sight and Sound*. 13: 8 (2002): 12–15.

Thornburn, David. 'Television Melodrama'. In Horace Newcomb, ed. *Television: The Critical View*. Fifth, ed. New York: Oxford University Press, 1994. 537–50.

Twining, WL and PE Twining. 'Bentham on Torture'. *Northern Ireland Legal Quarterly* 24 (1973): 305–56.

Unger, Craig. *House of Bush, House of Saud: The Secret Relationship between the World's Two Most Powerful Dynasties*. London: Gibson Square Books, 2004; reprinted with new afterword, 2005.

Vardac, Nicholas. *Stage to Screen: Theatrical Method from Garrick to Griffith*. Cambridge, MA: Harvard University Press, 1949.

Vidal, John. 'Britain Bucks Trend by Falling in Love with SUVs'. *The Guardian*. 25 October 2005.

Virilio, Paul. *Speed and Politics: An Essay on Dromology*. New York: Columbia University, 1986.

Virilio, Paul. *Negative Horizon: An Essay in Dromoscopy*. Trans. M Degener. New York: Continuum, 2005.

Virno, Paolo. *A Grammar of the Multitude: For an Analysis of Contemporary Forms of Life*. Cambridge, MA: Semiotext(e), 2004.

Waller, Gregory A. 'Re-Placing 'The Day After''. *Cinema Journal*. 26: 3. (Spring 1987): 3–20.

Warshow, Robert. 'Movie Chronicle: The Westerner'. *The Immediate Experience*. New York: Doubleday, 1964.

Weeks, Janet. 'Secrets & Spies,' *TV Guide*. 3 November, 2001.

White, Rob. 'Channelling'. *Sight and Sound*. July 2002.

White, Ronald. 'Foreign Landscape: Non-U.S. firms manage most of the terminals at L.A.-area ports'. *The Los Angeles Times*. 12 March, 2006. http://www.latimes.com.

Wiegman, Robyn. 'Missiles and Melodrama (Masculinity and the Televisual War)'. In Susan Jeffords and Lauren Rabinovitz, eds. *Seeing Through the Media: The Persian Gulf War*. Rutgers, NJ: Rutgers University Press, 1994.

Williams, Betsy. "North to the Future': Northern Exposure and Quality Television'. In Horace Newcomb, ed. *Television: The Critical View*. Fifth edition. New York: Oxford University Press, 1994. 141–54.

Williams, Richard. 'Once Upon A Time Code'. *The Guardian Magazine*. 11 August 2000.

Woodward, Kath. 'Motherhood, identities, meanings and myths'. In Kath Woodward, ed. *Identity and Difference*. London: Sage and the Open University, 1997. 239–85.

Younge, Gary. 'Big, Not Clever'. *The Guardian*. 22 April 2003.

Žižek, Slavoj. *Welcome to the Desert of the Real*. New York: Verso, 2002.

WEBSITES

Anon. http://www.24 addict.com.

Anon. http://www.24ever.com.

Anon. http://www.24fanatics.com.

Anon. http://www.24weblog.com.

Anon. http://www.almeidaisgod.com.

Anon. http://bbcnews.co.uk.

Anon. http://www.imdb.com/keyword/real-time.

Anon. 'A Conversation with Richard Kline', *ASC Awards News*. (2005) http://www.theasc.com/awards/20th_news/kline_QA.htm.

Anon. 'Green Products: The SUV Question'. (2006) http://www2.cddc.vt.edu/digitalfordism/12greenprosuv.html.

Anon. 'Rice Defends US Policy'. *BBC News*. 5 December 2005. BBC. http://news.bbc.co.uk.

Anon. 'This one is titled "Play the Theme from Jaws"'. *Detroit Free Press*. 8 February 2006. http://freep.typepad.com.

Barber, John. 'The Phenomenon of Multiple Dialectics in Comics Layout (Theory 2)' (2002). http://www.johnbarbercomics.com/resources/pdfs/theory2.pdf.

Bloom, Harold. 'Reflections in the Evening Land'. 17 December 2005. http://books.guardian.co.uk.

Boyd-Davis, Stephen. 'News from Now Where? – The Digital Spaces of Television', (2003). http://www.chart.ac.uk/chart2003/papers/boyd-davis.html.

Briody, Dan. 'Profits of War'. 22 July 2004. http://www.guardian.co.uk.

Bush, George W. 'State of the Union Address by the President'. 31 January 2006. Reproduced at: http://www.whitehouse.gov/stateoftheunion/2006/.

'Calendarlive'. *Los Angeles Times*. 30 April 2003: http:// www.calendarlive.com/ tv/ratings/cl-et-tvratingstext30apr30.story.

Cole, David. 'Bush's Illegal Spying'. *Salon*. 20 December 2005. http://www. salon.com/opinion/feature/2005/12/20/spying/index.html.

Cozens, Claire. '24 Sponsorship Deal Spells Trouble for BBC'. 9 September 2003. http://media.guardian.co.uk.

Deans, Jason. 'US Idol Pushes Fox to Top of Ratings Chart'. 22 May 2003. http://www.mediaguardian.co.uk.

Drum, Kevin. 'Torture and *24*'. 22 February 2005. http://www. washingtonmonthly.com/archives/individual/2005_02/005701.php.

Drum, Kevin. 'Political Animal'. 22 February 2005. http://www. washingtonmonthly.com/archives/individual/2005_02/005701.php.

Environmental Working Group. 'SUV Report'. March 2003. http://www.ewg. org/reports/upsidedown.

Fleischer, Ari. 'Press Briefing By Ari Fleischer'. 7 May 2001. http://www. whitehouse.gov/news/briefings/20010507.html.

Fox.com/24.

Friend, Tim. 'Accident-prone "24" is torture for experts'. *USA Today*. 6 May 2003. http://www.usatoday.com/life/television/news/2003-05-05-bauer_x.htm .

Huffington, Arianna. 'Support Our Troops, Dump That SUV'. 14 November 2002. www.detroitproject.com.

Huffington, Arianna. 'Why Oil Sheiks Love A Good Hummer'. 25 November 2002. www.detroitproject.com.

Huffington, Arianna. 'Road Outrage: How Corporate Greed and Political Corruption Paved the Way for the SUV Explosion'. 8 January 2003. www.detroitproject.com.

Kennedy Jr., Robert F. 'Missing the Boat on Oil Security'. 12 February 2003. http://www.detroitproject.com.

Keveney, Bill. 'Fictional *24* Brings Real Issue of Torture Home'. *USA Today*. 13 March 2005. http://www.usatoday.com/life/television/news/2005-03-13-24-torture_x.htm.

Kim, Richard. 'Pop Torture'. *The Nation*. 26 December 2005. http://www. thenation.com/docprem.mhtml.

Lawson, Mark. 'Mark Lawson asks if *24* can work for a second time'. *The Guardian*, 21 December 2003. http://www.guardian.co.uk/tv_and_ radio/story/0,892319,00.html#article_continue.

McPherson, Tara. 'Transform Me, Please ... ' *Flow* 1:8 (2005): http://jot. communication.utexas.edu/flow/?jot=view&id=524.

Mercer, Mark. 'Simon Cowell Comes In 6/25/03'. 1996–2005. http://www.marksfriggin.com/news.

Motley, Clay. '"It's a hell of a thing to kill a man": Western manhood in Clint Eastwood's *Unforgiven*'. *Americana*. spring 2004 (3: 1): http://www.americanpopularculture.com/journal/articles/spring_2004/motley.htm.

Murray, Stuart. 'Hollywood and the Fascination of Autism'. Society for Critical Exchange, Conference on 'Autism and Representation', 28–30 October 2005. http://www.cwru.edu/affil/sce//Texts_2005/Autism%20and%20Representation%20Murray.htm.

Norris, Robert S and Hans M Kristensen. 'Global Nuclear Stockpiles, 1945–2002'. *Bulletin of the Atomic Scientists*. 58: 6. November-December 2002: 103–104. http://www.thebulletin.org/article_nn.php?art_ofn=nd02norris.

Plungis, Jeff, et al. 'Anti-SUV Movement Grows'. 10 January 2003. http://www.usatoday.com.

Rice, Condoleeza. http://www.whitehouse.gov/news/releases/2004/08/20040819-5.html.

Rich, Frank. 'We'll Win This War – on *24*'. *New York Times*. 9 January 2005. http://www.nytimes.com.

Ridge, Tom. 'Secretary Ridge Discusses Homeland Security in Las Vegas'. 19 April 2004. http://www.whitehouse.gov/news/releases/2004/04/20040419-1.html.

Rose, Frank. 'The Fast-Forward, On-Demand, Network-Smashing Future of Television'. October 2003. http://www.wired.com.

Sadowski, Yahya. 'No War For Whose Oil?' April 2003. http://mondediplo.com.

Talen, Julie. '24: Split-screen's big comeback'. 2002. http://www.salon.com/ent/tv/feature/2002/05/14/24_split/.

Vogt, Heidi. 'Fox's Payback for Sticking with '24"', *Media Life*. 17 January, 2003. http://www.medialifemagazine.com.

Weitner, Sean. '24, Fox, Tuesday, 9 p.m / 8 p.m. CST'. http://www.flakmag.com/tv/24-1.html.

World Factbook 2005. http://www.cia.gov/cia/publications/factbook.

Žižek, Slavoj. 'The depraved heroes of *24* are the Himmlers of Hollywood'. *The Guardian*. 10 January 2006. http://www.guardianunlimited.co.uk.

INDEX